America Beyond Black and White

CONTEMPORARY POLITICAL AND SOCIAL ISSUES

Alan Wolfe, Series Editor

Contemporary Political and Social Issues provides a forum in which social scientists and seasoned observers of the political scene use their expertise to comment on issues of contemporary importance in American politics, including immigration, affirmative action, religious conflict, gay rights, welfare reform, and globalization.

America Beyond
Black and White

❀   ❀   ❀

How Immigrants and Fusions Are
Helping Us Overcome the Racial Divide

Ronald Fernandez

The University of Michigan Press • *Ann Arbor*

2010   2009   2008   2007   4   3   2   1

A CIP catalog record for this book is available from the British Library.

Library of Congress Cataloging-in-Publication Data

Fernandez, Ronald.
    America beyond black and white : how immigrants and fusions are
helping us overcome the racial divide / Ronald Fernandez.
        p.   cm. — (Contemporary political and social issues)
    Includes bibliographical references and index.
    ISBN-13: 978-0-472-11609-6 (cloth : alk. paper)
    ISBN-10: 0-472-11609-6 (cloth : alk. paper)
    1. United States—Race relations.   2. United States—Ethnic
relations.   3. United States—Emigration and immigration—Social
aspects.   4. Immigrants—United States—Social conditions.
5. Minorities—United States—Social conditions.   6. Racially-mixed
people—United States—Social conditions.   7. Assimilation
(Sociology)—United States.   I. Title.

E184.A1F473   2007
305.800973—dc22   2007019355

A Caravan book. For more information, visit www.caravanbooks.org

To JACOB MORTON FERNANDEZ

A fantastic fusion of Colombian, French,
Irish, Japanese, & Spanish heritages

Acknowledgments

I owe a great debt to Luis Nieves Falcon (in Puerto Rico) and Rex Nettleford (in Jamaica). Like two brothers, they introduced me to their Caribbean worlds, and, in the process, they changed my life. With love, thank you.

Research for this book included visits to the Kennedy, Johnson, and Reagan Presidential Libraries. The libraries are true arsenals of democracy, staffed by archivists who always do everything they can to get scholars all available documents.

Rather than risk missing someone, I would like to say thanks to all the people who helped at the Intercollegiate Conference on Mixed Race Students, at the seventy-fifth anniversary meeting of the Japanese American Citizenship League, at the Unity Conference of Journalists in Washington, D.C., and at the Borderlands Conference in Laredo; to everyone who helped arrange the visit to the Arab American community in Detroit; to our dancer hosts in Jamaica; to the Hartford-based West Indian Foundation; to our many guides in Puerto Rico and Vieques; to our hosts in Mexico, San Diego, and Los Angeles; and to all the folks in Cuba, who, through four trips, extended a warm welcome and a wonderful introduction to Cuba's spectacular culture.

Antonio Garcia Lozada, Martin Espada, Elaine Cartland, and Susan Pease all offered comments about the manuscript in process. Their comments and criticisms were both helpful and necessary. So too the very thorough peer reviews commissioned by the University of

Michigan Press. The last chapter now includes a discussion of the 2005–2006 immigration debates because of a pointed suggestion by one of the reviewers.

At Central Connecticut State University, Paul Altieri, Steve Cox, Debbie Peterson, and Mary Wood also provided much needed assistance.

At the University of Michigan Press, Jim Reische is an editor who became a friend. He copyedited the manuscript with great skill and empathy. Jim is so good that he should serve as a model for anyone editing someone else's work. It was a pleasure to work again with Phil Pochoda, director of the University of Michigan Press. He and his staff operate with an enviable degree of both transparency and professionalism. Sarah Remington was always helpful, kind, and very efficient. Kevin Rennells coordinated the publishing process with great skill and much understanding. Finally, my thanks to Anne Taylor for an excellent copyedit of the manuscript.

Tammy Morton and Adam Fernandez helped me in countless ways, not the least of which was providing the idea for the book. Carrie and Benjamin Fernandez listened to their father's ideas with patience and a smile, even when I was guilty of acting too much like a professor.

This book would not exist without Brenda Harrison. She provided the book's original title. She acted as my partner at the presidential libraries; and she was also my partner on each of the research trips. There is no part of this book that has not benefited from her acute intelligence, curiosity, support, and love. I, of course, am alone responsible for any errors.

The book is dedicated to our grandson, Jacob Morton Fernandez.

Contents

Introduction

——— ✦ ———

Emilie Hammerstein has a problem. Her dad is German, her mother is Chinese, and she constantly gets the same question from total strangers: "What are you?"

Emilie generally responds in a polite manner, but once the intruders leave she questions herself as forcefully as the daily gauntlet of strangers. "I have often felt that the world is not ready for someone like me, someone who is a walking contradiction to their cultural definitions. They don't understand that it can be confusing for me to be constantly asked, 'What are you?'"[1]

Emilie's question—America's question—is one significant indication of an unprecedented challenge to U.S. culture. Millions of other American combinations share Emilie's sense of being a walking contradiction to the white/black dichotomy. In everyday life, U.S. culture still calls these (mostly younger) men and women "mixed-race" Americans. Many stoically endure that label, but others defiantly reject it and its everyday associates, negative markers like "half"; "exotic"; "tragic mulatto"; or, perhaps worst of all, "half-breed."

One term they do embrace is *fusion,* an idea I first became aware of at the 2004 National Student Conference on the Mixed Race Experience. Fusions argue that all human beings are ethnic combinations.

They believe that there is one race, the human race, and that the human race is, by definition, a ceaseless series of human unions. Fusions also deliberately refuse to use skin color as an important way to identify anyone on earth. They believe that, instead of being self-segregating barriers to interaction, somatic differences are delightful and diverse manifestations of the underlying and indissoluble unity of six billion people.

From the fusion's perspective, assimilation is a form of masochism: why embrace a society that lacks positive words to describe them? As "walking contradictions," these Americans try to reconfigure the culture. They want to instigate a mutiny. When the rest of us ask them, "What are you?" they respond with questions of their own. What kind of culture cuts people into mixtures and halves? Since even the smallest group of people manifests meaningful genetic differences, what is the basis for the idea of racial purity? How can anyone have the audacity to talk about me as a "mixture," when the idea of racial purity is as valid as the beliefs of the Flat Earth Society?

These questions will not disappear. On the contrary, the often contentious debates about the "racial" identities of figures like Senator Barack Obama and Tiger Woods suggest that the future promises more discussion than ever. Here are the Census Bureau's estimates for the next fifty years. As the Census Bureau indicates, "All other races" are growing at a rapid pace because, among other things, close to 60 percent of Asian Americans under the age of 25 marry outside of their ethnicity.[2] Emilie Hammerstein represents an integral part of America's future, and, in her need to find positive words to describe herself, Emilie and her cohort pose questions that may fundamentally reconfigure American culture. Put differently, Emile and her cohort hope to emancipate everyone from slavery's most lasting ideological legacy, the white/black dichotomy that, 140 years after the end of the Civil War, still defines Americans by what poisonously divides Americans.

All Other Races in 2000	7.1 million and 2.5 percent of our people
All Other Races in 2020	11.8 million and 3.5 percent of our people
All Other Races in 2050	22.4 million and 5.3 percent of our people

Emilie has company, lots of it. Like an obsolete computer running new software, American society crashes when confronted with the more than fifty million citizens who are incompatible with our operating system of racial beliefs. Latinos, Asians, West Indians, Arabs, Pakistanis, and Indians are neither black nor white; they can never fully embrace the culture, and it never fully embraces them because the nation's dictionary of racial definitions—what the sociologist Erving Goffman called our "grammar of conduct"—offers no accepted, much less positive, way to describe them. For example, many immigrants from Pakistan have darker skins than African Americans, but we never call them black. So, what are they? "None of the above" receives the check mark, because, from their perspective—one that they share with bronze-skinned Latinos, Indians, and Arabs—the operating system is a mystery, and so are they if they try to think in white and black.

Consider three provocative paradoxes posed by many of America's most recent immigrants.

- According to the Census Bureau, white people attacked America on September 11, 2001. That may sound absurd unless we remember that the U.S. Census Bureau defines "white as referring to people having origins in any of the original peoples of Europe, the Middle East or North Africa." From one perspective, this represents a reverse "one drop rule"; instead of one drop of black blood making you black, one drop of white blood makes you white, even if your skin is as dark as that of former Egyptian president Anwar Sadat. The Census Bureau helps makes our cultural rules, so, if we use it as a guide, the Arabs who executed the hideous attack on the World Trade Center were white men. The idea of "white Arabs" forces us to ask questions like these: are the census categories rational, much less valid? Or, are they, as some Arab Americans argue, "a peculiar fixation" of a culture so addicted to thinking in two colors that it must squeeze brown people into white boxes?[3]

- The United States is home to more than one million West Indian Americans, the majority from the Caribbean nation of Jamaica.

Jamaicans in Kingston or Ocho Rios certainly see the dark color of their skin but rarely dwell on it. Instead, Jamaicans use their nation and culture as all-important axes of social and personal self-esteem.

Jamaican pride is a delight to see but becomes a problem the moment a Jamaican lands in New York. Now they are black; of course, they already knew that. But until they arrived in the United States, no one told them that they were *only* black. The realization is often so jolting and uncomfortable that Jamaicans (and Trinidadians) resist assimilation. Instead, they ridicule American attitudes toward color by asking two sometimes very angry questions. How can dark-skinned people who use culture as an axis of identity assimilate into a society that only wants to define them by the color of their skin? And, why should they fit into American categories? If Jamaicans make skin color a secondary or peripheral consideration in judging themselves and others, maybe Americans should use Jamaicans as role models rather than vice versa?

- A final example comes from a question posed by one of my colleagues who had attended the 2004 Unity Conference of seven thousand "minority" journalists in Washington, D.C. Mexican, Puerto Rican, Japanese, Chinese, Indian, and Iranian professionals all agreed they were neither black nor white. Each group stood outside the dichotomy, but all still referred to themselves as "people of color." Stimulated by the immigrants' choice, my colleague wanted to know how Americans could ever create a color-blind society if immigrants were taught to use color as the primary basis for self-identification. Even more important, the immigrants' choice led my colleague to these perplexing conclusions: If Asians, Latinos, and Arabs were people of color, then white people had no color even though they and everyone else called them white. In essence, white was not a color, but *people of color only existed in relation to white people,* who did not get a color because they were white, which is not a color.

In this book, none-of-the-above immigrants are a blessing, never in disguise. In trying to comprehend or fit into the white/black dichotomy, Asians, Latinos, West Indians, Arabs, and (India) Indians ask us to rethink what the sociologists Robert and Helen Merrell Lynd called America's "of course" assumptions. Many immigrants suggest that our operating system of racial beliefs is weird or even a form of cultural insanity; and many of them are as eager for a full-scale mutiny as are Emilie and millions of other mixed-race Americans.

For the first time in U.S history, the white/black dichotomy faces a challenge, not from a small and insignificant minority but from the fastest-growing and arguably most vocal segment of the increasingly diverse American people. Consider the broad demographic outlines of America's future from the 2000 census.

Latinos in 2000	35.6 million and 12.6 percent of our people
Latinos in 2020	59.7 million and 17.8 percent of our people
Latinos in 2050	102.5 million and 24.4 percent of our people
Asians in 2000	10.6 million and 3.8 percent of our people
Asians in 2020	17.9 million and 5.4 percent of our people
Asians in 2050	33.4 million and 8 percent of our people
Blacks in 2000	35.8 million and 12.7 percent of our people
Blacks in 2020	45.3 million and 13.5 percent of our people
Blacks in 2050	61.3 million and 14.6 percent of our people
Whites in 2000	195.7 million and 65 percent of our people
Whites in 2020	205 million and 61.3 percent of our people
Whites in 2050	210 million and 50.1 percent of our people
All Other Races in 2000	7.1 million and 2.5 percent of our people
All Other Races in 2020	11.8 million and 3.5 percent of our people
All Other Races in 2050	22.4 million and 5.3 percent of our people

More than fifty million Americans and their children cannot or will not assimilate into American culture. In cities like Detroit (Arab Americans); San Diego (Mexican Americans); Edison, New Jersey (Indians); Seattle (mixed-race Americans); and Hartford (Puerto Ricans and Jamaicans), millions of new Americans busily engage in a series of parallel monologues. Working within their own ethnic groups, newcomers encounter what Harvard's Samuel Huntington calls "Anglo-Protestant culture," and, in the process of trying to comprehend how Americans think, Chicanos or West Indians regularly engage in tightly bounded acts of defiance. Each group provides more or less mutinous answers for its own members, but none seeks to provide a new cultural consensus for the nation as a whole.

This book argues that a new consensus can emerge if we consider what these parallel monologues tell us about U.S. culture as it is seen by none-of-the-above immigrants and fusions. Since a cultural mutiny is already under way, Americans have only two choices: understand why none-of-the-above Americans think as they do or stumble into a future that continues to define Americans by what divides them rather than by what unites them.

Some Americans will understandably question the need for a mutiny. Many of my students, for example, claim that they do not think in terms of race and ethnicity. They judge people by their character, not by the set of prejudices that guided their parents and grandparents. "Get over it," say many younger Americans. Why do we need to listen to multiculturalism lectures that only echo what we already think?

There has been substantial change over the last forty or fifty years. Many Americans are much more comfortable with difference than our predecessors were. But, to those who argue that a mutiny is unnecessary, I would ask these questions. If radical change is not required, why do the children of mixed-race marriages encounter some of the ugliest "racial" prejudice that America has to offer? Emilie Hammerstein's parents, a German man and a Chinese woman, married because they happily transcend the bigoted past; yet Emilie, as the child of color-blind Americans, every day faces the terrible discrimination and pain that occur because "halves" do not fit into a culture still dominated by race and the white/black dichotomy.

Put differently, if everything is OK, why was it necessary for Donna Jackson Nakazawa to publish (in 2003) a book titled *Does Anybody Else Look Like Me? A Parents Guide to Raising Multiracial Children*. This book helps parents protect their mixed-race children from the rest of us!

Let me repeat: substantial change has occurred, and the young-sters who argue that they no longer harbor prejudices are genuine. No one is lying. But the "get over it" attitude leads people to assume that, because they have changed, Americans have somehow leapfrogged over five hundred years of history without discarding some of its most basic and crucial forms of self-identification.

Here is my request. To those who argue that a radical reconfigura-tion is unnecessary, suspend judgment until we first analyze the debates taking place throughout the United States. Latinos, Arabs, and Asians, among others, argue that racial thinking is still a very vital part of everyday American life. Whatever we may think is happening, new immigrants still encounter a world aptly described by Senator Richard Durbin in congressional debates that occurred on March 27, 2006: "America has two great traditions. We are a nation of immi-grants and we are a nation intolerant of immigrants."

In the chapters that follow, *America Beyond Black and White* listens carefully to the series of parallel monologues now occurring in the dis-united states of America. The book also examines the history of vari-ous groups. This historical analysis serves three purposes: It helps explain the diverse and often negative reactions of these groups to American racial thinking; it underlines the continuing power of nine-teenth- and early twentieth-century U.S. history to still set the parame-ters of American beliefs about race, ethnicity, and the place of non-European immigrants in American life; and, finally, it helps "right" American history.

The history of none-of-the-above immigrants argues that, first, the melting pot is a myth and that, second, it is a myth that acts as a tow-ering barrier to any future sense of national unity. In the past, groups like Arabs, Indians, Mexicans, and Asians learned that American cul-ture never included their ethnic ingredients. Today, still faced with the rejection and confusion rooted in American history, millions of none-of-the-above immigrants deliberately isolate themselves from a society that treats them no better than it does Emilie Hammerstein and her seven million fellow fusions.

In essence, the immigrants, their (increasingly fused) children, and their experiences in the United States offer us an unprecedented chance to, all together, provide a radically imaginative answer to a question first posed by Randolph Bourne in 1916, "What shall we do with our America?"

That is the monumental question posed by none-of-the-above immigrants and mixed-race Americans. Should we abolish America's operating system of racial beliefs? Should we exchange the challenged metaphor of the melting pot for another ideal? And, if so, where do we all go from here? How, rooted in a more complete picture of U.S. immigrant history, can we create a world where Americans define one another by what unites them—their shared humanity— rather than by what divides them: the color of their skin and a descending scale of superior and inferior races?

We have meaningful cause for optimism, especially if we begin by accurately grasping how and why the United States of America fundamentally transformed its immigration laws in 1965.

One

A Historical Opportunity

❀

*Immigrants, Fusions, and the
Reconfiguration of American Culture*

The rat is dead, exterminated, in a nineteenth-century newspaper ad,
by a pest-control product called "Rough on Rats." For fifteen cents a
box, the poisonous pellets also cleared out mice, bed bugs, flies, and
roaches; nothing survived this pesticide except the Chinese coolie
carefully caricatured just below the dead pest. In the ad the Chinese
man relishes rats; he is about to pop a juicy specimen into his mouth,
and when he finishes his appetizer he can reach for the main course,
another fat rat suspended from his pants.

Above him is emblazoned an anti-immigrant slogan then popular
throughout the nation: "They must go." The Chinese need to leave
because they are rough on rats and rougher on the white race threatened by the Chinese immigrants who, in 1886, provided almost 90
percent of California's agricultural labor force.[1]

The conundrum is a constant of U.S. history. Groups of immigrants do the nation's dirty, dangerous, and demanding work. Then,
when they prove to be "incapable of assimilation," federal officials tell

9

them to disappear as quickly as the Chinese workers who were blown up creating tunnels for the transcontinental railroad.

Chinese immigrants also enjoy the distinction of being the first group legally barred from the United States. Congress initially forbade their entry in 1882. Ten years later Congress extended the Chinese Exclusion Act. In 1917, in the midst of fighting what President Wilson called "the culminating and final war for human liberty," Congress erased an entire continent. No Asians. No more.

Over time, Congress also slammed the door in the face of many southern Europeans. In the House of Representatives, members argued that the Italians, Greeks, Portuguese, and Spanish looked suspiciously like a cloud of "locusts." During legislative hearings, Congressman Albert Johnson told his colleagues that the newcomer crept up one block at a time; they swarmed neighborhoods and threatened to contaminate, through intermarriage, the sacred core of American culture.

That core was supposedly made up of English, Irish, and Germans. But, since 1897, three times as many people (ten million) had immigrated from southern as from northern Europe. Representative William Vaile of Colorado played the role of Aesop when he told his colleagues a fable about alligators and cats: "The cat looked the alligator over the very moment the alligator was brought into the house. The alligator snapped at the cat frequently; and the alligator kept growing larger and larger. The cat did not grow. And, finally, one day the alligator killed the cat."[2]

The cat was in danger because poverty had driven southern European alligators to America's shores and because Congress then practiced a form of what today we call affirmative action. In the early twentieth century U.S. immigration laws offered ironclad preferences for the close relatives of new American citizens. Family reunification allowed one immigrant to easily multiply into three or even five. And, since the relatives also had relatives, the newcomers kept coming, threatening to overrun one neighborhood after another.

To safeguard what Samuel Huntington had recently called "Anglo-Protestant culture," Congress passed laws in 1924 that institutionalized discrimination against prospective immigrants based on their ethnic origin. Chinese, Japanese, and other Asians were granted no immigration slots. As Congressman John Miller put it in December 1923, "we are fairly settled with the Chinese (and other Asians); they cannot come; they understand it; we understand it."[3]

Congress devised an ingenious statistical formula to exclude the southern Europeans. Every European nation received the same hypothetical annual quota: 2 percent to England, 2 percent to Spain. This appeared to offer a real measure of equality, but Italians, Greeks, and other new-seed immigrants had only arrived in large numbers *after* 1890. Congress set 1890 as the dividing line for their computations. The 1924 law dictated that a nation was allocated its immigration slots based on 2 percent of that nation's percentage of the American population *in 1890*. As a result, more than 60 percent of the slots went instantly to Britain, Ireland, and Germany, while the rest of Europe fought over the few remaining opportunities.[4]

Forty years later, President Johnson offered Congress this summary of the nation's immigrant preferences. Out of 150,000 immigration slots in 1964, two nations—Great Britain and Ireland—received 83,000 openings, "more quota numbers than are authorized for the entire rest of the world." Germany got 25,814 openings while the numbers for southern Europe included a mere 5,666 slots for Italy, 308 for Greece, 250 for Spain, and 438 for Portugal.[5]

In most years the three biggest recipients failed to exhaust their available slots; why would a multitude leave England or Ireland if positive social conditions prevailed? However, if you wanted a British or Irish maid, Congress acted quickly. Campaigning for LBJ's reforms in 1965, Attorney General Nicholas Katzenbach told a San Francisco audience that "an American citizen with a mother in Greece must wait at least five years—'and often longer'—to secure a visa which would allow her to join him here." But, if you wanted a maid from England or Ireland she arrived in four to six weeks.[6]

From 1924 through 1964, the restrictions against Asians remained quite tight. When Congress finally repealed the Chinese Exclusion Act in 1943, it set the new quota at 105 Chinese immigrants a year. Meanwhile, anyone from Korea, China, or Japan always tried to maneuver his or her way out of a prejudicial process known as the "Asia Pacific

Triangle": If, for example, you lived in Peru and traced even part of your ancestry to any Asian nation, entry into the United States nevertheless counted against the already miniscule quotas offered to nations like Korea, China, or Japan.

As late as 1964, Congress remained very rough on Asians. Attorney General Robert Kennedy forcefully told Congress that "the national origins system contradicts our basic national philosophy and basic values . . . it judges men and women not on the basis of their worth but on their place of birth . . . this system is a standing affront to many Americans and to many countries."7

The New Immigration Law:
All People Are Created Equal

President John Kennedy wanted to do the right thing. Documents in the president's library indicate that he and his advisers idealistically sought to end a policy of discrimination based on national origins. The existing laws were also such an easy target that our enemies constantly, and correctly, charged us with hypocrisy in the United Nations and other international forums.

Kennedy was also an astute politician, and he knew that even a failed attempt at reform would score political points. Among other southern European groups, Italians and Greeks endlessly lobbied for an end to the quotas, and they would certainly remember the Kennedy efforts when they pulled voting levers in 1964.

Congress initially resisted the administration's efforts, but Kennedy's assassination perversely catalyzed the need for change. With Lyndon Johnson assuming the presidency and the nation on fire for civil rights, legislators found it impossible to argue against changes that proposed to make all nations equal. The problem was still the 1924 law. Abolish it, of course, but replace it with what? To escape the worldwide opprobrium attached to the old law, the new one needed to avoid even a hint of bias against any continent, race, or ethnicity.

The solution Congress devised in 1964 still serves as the axis of U.S. immigration law: first come, first served. As White House official Norbert Schlei put it in an oral interview from the Kennedy Presidential Library, "the idea that we came up with—and I think essentially this was my idea—we should start with first come first served because that's an unanswerably fair kind of a basis."[8] Officials also agreed to maintain preferences for family members and to keep a separate line for immigrants with occupational skills needed by the American economy. But, essentially, Congress opened America's airports to the entire world. After the bill passed in October 1965, the rule became "first to fly into New York, Chicago, Miami, or Los Angeles, first granted residency."

Equality is a tough taskmaster. Theoretically, everyone gets a fair deal. Unfortunately, when the president's advisers checked the waiting lines for admission to the United States, they discovered that the institutionalized prejudices of 1924 lingered. Norbert Schlei told the Senate's Subcommittee on Immigration and Naturalization that "if first come first served were allowed to dictate the entire quota immigration policy, we would get ninety percent of our quota immigration from Italy, we would get about 8 percent from Greece, and we would get the other 2 percent from Poland and Portugal."[9]

Malcom X's warning was borne out; America's chickens were coming home to roost. So, to ensure equal opportunity for everyone, Congress imposed maximum limits on the number of immigrants that could come from any single country. In practice, Congress said that if a country received 10 percent of America's immigration slots, that was its maximum number. After reaching the limit, Congress required a new form of diversity; the rest of the slots were distributed to the world.

But not before Senator Sam Ervin (D-North Carolina) asked some controversial questions. Ervin liked the old rules so much that he still openly endorsed the system of national origin quotas. "I believe that we ought to give preference to those who have made contributions to America and not put them on exactly the same basis as people who have made little or no contribution to our population and no contribution to our development."[10] Among other things, Ervin was forgetting the Chinese contribution to the transcontinental railroad and

California agriculture. He also never asked how particular ethnic groups could contribute to America if, despite the melting pot ideology, no one ever allowed them into the pot.

Sam Ervin's arguments emphasized potential problems with assimilation. He believed that old-seed immigrants deserved affirmative action because of their contributions and because Greeks and Italians easily meshed into American society whereas Asian or African newcomers brought decidedly dangerous and dissonant beliefs, values, and ancestry.

Despite assurances from White House staff, Ervin argued that the new legislation threatened to introduce into American life the very people our ancestors so obviously despised. As early as 1790, U.S. immigration law had specified "free white persons" as the only group eligible for citizenship; after the Civil War, people of "African ancestry" also became acceptable, but bring in Indians and Asians and you once again opened the ancestry debate so forcefully silenced by the 1924 national origins legislation. For Ervin America only welcomed white people—that is, anyone from Europe, including (in 1965) the Italians, Greeks, Portuguese, and Spanish.

Because many other members of Congress shared Sam Ervin's reservations and prejudices, the White House took the offensive. The Johnson Presidential Library contains a copy of the document "The Road to Final Passage," distributed to all members of Congress; it reassured readers that people from southern Europe would be the "principal beneficiaries" of the new legislation. De jure, each nation did get an equal allotment of immigration slots; de facto, the new law somehow functioned like its prejudiced predecessor. Attorney General Katzenbach assured Congress that the "total" increase in immigration signaled no more than eighty thousand people a year, including Italians and Greeks who entered the United States in the name of family reunification.[11]

But Sam Ervin remained skeptical. To his old and experienced eyes, only "a man with prophetic powers" made precise predictions about the consequences of the proposed legislation. No one knew what tomorrow promised except Norbert Schlei and his colleagues. With all the arrogance of the "best and the brightest" Schlei assured

Congress that reform would produce only small changes in the ethnic composition of the American people. Pushed by Ervin, Schlei did finally concede that "the prediction becomes less certain as you go into the future,"[12] but the administration's statistical calculations were reassuring. Only southern Europeans meant to take advantage of the new law; Indians, Asians, and Latin Americans would return Uncle Sam's immigration invitation like a misaddressed envelope.

In October 1965, the House of Representatives passed the new immigration legislation by a huge majority; the Senate approved it by a show of voices sufficed; as Schlei later boasted, "they didn't even count because it was obvious that it had passed."[13]

Twenty-Five Million Immigrants

Norbert Schlei and his colleagues made a computational error. The predictions offered by the Kennedy and Johnson administrations proved to be incredibly incorrect. Here are some recent numbers.

- In 1970, recent immigrants (i.e., the foreign-born population) represented 4.7 percent of the American people. By 2006, the figure was 12.4 percent, the highest percentage since Congress closed the doors to "nonwhite" immigration in 1924.[14]
- Previously, the highest percentage of foreign-born residents to be counted in America in a single year was 14.7 percent, in 1910.[15]
- Over 50 percent of the foreign-born population arrived since 1990. The 7.9 million (legal and illegal) immigrants who arrived between January 2000 and March 2005 make that the highest five-year period of immigration in American history.[16]
- The overwhelming majority of these new immigrants come from nations and continents *negatively targeted* by the 1924 national origin legislation. Almost 26 percent trace their roots to Asia, and more than 50 percent come from the Caribbean, Central America, and Latin America. Another 8.3 percent are from "other regions," especially Arab and African countries. Only 14 percent of the newcomers hail from Europe.[17]

- Since 1970, the top ten nations sending immigrants include, from top to bottom, Mexico, China/Taiwan/Hong Kong, Philippines, India, Vietnam, El Salvador, Korea, Dominican Republic, Cuba, and Colombia.[18]

- One nation—Mexico—accounts for 27.7 percent of the U.S. foreign-born population.[19]

- In 2004, the nation's quota limit on immigrants totaled 432,373. Nevertheless, the United States admitted 946,142 legal immigrants in 2004. Fully 80 percent of the one-half million immigrants who came over and above the quota received preference as "the immediate relatives of U.S. citizens." Another 61,013 arrived as refugees (e.g., Cubans in Miami); refugees are not counted against annual quotas.[20]

- As of March 2005, more than 11.1 million undocumented immigrants were living in the United States. The figure in 2000 was 8.4 million undocumented migrants. More than 78 percent come from Mexico (56 percent) and Latin America, a group that makes up a significant percentage (12–14 percent) of the workers in food manufacturing, farming, furniture manufacturing, construction, textiles, and food services.[21]

- Immigrants live disproportionately on the East and West Coasts. Almost 45 percent of all Asians and 41 percent of all Latinos live in the western states. Another 22 percent of Asians and 19 percent of Latinos live in the East. Meanwhile, America's heartland contains relatively few immigrants.[22]

- Immigrants make up 26 percent of the people in California, almost 20 percent of the population in New York, and 18.4 percent in Florida. By contrast, only 4.4 percent of Georgians are immigrants, 3.9 percent of Iowans, 2.2 percent of Maine's residents, and a mere 0.95 percent of Mississippians.[23]

Even if we stopped all immigration tomorrow, the makeup of the United States wouldn't change, because the 1965 legislation irreversibly changed the ethnic composition of the American people. The future is here, and it is here to stay.

A Cuban's Critique of American Sociology

Desi Arnez's trademark call was a passionate Babalú! American television viewers of the 1950s never realized that they were welcoming an African god into their homes. Eating frozen Swanson dinners on plastic TV trays, Americans in the fifties were hearing an actor; Cubans were hearing pleas to Babalú-Ayé, the Nigerian orisha charged with causing and curing a multitude of human infirmities.

Babalú-Ayé retains his hold on the Cuban people. From Santiago to Havana, the artisan markets boast countless statues of Babalú and a spectacular array of other Nigerian orishas. However, Cuban culture deliberately hides the truth. Babalú pretends to be Saint Lazarus. Changó pretends to be Saint Barbara. And Yemayá is the Virgen de Regla, a dark-skinned Mother of God, holding, on the altar of her church, a light-skinned son, the baby Jesus.

Instead of assimilating into Cuban culture, the slaves in Cuba slowly reconfigured it, fusing Nigerian and Christian traditions into a religion called Santería. As of the summer of 2003, that religion was still adding new elements to its pantheon. On the outskirts of Havana, the altar of one Santera (priestess) boasted Christmas lights from Wal-Mart and, very prominently, a blond Barbie doll, in all her bleached beauty.

Desi Arnez came from a spectacular culture, a culture that offers fresh and important theoretical insights into the nature and consequences of immigration. According to Cuban anthropologist Fernando Ortiz, when masses of new immigrants entered the United States after 1890, social scientists continually focused on assimilation, on immigrants becoming *similar* to the already existing host culture. Assuming a perfect transition, the immigrants not only acquired a new culture but lost the old one. Italian, Greek, or Spanish traits "disappeared" so completely that immigrants and their children unconsciously melted into the American mainstream.

In the early twentieth century, assimilation became a moral imperative. Anxiety about the arrival of millions of southern European immigrants produced a movement to restrict immigration and a simultaneous movement to Americanize the new-seed immigrants. Theodore

Roosevelt and Woodrow Wilson both preached Americanization with such passion that they used the stars and stripes to "swat," like flies at a picnic, any immigrant who used a hyphen (e.g., Italian-American or Greek-American). Each president demanded a lusty embrace of the host culture, which *already* contained all the right ingredients. Immigrants entered the pot only when, through a transforming process resembling a baptism, they finally became real Americans.

Ortiz and Cuban scholars also debated the assimilation of newcomers to the Spanish Caribbean during these same years, However, instead of viewing assimilation as a moral imperative to join the existing culture, they found that many Cubans relished creative interactions with the Spanish, Africans, Portuguese, Americans, and, in the nineteenth century, more than 150,000 Chinese. The island today boasts nineteen different species of orange trees of Chinese origin, and a common saying of Cuban street vendors is *"naranja china dulce"* (sweet Chinese orange). Cubans also use musical instruments with deep roots in China.[24]

Cuba acted like the cultural crossroads of the Americas. Students of its culture observed such rapid change that they devised a new term, *transculturation,* to describe it. Transculturation spotlights, as in the fusion of Nigerian and Christian religions, the process of cultural creativity that always occurs when different ethnic groups interact for significant periods of time. It treats people as imaginative forces in the reconfiguration of interacting cultures.

Because interacting ethnicities always produced cultural creativity, Fernando Ortiz argued that beyond the two phases of immigration highlighted by American social scientists—the disappearance of the old culture and assimilation into the new culture—immigration also and always produced a third phase. Overlook cultural creativity and you ignore the role of immigrants as consistently inventive forces in the reconfiguration of the host culture. Immigrants could change Cuban or American culture as much as it changed them.[25]

Ortiz never made precise predictions about the inevitability of assimilation or of cultural reconfiguration. Instead, he lovingly focused on the transformations produced by Cuba's incredible mix of immigrants. No one process necessarily dominated or eliminated the other. But his critique raised important questions: if a culture closed the door to new-seed immigration—as the United States did in 1924—immigrants would likely assimilate more readily into the host culture. What is the alternative if fresh doses of old-world culture are impossible to obtain? Alternatively, when you open your door to the world, chances are that the host culture will witness a good degree of resistance to assimilation and experience instead varying degrees of cultural creativity.

Despite Ortiz's insights, American sociology often remains a prisoner of the assimilation norm. Even accomplished scholars like Alejandro Portes and Ruben Rumbaut, while stressing that "rapid integration and acceptance into the American mainstream represent just one possible alternative," still use assimilation as the "master concept" and argue that alternative responses represent a "segmented" (partial) assimilation or, even worse, a dissonant assimilation. Like a fusion measuring itself against the white/black archetype, alternatives to assimilation are still regarded as jarring, inharmonious, or "dissonant."[26]

Rooted in the work of Fernando Ortiz, this book argues that nothing is necessarily normal when it comes to the immigrant experience. Analysts must be prepared to see three general responses—loss of the original culture, assimilation, and transculturation—and understand that the likelihood of any one is relative to a variety of variables. Thus, the following table indicates the overarching variables that affect the probability of immigrant assimilation to, or immigrant reconfiguration of, the host culture. My umbrella argument is that the challenges posed by none-of-the-above immigrants and mixed-race Americans mesh—they enjoy a positive dialectical relationship—with a number of social conditions that also nurture and sustain transculturation, that is, the cultural creativity that always occurs when two or more cultures interact for significant periods.

Evidence of cultural reconfiguration is as easy to find as the local Burger King. In Albuquerque, a stop for a cup of coffee offered alternatives not available in Connecticut. The fellow in front ordered a Whopper with no sauce. He wanted green salsa instead, so the clerk matter-of-factly dipped into a waiting container and reconfigured, with Mexican fire, a previously all-American burger.

The ethnic food aisles of U.S. supermarkets also prominently demonstrate the impact of recent immigrants on American food habits. If you pass by the salad bar in a supermarket in Abilene, Kansas, as well as on both coasts, you may well see a sushi bar, raw ocean fish for dinner on two coasts and in the heartland.

New food preferences are an easy, obvious, and, in many instances, welcomed reconfiguration of U.S. culture. The city guides offered by most hotels break down restaurants by both price and ethnicity. Moreover, given the popularity of the Food Network channel on American TV, no viewer wants the "iron chefs" to assimilate into American culture. On the contrary, Americans have enthusiastically supported chefs who fuse the world's most diverse ingredients into delicious and distinctly reconfigured dishes.

But, when we move from food to politics, not to mention race and ethnicity, the welcome mat often disappears. Instead of appetizing alternatives, Latinos, Indians, Asians, Arabs, and mixed-race Americans are regarded as threats that strike at the very core of America's traditional wisdom. However, as the mixed-race population suggests, a challenge to U.S. culture is not only well under way, but it receives direct and indirect support from a series of seven contemporary social conditions, all conducive to a revolutionary reconfiguration of U.S. beliefs about race, ethnicity, and the consequences of immigration.

TABLE 1.   Probability of Cultural Loss, Gain, and/or Creation

The probability of cultural reconfiguration substantially increases as a society moves from assimilation and its associated variables to multiculturalism and its associated variables.

Attitude of Host Society	World/Regional Attitude toward the Host Society	Prejudice against Immigrant Group	Preexisting Ethnic Community's Attitude toward the Host Society	Interest and Efforts of the Immigrant's Country of Origin
Assimilation	Positive	Low	Positive	Weak
Laissez-Faire	Neutral	Moderate	Neutral	Moderate
Multiculturalism	Critical	High	Negative	Strong

Note: The initial stimulus for this table came from my reading of Alejandro Portes and Rubén C. Rumbaut, *Immigrant America* (Berkeley: University of California Press, 1996), esp. 89; the table is also firmly rooted in the ideas of Fernando Ortiz, especially his discussion of transculturation.

In sharp contrast to the immigrant influx of the early twentieth century, post-1965 immigration occurs under social conditions that greatly facilitate not assimilation but the cultural creativity that Fernando Ortiz calls transculturation. These conditions will exist into the indefinite future. Thus, America can seize the moment as a historic opportunity; or, as the following chapters show, it can continue the series of divisive, parallel monologues that now dominate U.S. discussions of race, ethnicity, and the consequences of immigration.

New Conditions, Historic Opportunities

Condition number one is the great success of the multicultural movement; as sociologist Nathan Glazer wrote in 1997, we are all multiculturalists now. Glazier meant that long efforts by "minority" cultural groups to attain equal recognition had been so successful that even social conservatives "now accept a greater degree of attention to minorities and women and their role in American history and social studies and literature classes in high schools." Glazer argued that the victory of multiculturalism was so complete that "those few who want to return American education to a period in which the various subcultures were ignored, and in which America was presented as the peak and end-product of civilization, cannot expect to make any progress in the schools."[27]

In January 2005, the Web page of the Charlotte-Mecklenburg (North Carolina) Board of Education defined multiculturalism as "education that recognizes values and affirms diversity in a pluralistic environment." Continuing, the board encouraged an education that includes "respect for people of all cultures, plus the development of positive and productive interaction among people and experiences of diverse cultural groups."[28] In 1916, schools preached and practiced a focus on 100 percent Americans. In 2005, we seek to respect all cultures and, at least theoretically, to learn from them as they learn from us.

Condition number two is the critical aspect of the multicultural movement; thus, the Charlotte-Mecklenburg Board of Education emphasized that multiculturalism "demands an understanding of historical, political and economic bases of current inequities." Students learn about the harmful as well as the positive "achievements of American culture." Former heroes become villains; from a Latino perspective, the Spanish American War was the Cuban War for Independence, and the "rough riders," instead of being liberators, were oppressive instruments of U.S. imperial policy.[29]

The result of the critical impact of multiculturalism is that contemporary requests for assimilation occur when Western civilization in general and U.S. culture in particular experience constant criticisms from a variety of different directions. Being Eurocentric is a fault and, long before 9/11, American culture often acted as a magnet for critiques of Western imperialism, arrogance, and prejudice.

Historically, it was much easier for immigrants and their children to identify with U.S. culture. Especially in the Southwest, many Mexicans proudly embraced their Spanish heritage, calling themselves "Hispanos" in a deliberate effort to champion U.S. culture and its allegedly European biases. Well into the 1950s the Mexican-based organization League of United Latin American Citizens (LULAC) "insisted that Mexicans should be free from discrimination not because discrimination was wrong but because they were white."

In 2006, Chicano studies students now learn about Aztlán, a "mythical" geographical area that "implies a new genealogy for the Chicanos, one in which their ancestors, commonly considered the descendants of Aztecs, are transformed into the Aztecs forebears." In a very imaginative manifestation of cultural reconfiguration, the Chicanos (who were once white) now define themselves "as the primordial Americans" and "the original Mexicans."[30]

The now institutionalized antagonism to U.S. culture makes it harder to assimilate and much easier to engage in an ongoing process of cultural creativity. In *Brown Tide Rising*, Otto Santa Ana discusses a new social identity that has suddenly appeared in California. The identity is "Americano," and the accent is on the "O."

Condition number three is the number of "family-sponsored" immigrants who legally enter the United States. This figure started to grow precipitously after 1965, and in 2004 fully 66 percent of the roughly one million legal immigrants arrived because of their family preferences. A full 406,074 of these family members were admitted over and above Congress's theoretical "annual numerical limitation," which was 432,373 in 2004.[31]

The large majority of these immigrants have new-seed origins, including the annual 55,000 diversity immigrants who sponsor family members from ethnicities "underrepresented" in the American immigrant pool. Eligible nations include, in Europe, Bulgaria and Turkmenistan; in South America, Suriname, Dominica, and Grenada; and, in Africa, Botswana and Senegal. Over time, these immigrants will increase the mix of nations that engender cultural creativity as they simultaneously add the immigrants who, as with Indians or Chinese, make it harder for sponsoring family members to assimilate into U.S. culture.

Family preference immigrants represent the language and culture left behind. By themselves, grandparents, uncles, aunts, brothers, and sisters can be a significant impediment to the assimilation of the second and third generations. But, in 2007, these immigrants enter a multicultural society that criticizes U.S. culture as it simultaneously reexamines the history of America's treatment of Asians, Latinos, and Arabs. In a dialectical fashion, the social conditions fostering creativity nurture and sustain one another. At times, those who preach assimilation seem to be talking to the converted, not to the new immigrants and the long line of family-sponsored permanent residents.

Condition number four comprises the attitudes and efforts of the immigrant's country of origin. In recent years, a number of nations (e.g., Mexico, Brazil, Portugal, the Dominican Republic, and India) have significantly increased the variety of consular and other resources available to their expatriate communities. The programs range from dual citizenship with voting rights to special mortgages and housing for returning immigrants. Portugal "registers and attempts to maintain ties with nearly 4.3 million Portuguese and people with Portuguese ancestry living abroad." Meanwhile, the Dominican Republic established "Casas de Cultura" in all areas with sizable Dominican populations. As the Dominican counsel in Boston boasted, "Since we arrived here one of our main tasks has been to penetrate the Hispanic community, especially the Dominican community . . . In all the Hispanic events that have been held in Massachusetts, the Dominican consulate is involved."[32]

In many instances, the motivation is the remittances sent by the immigrants; these funds now total 17 percent of the gross domestic product (GDP) in Haiti and 10 percent in the Dominican Republic. Whatever the government's motivation, though, to the extent these programs are successful assimilation is less likely and so too the loss of everything from language to cultural customs.

Condition number five is as plain as the Statue of Liberty seen from the New York harbor: Many millions of new immigrants come from nations formerly forbidden entry into the United States. From 1920 to 1965, we excluded people from countries such as China, Japan, India, and Korea. As the Supreme Court told Takao Ozawa in 1922, a Japanese national could not be a U.S. citizen because "the appellant was clearly of a race which is not Caucasian and therefore belongs outside the zone (of acceptability) on the *negative* side" (emphasis added).[33]

With Asian and other contradictions to the white/black dichotomy deliberately excluded from the United States, the culture never needed to change or challenge its grammar of racial conduct. We continued to think and talk in only two colors, and the forty-year contradiction is that, even though we legally abolished our ethnic origin prejudices in 1965, we continued to use—what choice was there?—the racial language that, by definition, depreciates the humanity of Asian and other none-of-the-above immigrants.

Remember that the words matter and that it is not a question of political correctness. The words matter because they deliver the beliefs and values that teach all Americans to place whites in the end zone and everyone else in a zone of racial negation. That is a problem for the millions of none-of-the-above immigrants who explode the parameters of the white/black dichotomy; and it is a continuing problem for many millions of accessible "white" and "black" Americans.

Emilie Hammerstein must listen to the perpetual question "What are you?" because many "white" and "black" Americans agree with her self-perception: She is a "walking contradiction" to American beliefs. However, for those of us willing or seeking to create a different culture, Emilie and none-of-the-above immigrants create a situation in which her question is simultaneously our own. Especially in a multicultural environment, whites and blacks can also grasp the handle that opens the door to cultural creativity, to a future that refuses to make white the default category of America's racial life.[34]

Condition number six is the harshly critical reaction of ethnic groups who once played a passive or offstage role in American society. The multicultural movement induces self-criticism of the United States; and then, as Mexican, Chinese, Japanese, Indian, and Korean Americans begin to reexamine the past, they discover a history that challenges the melting pot ideology. All over the United States, college students now take mandated diversity courses that examine ads like "Rough on Rats"; the justifiable anger that many of them feel then fuels further criticism of Eurocentrism. Yet again, one social condition acts back upon the other with such effectiveness that it is often impossible to separate the chicken and the egg.

In *Asian American Dreams,* Helen Zia talks about the "emergence of an American people." Asians are emerging from a period of passivity, and, like the Chicanos, they are asking hard questions about a formerly hidden part of U.S. history. Zia, for example, reminds her readers that the Chinese helped build the transcontinental railroad, but when it came time for the completion ceremonies, no Chinese appeared on the podium. On the contrary, they walked back to San Francisco because Chinese people "were forbidden to ride on the railroad they built."[35]

Such memories and perceptions undermine respect, not to mention admiration, for U.S. culture. The critiques they produce stimulate not a desire for assimilation but, at times, a literal craving to reexamine and "right" *all* aspects of America's past in a manner that transforms our image as "old stock" Americans and our appreciation for old and recent immigrants.

Condition number seven is another accident of history: the arrival of newcomers as the nation struggled to deal with the short- and long-term consequences of the civil rights movement. First African Americans and then Latinos, Asians, women, gays, the handicapped, and a variety of other groups sought to redress their grievances. Equal opportunity became everybody's right; simultaneously, the federal government made up for the past with a variety of affirmative action efforts. Agencies soon allocated federal funds based on the number of minority citizens in a particular locality. As a way of precisely measuring the population, the Nixon administration issued Statistical Policy Directive 15. Are you white, black, or do you need or want another box? In the seventies public and private organizations suddenly requested that employees and clients identify their racial and ethnic classification. Federal officials even invented something called "Hispanics." Yet we soon discovered a widening proliferation of other labels as some people rejected the imposed categories. Latinos told Washington exactly what it could do with the Hispanic label.

In the name of equality opportunity, Statistical Policy Directive 15 forcefully strengthened the divisive white/black dichotomy at the very time the nation welcomed immigrants who could never find the boxes they needed. Indians, Mexicans, and mixed-race Americans explode the nation's racial categories, yet we reaffirm their status as inconsequential "others" every time they fill out an employment or government form. As Soledad (from Colombia) puts it, "whoever did this made a lot of mistakes. Whoever did the census wasn't educated about race. Because how could someone who is really black but speaks Spanish write down that he's black. I kept wondering about that."[36]

She is still wondering; so are the rest of us. In our collective confusion, we stumble from one pole to the other. At Tufts University, students are encouraged to choose two boxes from 27 different racial and ethnic options: the menu offers 351 possible combinations. Schools like Bard and Davidson College symbolize the other extreme: allowing students to fill in whatever they wish under the heading.[37]

In an ideal world, self-definition would be the norm. In real life, we need to share the same or similar assumptions about one another. Without shared assumptions, Americans talk past rather than to one another. So, keeping Tufts University's 351 possible combinations in mind, here is my conclusion. The seven social conditions I describe in this chapter mesh with the desires of mixed-race and none-of-the-above immigrants. The short-term result is a mutiny in action; the end result could be a voluntary and revolutionary reconfiguration of American culture.

Latino, Asian, Arab, and Indian Americans offer this country a unique, historic opportunity. They suggest that we need to seize the moment collectively because, for the first time in four hundred years, we can challenge the divisive legacy of slavery and create a New World dramatically different from the one envisioned by men like Columbus and Cortez.

The chapters that follow analyze the parallel monologues now occurring throughout the United States. Some are exciting; some divide us more than ever. My aim is to show how the monologues can be turned into dialogues and, in the final chapter, to show how we can transcend separateness by allowing three hundred million Americans to express their ethnic differences while embracing a definition of *American* that enthusiastically includes each of us, all the time.

Two

Dead End

— ✦ —

The White/Black Dichotomy

The Shahid Case

Was Jesus white? This may seem like a preposterous question, but in 1913 the federal district judge Henry Augustus Middleton Smith needed to devise an answer to this divine conundrum. Faras Shahid, a native of Syria, a Christian, and "in color, he is about that of a walnut," proudly stood before the Eastern District Court of South Carolina with a simple request: I come from a part of the world that gave birth to the son of God; can I be an American? Am I one of the "free white persons" eligible for citizenship under the laws of the United States of America?[1]

Judge Smith started his answer by complaining about the law. "The statute as it now stands is most uncertain, ambiguous and difficult of both construction and application." Some judges, for example, used the word *Caucasian* to describe white people; but Judge Smith correctly stressed that the word *Caucasian*—not to mention the word *race*—became popular long after the Founding Fathers decided to exclude everyone except "free white persons."

Since neither the law nor science offered the judge any sensible guidelines, he decided to rely on conventional American prejudices. "The meaning of free white persons is to be such as would naturally have been given to it when used in the first naturalization act of 1790." Thus, the judge artfully drew a circle around Europe and argued that only Europeans could be white in 1790 and hence in 1913. Smith's "construction of the statute would exclude from naturalization all inhabitants of Asia, Australia, the South Seas, the Malaysian Islands and territories, and of South America, who are not of European descent, or of mixed European and African descent. Under this definition the inhabitants of Syria would be excluded."

The judge understood the implication of his decision. The son of God could not become an American citizen. However, "if the people of the United States, through their representatives in Congress, see fit to exclude by law from citizenship the most worthy and spiritual inhabitants of the globe, it is not for the courts by judicial legislation to gainsay that law, and substitute for it what in their opinion may be more appropriate and reasonable legislation."[2]

In ruling against Shahid, Smith enforced the notion that the United States was a white, Christian nation capable of excluding even Jesus Christ. His was the conventional wisdom in 1913. And it still is today; because, just like the Honorable Henry Augustus Middleton Smith, we still have no idea who, exactly, is a white person; nor do we know, ninety-three years later, what color a Syrian is. "Common sense" prejudices still dominate in part because, in 2006, many Arab Americans still clamor for a separate minority status; to American eyes, they are neither white nor black. Instead, they are "invisible," and many of them resent it. Meanwhile, many of the rest of us try to be color-blind even as we simultaneously use the white/black dichotomy to box out millions of recent immigrants from non-European nations.

The white/black dichotomy was and is the crucial axis on which old-stock Americans base their negative judgments of fifty million none-of-the-above immigrants and seven million fusions. This dichotomy and its exclusionary mandates explode the historical and contemporary legitimacy of the melting pot metaphor.

So, before we examine the mutinous responses of immigrants and fusions, we will first analyze the social constructs that, in the process of assimilation, immigrants are supposed to embrace. Those white and black constructs often produce what sociologists Peter Berger and Thomas Luckmann call "cultural dehumanization"; in everyday life, a set of cultural beliefs become so taken for granted that people forget or never learn that all ideas and values are only human creations. Like they do for the weather, people stoically accept the beliefs they receive rather than learn that nothing is set in stone, even the white/black dichotomy.

Sociology teaches that all social constructs can be challenged or even demolished. But to do that in an effective manner we must appreciate the origins of the racial beliefs created by white people and, astonishingly enough, still passionately embraced by black people. As Debra Dickerson stresses in *The End of Blackness*, "no one believes as fervently in the one drop rule as blacks do."[3]

In Plain Black and White

The journalist George Washington Cable saw her on an Alabama train in September 1884. "Neatly and tastefully dressed in cool fresh muslins," the black mother and her three- or four-year-old daughter entered the train, squeezed through to the Negroes-only car, and, "very still and quiet," sat in two corner seats until a "revolting" group of chained black convicts interrupted the other passengers as they came on board. Headed for the mines, some two hundred miles ahead, the twenty or so bound and cuffed convicts threatened to wake the child and anyone else on board with the loud "clanking of their shackles and chains."

These prisoners wore no striped uniforms. Dressed in "filthy rags," they instantly filled the car with "vile odors." A white onlooker noted that it "stank insufferably," returning to the safety of his car. The mother approached the conductor, requesting permission to move to the white car. He refused her a passport, explaining that moving would only be possible if she worked as a servant for a white family. Instead, she and her child remained, along with the convicts, prisoners of hate.[4]

In 1884, the American system of apartheid made absolutely no allowance for simple common decency. "The hot branding iron of ignominious distinctions" was as fundamental a feature of life in Alabama as southern hospitality. Writing in the *Century,* a national monthly, Cable courageously challenged the system imposed by whites on blacks, calling southern customs "crude, invidious, humiliating and tyrannous." Only "driveling imbeciles" defended segregation, an evil that extended its tentacles to every state in the union. Cable listened to Yankees' pious excuses, but, as he reminded his readers, if they craved honesty, they should always remember this fact: "These six million freedmen are dominated by nine million whites immeasurably stronger than they, *backed by the virtual consent of thirty-odd millions more.*"

The dress and comportment of the woman and child on the train clearly signaled their middle-class status. Yet the apartheid system cut six million blacks down to the exact same level. Neither social class, gender, age, education, religion, nor any other variable mattered when the conductor played the white trump card.

Cable wanted to know why. What produced this world of "ignominious distinctions"? To understand it, an outsider needed to know that a Negro "came to our shores a naked, brutish, unclean, captive, pagan savage, to be and remain a kind of connecting link between man and the beasts of burden." While savages always had trouble when they confronted civilized people, their interactions in the New World produced unique problems. Southerners manfully represented "a superb race of masters"; first in the colonies and then in the United States, the best met the worst, with no one giving forethought to the consequences of sustained contact between the polar opposites on the evolutionary tree.

Cable forcefully opposed prejudice against African Americans. His 1885 article provoked immediate and sustained controversy. In explaining the system, however, he used only one number. "As a social factor he was intended to be as purely zero as the brute at the other end of his plow line." Every now and then, the masters did "mingle" their blood with that of the savages; whites raped or otherwise forcefully imposed themselves on black women, but this "worked no change in the sentiment; one, two, four, eight, multiplied or divided into zero still gave zero for the result."

Negros were human zeros; no dose of white blood ever changed their being and nothingness. But after the Civil War ended, six million former slaves were suddenly endowed with the inalienable right to life, liberty, and the pursuit of happiness. How in this new climate could whites keep mother and daughter in the black car? How could they justify the forced intermingling of a decent, law-abiding woman with a group of convicts?

Cable made a point that is crucial for any understanding of our cultural legacy and its twenty-first-century effects. The new system—Jim Crow—*dramatically intensified* the already divisive consequences of the white/black dichotomy. For all its horror, the plantation system sometimes sanctioned a "patriarchal tie and its really tender and benevolent sentiment of dependence and protection." War destroyed that sentiment and nothing replaced it; a Negro was now less than a zero. Instead of the Civil War making the two-color dichotomy less important, Jim Crow made it more so. Generations of old and new immigrant Americans would learn to rely on white and black as the essential guideposts of thought and action. Post–Civil War America now devised an endless series of rules that deliberately demeaned blacks and elevated the status of even the most contemptible white people.

Henry Grady, the editor of the *Atlanta Constitution,* responded to Cable's critique with an article entitled "In Plain Black and White: A Reply to Mr. Cable."[5] Grady, the self-appointed representative of the "New South," welcomed the opportunity to explain postwar southern manners. In preaching constitutional equality, Cable placed the laws of man over the laws of God. If people mixed whenever they wished, "mere prejudice would not long survive perfect equality and social intermingling; and the prejudice once gone, intermarrying would begin."

Grady openly walked into a minefield of contradiction and confusion. If a God-given instinct prevented "intermingling," how could it occur? And was Grady trying to prevent interaction or preserve prejudice? Apparently, despite our God-given dose of instinctual resistance, people proved to be so unreliable that they actually got to know one another, with the awful prospect that "mere prejudice would not long survive." This possibility petrified the New South, so Grady made a transparent statement of fact. "We add in perfect frankness that if no such instinct existed, or if the South had reasonable doubts of its existence, it would, by every means in its power, so strengthen the race prejudice that it would do the work and hold the stubbornness and strength of instinct."

Henry Grady succeeded. His ideas are still central in our cultural inheritance 120 years later. Grady's template of separation still functions, all too often, with the force of instinct, an "instinct" based in distinctions of white and black.

Consider the behavior of the actor Michael Richards, from the television show *Seinfeld,* when, in late 2006, he spewed racial venom at a heckler in a California comedy store. He could have called the fellow a jerk or a fool. Instead, he saw color, reached into his cultural preconscious, and reacted with hate. This is the dehumanization highlighted by sociology. Richards used skin color as a traffic sign. He obeyed the racial rules, poisonously attached to the cement, like beliefs, that keeps the signs in place. When a contrite Richards later sought explanations for his contemptible behavior, he only needed to look at history. His racial tirade shows that, in 2006, the words *white* and *black* still function as echoes for the beliefs of men like Henry Grady. Forget that fact and we forget the first reason that many none-of-the-above Americans argue that the dichotomy is a national dead end. *Thinking in white and black perpetuates, however faintly and unintentionally, the beliefs, values, and practices of the very worst representatives of U.S. culture.*

Slavery gave expression to the dichotomy, but after the Civil War the New South and the rest of the United States significantly strengthened the old prejudices by using the words *white* and *black* as guideposts to "intermingling." The hate embodied in the distinctions has certainly dissipated, but the cultural poles of our thinking remain, as Henry Grady put it, in plain black and white.

Even if we all move to the center, the poles set the limits of our sociological imaginations. Thus, none-of-the-above immigrants argue that we need to consider bulldozing the poles, if only because every time an immigrant learns to think in white and black he or she symbolically sustains, in the new millennium, the future redesigned in the New South.

Mountains, Myths, and the Concept of Race

German naturalist J. F. Blumenbach liked skulls. He precisely and lovingly scrutinized their every nook and cranny, their shapes, their colors, their folds, their size, and their capacity. When he examined bony remains, he rigorously performed every available analytical test. Having paid his debt to science, Blumenbach let his imagination run wild, right to the Caucasus Mountains. Like Christian theologians who once argued that the earth was the center of the universe, Blumenbach pointed to his beloved mass of rocks as the probable origin of all humankind. The Caucasus was the racial axis of the universe, and its southern slopes "produced the most beautiful race of men."[6]

Of course, Chinese, Indian, Egyptian, or Mexican people embraced their own standards of beauty. And scholars studying other collections of skulls produced different results. But Blumenbach's pictures were worth far more than words. In an 1865 edition of the *Natural Varieties of Mankind,* the five black and white skulls form a racial pyramid. On the top sits the head of a "Caucasian," named after "the ark of Noah" once stranded on Mount Ararat. Presumably from the mountain's southern slopes, the skull was presented as the apex of a scale of "degeneration"; people slowly got uglier (not less intelligent or morally deficient) as one moved from the Caucasian peaks to the Oriental and African flatland.[7]

In the mid-nineteenth century, Blumenbach's concept of race fit like a white glove over the ignominious distinctions established by slavery and the Jim Crow system. Science suddenly provided powerful new reasons to cherish the old dichotomy of black and white.

Judges used the new "knowledge" to justify a wave of segregationist decisions. When Congress established the first naturalization laws in 1790, it limited citizenship to free white persons. Neither the modern concept of race nor even the word *Caucasian* existed at the time. But, eighty years later, educated Americans accepted the concept of multiple races in general and Caucasians in particular. When a judge now considered someone for citizenship, he needed to know if whites and Caucasians were synonymous. Did race trump skin color as a cause of exclusion? How many races were there? Did Congress mean to say no to everyone except those who traced their roots to the southern slopes of the Caucasus Mountains? Or, was the label "white" even more inclusive?

When Ah Yup, "a native and citizen of the empire of China," applied for naturalization in 1878, he became the human guinea pig for a forty-year series of "prerequisite cases."[8] As Judge Sawyer of the Circuit Court of California stressed, this was "the first application made by a native Chinaman"; the courts needed to tell the nation "if a person of the Mongolian race is a white person within the meaning of the statute."

Judge Sawyer began by affirming the problem with the color white. It "constituted a very indefinite description of a class of persons, where none can be said to be literally white, and those called white may be found of every shade from the lightest blonde to the most swarthy brunette." That said, Judge Sawyer turned to "common popular speech" and argued that, "as ordinarily used everywhere in the United States, one would scarcely fail to understand that the party employing the words 'white person' would intend a person of the Caucasian race."

Sawyer used Blumenbach as his scientific standard for defining whiteness, slipping the looser-fitting label of Caucasian over the indefiniteness of human color; he summarily rejected Ah Yup's petition because "I am of the opinion that a native of China, of the Mongolian race, is not a white person within the meaning of the act of Congress."

In making this decision, Sawyer formally initiated the legal creation of millions of "others," millions of what we today call none-of-the-aboves. After the Civil War, persons of African ancestry acquired the right to citizenship. But by limiting that right to Caucasians and people of African descent judges like Sawyer helped create a culture that deliberately excluded what Blumenbach called the "uglier" races. Conventional wisdom soon came to regard lesser races as such inferior peoples that they needed to be prevented from infecting Caucasians.

In many of these cases scientific race trumped color; in others, such as the Shahid case involving Jesus, color trumped race. But no matter which set of prejudices won out, racial thinking was woven ever more deeply into the fabric of American culture. At least seven generations of Americans learned that races actually exist, a reality that makes it much harder to dispense with white and black thinking. As we will see subsequently, race is a scientific fallacy, yet every time we use the word we reaffirm the supposed distinctions between whites, blacks, and other races; worse still, these supposed differences are too often translated into value judgments of those around us.

Like Jim Crow, the idea of race reinforces and rejuvenates the thinking of slave masters because it legitimates the idea of homogeneous, biological groups. Slavers created the white/black dichotomy, but Blumenbach and the social Darwinists claim to have traced its roots back to the laws of nature and the survival of the fittest. The worst people got the best scientific support for the ugliest prejudices of American society.[9]

As journalist Ellis Cose wrote at the turn of the twenty-first century: "For most of us, race is simply accepted as a given, and on faith, no more subject to questioning than the reality of our existence."[10]

To the extent that Cose is correct, all Americans remain prisoners of a concept devised by a man fixated on the southern slopes of the Caucasus Mountains. So, fusions and none-of-the-above immigrants argue that we do have a choice: blindly follow Blumenbach or use our minds to replace race with a concept that accurately reflects the nature of the globe's more than six billion inhabitants.

The Concept of Race

The idea of race is rooted in the unprovable assumption that once upon a time "huge numbers of people, distributed over broad masses of land, were biologically fairly homogeneous within their group and different from the (relatively few) other groups."[11] Make this assumption and you instantly make another: people are mixed, mongrels, impure, half-breeds, or mestizo because you unite two supposedly homogeneous groups. Over time, half-breeds became the worst made-in-America creation of all. And the problems of mixed-race students trace their roots to the erroneous idea of racially homogenous groups.

In the United States, color remains the principal standard by which people separate themselves into homogenous, racial groups. Color retains its hold even though molecular biologists have indisputably shown that, of our fifty thousand to one hundred thousand gene pairs, less than fifty have anything to do with the color of our skin. Some biologists put the number of important pairs at six to ten. Even figuring conservatively, that translates into a conception of race based on .001 percent of our total genetic endowment.[12]

From the dawn of racial thinking, the crucial question has always been the same: what physical traits (skin color, eyes, height, and hair) are most important in defining racial groups? Where do you draw the line between one group and another? Blumenbach posited five races, but other systems have described anywhere from twelve to one hundred. The breaks are as subjective as the criteria employed, and all categorizations fail because it is impossible to find the homogeneous biological groups assumed by the race concept. Estonians in eastern Europe boast blood types that are "nearly identical" to those of the Japanese. A study of Germans found that their blood types turned out to be "virtually the same" as a large sample of New Guineans. And 70–80 percent of light-skinned Scots, dark-skinned central Africans, and brown-skinned Aborigines all have type O blood.[13] For homogeneous groups to exist, genetic endowments need to be "concordant." For example, American thinking teaches that dark skin color and curly hair go together. However, many Indians from South Asia have dark skin and straight hair.

There is frequently more variation within supposed races than between them. In 1931, a researcher spilled phenylthiocarbamide (PTC) on a laboratory floor. Some of his colleagues instantly complained about a bitter taste in their mouths; others were ready to rush to lunch. Eventually anthropological research was able to divide the world into those who sense PTC and those who do not. The tasters make up anywhere from 15–40 percent of the population of Asia, but

Japan has twice as many nontasters as China and more than three times as many as Malaysia. Meanwhile, the percentages of American and Japanese tasters are quite similar.[14]

The problem with using skin color or eye shape as racial indicators is that the traits we see do not match up with the traits that remain hidden to the naked eye. Despite superficial differences, humans are remarkably similar. "All humans are identical for fully 75% of the human genome. This is a higher percentage than in chimpanzees."[15] In a world devoted to the truth, we might regard our physical differences as magnificent expressions of an underlying, indissoluble unity. Instead, we perpetuate the poisonous white/black dichotomy.

In the United States, whites and blacks alike often learn to see Africa as full of black people. Sometimes they are savages; sometimes they are civilized, but, whatever their statuses, Africans are black. Yet, as Jared Diamond notes in *Guns, Germs, and Steel,* when the European colonists first invaded Africa, the continent actually harbored significant somatic differences; and if we recall that "one-quarter of the world's languages are spoken only in Africa, the truth is that *no other continent approaches this human diversity.*" We forget or never learn that Winston Churchill and his fellow colonists killed off most of the Hottentots, whose real name is the Khoisans. Some still live in southern Africa, where their yellowish skins and "almost oriental" features mock the notion of a one-color continent. Egyptians, Moroccans, and Algerians defy racial stereotypes as well, and 250 miles to the southeast of Africa is the island of Madagascar, home to a significant number of people from Borneo. Somehow, seafarers from Indonesia crossed 4,000 miles of ocean, settled in Madagascar, and created a fused group of people whose features suggest Southeast Asia rather than the color and facial homogeneity taught in the United States.[16]

Race is a very expensive illusion. It nourishes and sustains the false assumption of homogeneity, masking ignorance—witness Africa—about the world that is actually there. We inherited a mountain of Caucasian nonsense, but even scholars who agree that race is a social construct see radical change as a utopian dream. From this perspective race is such an axis of modern thought that we cannot get beyond it. Our only sensible option is to accept race "as a dimension of human representation rather than an illusion."[17]

This is dehumanized, sociological nonsense. Recall the "Rough on Rats" advertisement about Chinese immigrants. As a human representation, how many of us would assent to its use? So why fight the stereotypes? Why change the language? And then refuse to challenge the concept that reinforces the worst thinking of the worst Americans?

Race forcefully supports the white/black dichotomy as it systematically excludes, in the twenty-first century, the same people it excluded in the nineteenth century. Remember Ah Yup. The judge refused his petition because he was neither a Caucasian nor a person of African descent. When we placed the white glove of race over our traditional prejudices, we married skin color to an alleged biological grouping. Caucasian became the archetypical category for judging the world, and we said no to most of it because Asians, Indians, and Arabs were outside the zone of acceptability "on the negative side." We can never become whole until we bury the concept of race where it rightfully belongs: on the southern slopes of the Caucasus Mountains.

The United States of Demographic Extremes

In geographical terms, the United States represents stark demographic contrasts. Here are some 2004 U.S. Census numbers from the Northeast: Maine, 97 percent white, 0.5 percent black; New Hampshire, 96 percent white, 0.7 percent black; Vermont, 96.8 percent white, 0.5 percent black; Massachusetts, 84.5 percent white, 5.4 percent black.

The southern states look quite different. In 1865, the vast majority of African Americans lived in the South. In 2004, 55 percent of African Americans lived in the South, and this percentage is still rising: Georgia, 65 percent white, 29 percent black; Alabama, 71 percent white, 26 percent black; Arkansas, 80 percent white, 16 percent black; Mississippi, 61 percent white, 36 percent black; and Louisiana, 64 percent white, 33 percent black.

Midwestern numbers often tend to mirror the statistics from the highly segregated Northeast: Iowa, 94 percent white, 2 percent black;

Minnesota, 89 percent white, 3.5 percent black; North Dakota, 92 percent white, 0.6 percent black; South Dakota, 89 percent white, 0.6 percent black.

Whether by intention or accident, in many midwestern and northeastern states, the concentration of whites is so extreme that whites have few opportunities for a meaningful encounter with blacks. The assumptions embedded in the dichotomy are likely to dominate their assessments of blacks because they never or rarely meet the very people who could challenge what the culture teaches.

In Maine, the *Portland Sunday Telegram* openly expressed this concern: "Imagine the white Maine kid growing up in an all-white community, going to a virtually all-white university or college, getting a job in an all-white establishment, and someday leaving the state to learn that most of the world is composed of people of color . . . the culture shock could be severe."[18]

Friends of ours from Portland came to visit us in Connecticut during the O. J. Simpson trial. Driving through Hartford, our friends' then eight-year-old daughter saw an African American man who was wearing black leather gloves. She yelled, "Look, Mom, there's O.J." Given this level of learned ignorance, the dichotomy often or even always directs behavior because it is the only perceptual tool, the only filtering device, offered by the child's culture and his or her everyday experiences.

In the South, everyday interactions take on a different tenor. In *Sons of Mississippi* (published in 2003), Paul Hendrikson discusses rituals associated with University of Mississippi football games. "Until a few years ago it was commonplace for Rebel fans in Vaught-Hemingway Stadium to wave their Confederate battle flags after great plays. You'd even see the little flags being waved during the playing of the National Anthem before the first whistle. Recalcitrants still do it." They also still join and support whites-only golf clubs and talk like this. In his cotton mill, Scott Middleton said, "we work blacks here." A second later he also said, "I didn't mean it to come out that way. I'll apologize for that. Sounds like plantation stuff."[19]

In discussing the consequences of our history, analysts understandably focus on the extraordinary levels of continuing, intentional racial segregation. They devise white and black isolation indexes and then measure cities accordingly. Despite some improvements, the picture they paint is not a pretty one. Even in our most cosmopolitan locales, blacks and whites often remain quite isolated from one another.[20] However, by focusing on deliberate segregation, we miss its "accidental" companion: regional segregation between southern states dominated by whites and blacks and much more homogeneous midwestern and northeastern states where living patterns assure few everyday contacts between whites and blacks.

However unintentionally, our demographic extremes make the white/black dichotomy more crucial than ever. Despite great progress over the last forty years, the color white still governs as the racial thinking of blacks as much as whites and others. As Bruce Jacobs lamented in *Race Manners,* "we strain our eyes looking for color and in the process lose all our other senses."[21]

Whites Are . . . White

What is a white person? I asked at least fifty white people in Connecticut to answer this question: Without writing a term paper, just tell me the everyday meaning of a white person in ten, fifty, a hundred words. My aim was to get streetwise answers from people across a wide variety of educational and occupational levels.

The responses were surprising. Many respondents expressed a genuine sense of bewilderment. Apparently, no one had ever posed this question before. "Gee, I never thought about that," they would say. "What an odd question to ask." Some people attempted a humorous answer: "A white person is someone who stays out of the sun." Others responded by striving for political correctness: "A white person is just like anybody else. How's that?" Some folks focused on geography: A white person "is someone of European ancestry." Or, "Image conjured up by a white person: light skinned, speaking European-based language and with European physical features (i.e., not a light skinned African)." Negatives figured in the responses of other people. "A white person is someone who is not black or red skinned." Or, "A white person is someone who is not black and is of white skin color."

The distant past was revived in many responses. "A white person is a Caucasian." Or, "A white person is generally an individual whose parents were both Caucasian or whose parents' lineage may not have been Caucasian but over many generations and through successive marriages and intermarriages predominately with Caucasians produced individuals considered white." When asked about the origin of the term *Caucasian* even many very well-educated respondents knew nothing about Blumenbach and his love of the Caucasus Mountains. People repeated what they learned in school. More than two hundred years after he borrowed the name from Noah and his ark, Blumenbach's nomenclature still provides the right word for a white person.

In all the responses, two consistencies seemed most important. First, virtually no one had ever given the meaning of the term *white* any serious thought. Like the sky, it was an omnipresent feature of social life but only the concern of specialists. Second, no one—not one person—had any nice things to say about white people. Language, culture, architecture, democracy, art: No one attached any positive achievements to the word *white* or the people called white. For my Connecticut respondents the color seemed to be a giant vacuum, devoid of meaning or content. An alien might conclude that, given their lack of positive attributes, no one would want to pal around with white people. They apparently offer nothing interesting, stimulating, creative, or important to potential friends or acquaintances.

White people are nothing. Yet white people run the United States. It is a puzzle with a solution. On the one hand, whiteness is one of the most positive and powerful ideas in America. Yet most whites rarely think about—or ask others to think about—the beliefs, values, and *privileges* associated with the word. The color is instead "an invisible knapsack"[22] of cultural content; arbitrarily acquired at birth, it is worn by whites from the cradle to the grave. We unthinkingly dip into the bag when we need to define a situation, and we rarely challenge the culture, even when it offers contradictory and ridiculous information. For example, whites may disparage dark-skinned people yet pay substantial amounts to get a tan and possible skin cancer. Apparently, there is a difference between the shade of brown that attracts the opposite sex and the shade that deserves prejudice and discrimination.

One way to focus on the contemporary cultural content of the word *white* is to use the philosopher George Herbert Mead's notion of self-concept. Simply put, a self-concept is what you think of you about a particular characteristic. Saying "I am white" may not sound like an arrogant and obnoxious declaration of superiority until you examine the four types of information simultaneously warehoused in this or any other self-concept. White says something about you; about others; about behavior (what whites and blacks do); and about life's prospects, that is, what whites and nonwhites should and can expect.

The words *white* and *black* function as terribly efficient storehouses of cultural knowledge. The dichotomy is not crucial in and of itself; it is crucial because, like the script for a play, the words *white* and *black* tell us how to think and behave in countless social situations. At its worst, we see black and think white.

Start with the supposedly simple self-image. When I say I am white, I use the color to say something about myself. Perhaps it is a response as succinct as the comments of my respondents: "I am white, that is, a Caucasian" or "A white is someone who is not black." Either way, in saying I am white I also simultaneously draw in, like a magnet, blacks and others. In social life, opposites not only attract; they need one another to exist. Short assumes tall; fat assumes thin; young assumes old; and, in the United States, white assumes black and especially "nonwhite."

The identity white divides and conquers because, as the default category of American "racial" thinking—recall the Crayola crayon boxes that once had a "flesh tone" selection—it partitions the society into one archetypal group and the rest of us. Even so-called people of color only exist in comparison to the assumption that white, which looks like a ("flesh tone") color in everyday life, is not a color in everyday life.

As we walk through a day's experiences, the supposed negative content of white (i.e., I am not black or Asian or Indian) turns into a perpetual positive, because the denotation of white is clear: Whites have what I lack; whites are *the* designer original, while the rest of us are knockoffs.

Whites only exist in comparison to a negative. It rarely sounds men-

acing until we turn to the crucial connotation of the label "non-white."
As Albert Murray told us more than thirty-five years ago, "thus are all
the fundamental assumptions of white supremacy and segregation
represented in a word, in one key hyphenating and hyphenated
word."[23] Murray continues: "When your yes-am-is-are white U.S citizen
says non-white, he has said it all and given away the game. What he forgets, and much too easily, is the fact that, as the self-chosen model
from which the non-white variant is a bad departure, he himself, more
often than not, is self-identified, self-certified, and self-elected. He also
forgets that he is self-esteemed—and for the most part only self-
esteemed."

White people forget that, by definition, they always carry on their
backs the invisible knapsack of privilege, pretension, and self-esteem.
No matter how well intentioned, no person defining themselves as
white can escape the knapsack and its assumptions. The assessments
of positive and negative self-worth attach themselves to the
white/black dichotomy and cannot disappear unless we consciously
confront the level of dehumanization produced by our contemporary
cultural inheritance.

Caspar the Moor

In a series of medieval artworks, King Caspar the Moor suddenly
appeared not as a follower of the Three Wise Men but as the wisest
man of all. In a 1540 Dutch portrait, the coal-black Caspar appears as
"elegant, eager, and well-dressed." In the late fourteenth and entire
fifteenth centuries actors blackened their faces as Caspar. He was the
spokesman of the Three Kings, and many inns took the Moorish king
as their trademark. Caspar and the American Sambo existed on different continents because, prior to the slave trade, many Europeans
accepted "an iconography in which black Africans received a positive
representation."[24]

Caspar was a Moor; and, until the onset of Portuguese slavery,
many European cultures employed "Moor," an ethnic and religious
label, to define visitors, soldiers, or immigrants from Africa. "Black"

replaced "Moor" when the Portuguese captured "pagans"; in reality, they captured cultured people from preliterate tribes, who shared few if any of the religious and ethnic characteristics of the Moorish/Muslim cultures. The Portuguese began to use "black Moor and black-amoor" to aggregate the two groups; eventually they and other slavers dropped the ethnic label and focused on color as the key way to distinguish between themselves and the new, preliterate slaves.[25]

Initially, the New England colonists used ethnic, national, religious, or social categories (free, indentured servant) to identify one another. Over time, this vocabulary changed in response to the colonists' need to classify, *from their perspective,* the slaves they imported. Like some Spanish priests in the Caribbean, colonists could see Indians and Africans as equal creatures of God, but the English chose to create a double negative—"white as not nonwhite"—because, among other things, the colonists sought to justify the horrors of slavery. In rationalizing the new world of masters and slaves, the English sanctioned a typical form of self-centeredness. They labeled outsiders from the perspective of the insiders and created a subhuman category—"blacks"—even before they created whites.

At the beginning of the eighteenth century, writers seeking to classify groups of humanity faced the same problem I had in Connecticut: whites lacked any positive, distinguishing characteristics. Nobody said nice things about white people. Historian Scott Malcomson stresses that whites were nothing because the colonial classifiers of humanity lacked plausible options. To give whites specific characteristics "raised the specter of relativism." One group might be as good as another. So, rather than make whites like the rest of humanity, whites used their nothingness to justify their status as the human role model. "At the birth of the republic whiteness was a concept shaped by a set of absences. The sum of what you were not—Indian, black, slave—made you what you were." That is, nothing, a white person.

The Declaration of Independence presented a problem to this way of thinking. If all men were created equal, how could the Founding Fathers justify the subjugation of millions of Africans? Jefferson, Monroe, Madison, and others were up against a wall that they themselves had built out of reason, natural law, and inalienable human rights. Theoretically, it created an impediment to a nation full of slaves and a world full of nonwhites.

Caught in this contradiction, the Founding Fathers decided to blame the English. In an imaginative, ironic reversal of thought, the insiders—the English—became the outsiders. In 1676, the English labeled blacks outsiders from their self-centered perspective; and, in 1776, the new insiders—the Americans—redefined the English from their own, equally self-centered perspective. As Monroe noted, slavery "is an existing evil which commenced under our colonial system, *with which we are not properly charged*" (emphasis added).

The contradiction still existed; if all people were equal, then the white/black dichotomy stood as a terrible example of institutionalized inhumanity. Since slavery could never be justified by a mind interested in consistency, a group of American revolutionaries sheepishly accepted the ideas of their inherited culture. They censured the English for their poisonous prejudices against the original thirteen states, yet they continued to think and act like the English when it came to slavery because any challenge to the double negative—white is not nonwhite—thoroughly undermined the cultural rationalizations and the economic system, created by Portuguese, English, and American slave masters.

We can face this history, or, like the Founding Fathers, we can ignore it. However, to honestly confront our cultural inheritance is to acknowledge the everyday consequences of the dichotomy. Whites are nothing and everything; nonwhites are the more or less awful negative against which everything is measured. As one of my respondents put it on May 18, 2004, "a white person is someone who is not black and is of white skin color."

The Sincere Fictions of White People

So far, this analysis includes four embedded layers of cultural reality: the dichotomy created by slave traders; the everyday life shaped by Jim Crow; the "scientific" concept of race; and, with Judge Smith's banishing of Jesus, America's resistance to immigration by many nonwhites.

But we live in contemporary America. What do we know about what white people in 2007 believe about themselves and about black people?

To answer that question, some researchers begin with a simple question: How many white people claim a black person as a good friend? In one survey, 60–90 percent of whites claimed to have a black person as "a close personal friend." Given the high degree of segregation in modern-day America, this figure seemed implausibly high. Since the survey asked the respondents no follow-up questions, analysts were stuck. They simply reported what white people said. In another study, when 42 percent of whites said they had a close friend who was black, analysts followed up by asking for the person's name. Only 6 percent of whites knew the name of the black person "they felt close to."[26]

In other words, most of these "friendships" were a white lie. Living in a society that most people, at least publicly, endorse as color-blind, whites wish to appear open minded. They lie to the researchers in order to avoid the appearance of prejudice.

But a fiction is more damaging than a lie. The liar is generally aware of his or her falsifications. The person living with a fiction honestly believes something that is false. Reality never shatters what Berger and Luckmann call "false consciousness" because preconceived beliefs direct both perceptions and evaluations of self, others, and society. Lies are a nonissue; self-delusion is the culprit when earnest fictions make an appearance.

In *White Men on Race,* Joe Feagin and Eileen O'Brien contend that many Americans endorse a series of significant fictions about relations between whites and blacks. More than two hundred million people are allegedly implicated in those fictions; whites share them with varying degrees of salience, conviction, and uniformity. Whites are also confused, the authors claim, because the fictions simultaneously include these beliefs: whites are "color-blind, privileged and victimized."[27] This apparently contradictory combination begins with the belief that contemporary whites are increasingly color-blind.

This claim comes with an obvious problem: How can any American, even one committed to significant change, claim to be color-blind when we all use the colors white and black as primary forms of self-identification? By definition, the dichotomy and its offspring—for example, nonwhites and people of color—make color blindness impossible; yet many white Americans sincerely believe that skin color is *already* an insignificant factor in their lives and the lives of black people. What seems to happen is that whites correctly see substantial positive change—compared to, say, 1960—and then conclude that color is no longer an issue. Many whites try to not see color in a society that constantly forces them to do so. It is an insuperable task and a sincere fiction because, besides the limitations imposed by our grammar of conduct, the poisonous beliefs attached to the words *white* and *black* still contribute to so much ugliness.

Take, for example, what real estate agents call a box. It can be cardboard, or it can be an old suitcase. What is important is its contents: "Diplomas, artwork, books, music, and especially all the family photos—anything that can identify the family as black." Homeowners hide the box in a remote part of the house, and they hide themselves, as well. They retreat before prospective buyers arrive, because if a black family wants to sell a house in a predominantly white neighborhood, "they are often advised by friends or their real estate agent to put everything identifiably black—any vestige of who they are—in the box. Otherwise white people may not buy the house."[28]

Take another example and a fact confirmed in many of my own interviews. According to Ellis Cose in *The Rage of a Privileged Class,* blacks who do go out in public often feel compelled to dress better than the rest of us. I, as a supposed white person, can go to a place like Home Depot unshaven, in my torn and tattered work clothes. But, to avoid being singled out as a possible shoplifter, black customers wear dress clothes, even ties, to purchase anything from drills to Sheetrock, from an appliance at Wal-Mart to the food at the local supermarket.

And yet many whites sincerely believe that they live in a color-blind society. As Debra Dickerson stresses in *The End of Blackness,* it is a fiction, made worse by the whites who argue that, if color *is* still a force in American life, black people must receive the blame. All they think about is race. Blacks allegedly see problems where none exist. If they would just forget about race and color our problems would disappear.

This is at best bizarre. For more than four hundred years, whites constructed and sustained a culture that judged people by the color of their skin. To tell blacks to stop thinking the way whites have forced them to think is to forget the past four centuries and their significant impact on the present. "For centuries, race affected every aspect of American life; now we are to believe it affects nothing."[29]

Besides the fiction of color blindness, many whites also believe that they are simultaneously privileged and victimized. The privileges come from being white in a supposedly color-blind society. A 2002 FBI Diversity Report indicated that whites felt quite free to express differences "due to cultural backgrounds," while blacks felt more constrained. The FBI explained the difference this way: "white men, having essentially created the culture of the organization, are more comfortable working in it."[30]

Despite the FBI reality, whites believe that they are privileged *and* victimized by a society that blames them for the past and that seeks to make up for that past by giving unfair affirmative action advantages to minorities and especially blacks. In my interviews, many whites instantly offer stories about the incompetent black person who got a job; whites also love to describe ideal-type corporations or public agencies that do not and have never existed. In a society that teaches its children that "it is not what you know but who you know," the advantages of contacts apparently disappear when it comes to black people. Merit is the rule, and no one should get a job unless he or she is fully qualified.

However, the FBI study concluded that informal networks were crucial to successfully climbing the bureau's ladder of advancement; even more important, despite the sincere fiction of merit-based advancement, the FBI "does not have an effective performance evaluation system. Virtually all components use a pass/fail evaluation system . . . through this and other results it is apparent that the management does not take evaluating employee performance seriously." Instead, managers "by nature tend to favor applicants with experiences, backgrounds and identities similar to their own."

This is the real world; yet, when I referred to this study in one of my classes, many white students refused to accept the FBI's assessment of itself. Jobs must have been allocated on the basis of merit despite the FBI's self-criticism and despite students' own experiences with university preferences for athletes, legacies, and those with cash or friends. At our Division 1 school, athletes—and only athletes—enjoy the luxury of a separate library facility reserved for them *and their tutors*. Those tutors help the athletes with their papers and homework, and they monitor the athletes' class work by calling faculty to check on the athletes' grades and participation.

Such institutionalized preferences are normal in our society. In addition to allotments for athletes, preferences exist for veterans and for those with workplace seniority; and, in the service of family reunification, America boasts a century-long tradition of offering significant preferences for immigrants with family members already in the United States. Merit never enters the process because the only criterion is the immigrant's familial link to the sponsoring American citizen.

Finally, if professors are honest, they will explain that in many job searches everyone knows the winner before the search takes place. Instead of offering advantages to whites and other minorities, affirmative action is often a farce because minority candidates are only included so that the committee can say they tried but the winner (a college buddy, a colleague's wife) was clearly more qualified.[31]

All too often, when reality meets the sincere fiction of merit-based employment, whites choose the illusion. Like my students, they deny the obvious fact of the importance of subjective factors in achieving personal and organizational success.[32]

When he wrote "In Plain Black and White" in 1885, *Atlanta Constitution* editor Henry Grady worried about the intermingling of the races. Whites and blacks needed to avoid the contacts that led to intercourse, children, and even marriage. In 2006, love and family remain bellwethers of social change. When asked about the extent of continuing discrimination, whites downplay its effects. Blacks are imagining what no longer exists or what exists only in isolated instances. And when it comes to marriage, many whites give responses that seem to mirror those they gave about having close black friends. In one survey, 80 percent of students indicated approval of interracial marriages.

However, when in a smaller group, speaking at length, more than 60 percent of whites changed their minds, citing, among other things, the discrimination that "interracial" couples would inevitably experience. As one father put it, "I would worry about the cultural differences, mainly whether younger adults and all have thought through the various issues in all that they may face from such mixed marriages. And whether, when those issues would eventually . . . arise, they are going to be capable and mature enough to handle it."[33]

When the belief that we have already achieved equality runs headlong into the possibility of a "mixed" marriage, the discrimination that supposedly did not exist suddenly rears its ugly head. It is a contradiction with deep roots in the thinking of Henry Grady and J. F. Blumenbach. The notion of mixed marriage assumes the existence of "pure or homogenous" groups; and the significant resistance expressed by fathers, mothers, and other relatives is still so strong that only 2.5 percent of whites cross the color line.[34] That number is higher than it ever was in the past—remember the fusions—but still suggests the power of Grady's "New South" to the new century.

Overall, the fictions and contradictions of many contemporary whites suggest an unwillingness to challenge seriously the dichotomy; the concept of race; or the thinking that created Jim Crow and the exclusion of Chinese, Japanese, Korean, Syrian, and other "alien" groups.

Whites remain the designer original, and the dichotomy and its attached beliefs ensure that the idea is protected from challenge. Paradoxically, forty years after the civil rights movement, black thinking is perhaps more dominated by whites than ever before. From Louisiana to California, blacks allegedly use whites as such a negative role model that whites dominate black culture even when—or especially when—blacks see whites as the devil incarnate.[35]

The Sincere Beliefs of Black People

In May 2004, Bill Cosby made an important speech at a National Association for the Advancement of Colored People (NAACP) convention celebrating the fiftieth anniversary of *Brown v. Board of Education.*

Cosby told the black-tie audience, "ladies and gentlemen, the lower economic people are not holding up their end in this deal. These people are not parenting. They are buying things for kids—$500 sneakers for what? And won't spend $200 for Hooked on Phonics."

"They're standing on the corner and they can't speak English," Cosby continued. "I can't even talk the way these people talk: Why you ain't, Where you is . . . and I blamed the kid until I heard the mother talk . . . Everybody knows it's important to speak English except these knuckleheads . . . You can't be a doctor with that kind of crap coming out of your mouth."

Cosby ended his speech by focusing on crime: "These are not political criminals. These are people going around stealing Coca-Cola. People getting shot in the back of the head over a piece of pound cake and then we run out and we are outraged, (saying) 'the cops shouldn't have shot him'. What the hell was he doing with the pound cake in his hand?"

On the podium, NAACP notables sat "stone-faced." Theodore Shaw, head of the organization's Legal Defense Fund, quickly told the audience "that most people on welfare are not African American, and many of the problems his organization (the NAACP) has addressed in the black community were not self-inflicted."

In the street people got angry. Using the Web, scores of African Americans jumped to Cosby's defense, praising what they perceived to be a genuine display of honesty and courage. A poster named Fuzzy Rider wrote, "lot of folks have been thinking this for a long time, but have been prohibited from speaking by the 'crypto-fascist' politically correct crowd. How can we ever solve a problem if we are not even allowed to talk about it without being vilified?"[36]

This instant response sentiment echoed a theme by John McWhorter in *Authentically Black: Essays for the Black Silent Majority.* He argues that black America is "permeated by a new kind of double consciousness": In private blacks applaud "personal initiative" and self-determination; in public blacks "dutifully take on the mantle of victimhood" in order to avoid alienating or arousing the media leaders of the black community.[37] No one wants to hear the accusation "you're a sellout" (to whites) or an Uncle Tom, so blacks supposedly embrace victimhood even though, like Cosby, they accept varying degrees of responsibility for the problems of African Americans.

In the debate that followed Cosby's comments, Regiwi, who identified himself as a forty-year-old black man, asked, "aren't we sick and tired of being sick and tired . . . I don't want to hear the tired excuse that white people are holding us back . . . we have to CHECK, CHANGE AND UNCHAIN OUR MINDSET, NOW FROM NEGATIVE TO POSITIVE." Another poster who used the tag "Macker" wanted to "see how fast it takes for the NAACP to demonize Doctor Cosby as an Uncle Tom." And still another writer summed up the entire argument in this fashion: "the tensions . . . are between the (this may sound strange) whitecentric, who see white people as the root of all problems . . . and those who are of the personality responsibility mindset, who believe that many problems are self-inflicted, and can be *solved by the black community*."

One powerful segment of the black community—the so-called whitecentrics—blames whites for every black problem, and, more ominously, they define themselves over and against white people. Parents actually resist sending their children to Harvard because, in the words of one parent, "I don't want her to lose her identity." Exposure to so many whites will presumably decrease her level of blackness, so, given the presence of whites, blacks stay home.[38]

Whether by design or by accident, Bill Cosby pressed some very hot buttons. African Americans are no more homogeneous than any other ethnic group: a fierce debate is taking place within the black community. But only one thing is clear. You can passionately reject a culture, yet that culture can still determine your thoughts and actions. If you define blackness as "opposition to whites at all costs,"[39] then, perversely, you only define your behavior in opposition.

For those interested in freedom, it is arguably a perverse outcome: The power of an inherited culture is often greatest when we passionately reject it.[40] I do this because you do that; you are still in charge because my behavior is rooted in a rejection of you. Greater freedom rests on evaluating the culture I received and my reaction to that culture. I am far less free if the only positive thing in my life is using you as the eternal negative. As Cornell West wrote in *Race Matters,* "mature black identity results from an acknowledgment of the specific black responses to white supremacist abuses and a moral assessment of these responses such that the humanity of black people does not rest on deifying or demonizing others."[41]

No one can ascertain exactly how much of contemporary black thought is "whitecentric." But a series of books argue that it is clearly dominant among America's black leadership. If that is so, the white/black dichotomy is a black hole and in that hole Henry Grady is smiling his diabolical smile.

White Norms for Black Deviation

Let's suppose, with John McWhorter, that a Jewish person and a black person move from the Bronx to Westchester, from the inner city to the weed-free suburbs. Each leaves his roots, and each weathers criticism from those who remain. The Jewish criticism may center on loss of attachment to "real" religious roots; the presumed switch from orthodox to reform Judaism generates so much criticism that some rabbis actually argue that the suburbanite is no longer Jewish. Losing orthodoxy means losing your Jewish soul.

But the black suburbanite hears a different insult: "You're still black." You can run but you cannot hide: no class, religious, or educational climb alters your personal or social status in American society. "You're still black," with the unstated assumption "that the person considers himself or herself not simply different from, but *better than,* black people" (emphasis in original).[42]

It is a sharp contrast. The Jewish person risks losing his ethnicity; the African American carries his with him forever. Blackness is a "stain" that cannot be removed. The insult is fired with such precision and fury that some black scholars argue it underlines a fundamental truth: black people believe what the dichotomy teaches. Anyone leveling the ultimate insult presumably thinks that whites are better than blacks. They never disown the suburbanite; they "stick it to him" by using an implied comparison. "You're still black" because you are not white—and never will be.[43] With the insult, whites direct the action even when blacks focus not on whites but on themselves.

W. E. B. Du Bois addressed this dilemma in *The Souls of Black Folk.*

Published in 1903, the book opens with Du Bois asking himself a question—"How does it feel to be a problem?"—and answering that American culture offered a black person "no true self consciousness but only lets him see himself through the revelation of the other world." By definition, blacks experienced "the peculiar sensation of a double consciousness," a "sense of always looking at one's self through the eyes of others, of measuring one's soul by the tape of a world that looks on in amused contempt and pity."[44]

Well into the 1960s this cultural contempt included media portrayals of black people as stupid—Buckwheat in the *Our Gang* comedies—or as servants for their white employers. The civil rights movement finally demanded positive representations of African Americans in the media, but, at the height of the movement for change, social science stepped in and, just as it had done in the nineteenth century, provided evidence justifying the worst portrayals of black people.

No one understood this better than Albert Murray in *The Omni-Americans*. Murray lambastes blacks and whites with equal vigor, yet reserves special anger for social scientists and those gullible enough to accept, like sheep, their scientifically proven and negative judgments of black people. Murray forcefully argues that social scientists create straw men by focusing on white norms and black deviations. The subject could be SAT scores, out-of-wedlock births, crime statistics, or the nature of the family; but whatever the issue, social scientists compiled data on white people, compared them to the data for black people, and then described blacks as deficient.[45]

In response, Albert Murray stresses an obvious fact: White people certainly deserved the lion's share of the responsibility for the conditions faced by black people—remember that Murray is writing in the mid-1960s—yet whites used the work of social science data to show that blacks were the abnormal group. Given hundreds of years of discrimination, blacks could never compare favorably to whites on, for example, rates of college graduation, yet the social scientists, dutifully following the logic of the dichotomy, compared blacks to whites and highlighted black failures.

Even "decent white people" played with a stacked deck. But Murray reserved a bit of extra outrage for the "naïve Negro spokesmen" who raised their voices in a "moral outcry." Black deficiencies proved the need for reform; compared to whites, blacks looked like losers, and their naive representatives rode high on the hot air of academic justifications.[46]

Murray did something radical. He compared white people to white people. Citing "the incredible provincialism of white social science technicians (and their Negro protégés)," he emphasized that the celebrated white norms of "material affluence and power" were "the very features of American life that the greatest artists and intellectuals (think of novelists like F. Scott Fitzgerald or Sinclair Lewis) have always found most highly questionable if not downright objectionable." Would black people be rewarded if they behaved like Babbitt or worshiped money like the characters in *The Great Gatsby*? Social scientists simply cited numbers and forgot that the winners in the money game often used the most despicable tactics to achieve success. Should blacks imitate that? Would that make them normal instead of deviant?

Murray also notes "the norms of citizenship which are based on the national ideals as established by the Declaration of Independence and the Constitution. The Constitution not only expresses principles of conduct that are valid for mankind as a whole; *it is also the ultimate official source for definitions of desirable and undesirable American behavior.*" Judged against their own standards, white people failed.

In 2003, the then eighty-seven-year-old Murray received a distinguished artist award from Tuskegee University. He deserved it. The problem is that forty years into the civil rights movement many black and white leaders have forgotten or ignored his admonitions. Using the false comparison of white norms and black deviations, "naive" black leaders transformed the notion of "victimhood from *a problem to be solved* into an *identity in itself.*"[47]

Whites Rule Black Minds

Bruce Jacobs and his cousin waited for the light to change at a San Francisco crosswalk. The white woman, in the car nearest the two black men, "nervously" eyed them and then "conspicuously leaned over and locked her door." Jacobs, "stung" by the woman's action, wanted to give his cousin an earful about white people. But his cousin stopped him in midsentence, saying, "Who cares? She's worried. I'm not."[48]

His cousin's remark prompted a flash of understanding: "My preoccupation with her perception of me," he later wrote—"my need to see how she saw me—was a surrender of the self." In short, the essential argument of many black critics of black culture is that most of its most renowned leaders abjectly surrender themselves to whites. Obsessed with three themes—victimization, separation, and anti-intellectualism—black leaders define themselves in opposition to whiteness, and, as they compete "for white approval or a white apology," they play the game on the master's terms.[49]

In this surrender of self, a victim requires a victimizer. When a black leader demonizes white people he or she keeps whites "at the center of the black agenda." If only because many whites now also see themselves as victims, stressing the injured party theme is far less effective than it used to be. Each half of the dichotomy screams at the other, locked in a four-hundred-year-old battle.

The deeper problem is that, however accurate the charge, making white people the victimizer gives white people the power to change black lives. The awful logic of the argument goes something like this. If white people produce the problems, only white people can produce the change. As a victim I am "largely powerless" to transform my own life, and, lacking power, failure is a self-fulfilling prophecy. Since whites will not change, how can I?[50]

The need for separatism again puts whites at the center of the black agenda. McWhorter tells a story of having lunch with a black friend. He was carrying a copy of *Jane Eyre,* and she noticed it. "Oh, I'd never read anything like that," she casually remarked. She preferred to read only books written by and about her own people. Once again, a very intelligent black person defines herself by her distance from anything white. Balzac, Zola, Camus, Nietzsche, Dickens, Dreiser, Fitzgerald: Albert Murray clearly read everybody, yet members of the present generation endlessly recreate a blacklist of only white books.

The final theme—anti-intellectualism—can be clearly traced in the response to the Cosby speech. Steven Armstrong, a teacher for twenty-five years, wrote, "During my career, I met many talented black men.

However, in the vast majority of the cases this talent did not match their performance. For example, I asked one young man, 'Why don't you do your homework?' His response, 'I can't let my friends see me with a book! They will say I'm selling out, trying to be white.'"[51]

The rejection of school and academic excellence is rooted, yet again, in a rejection of whites. Even at the finest universities, black students actually doubt that a youngster who excels is "authentically black." Black men or women admitted to Berkeley on the strength of their record are subject to suspicion from their peers that they were admitted via preferences because excelling at such a high level means having abandoned the black community. In essence, "black students are not *supposed to* be star students, because then they're not exactly black, are they?"[52]

A thorough, nationwide report by the Kaiser Family Foundation in June 2006 confirms many of the chat room conclusions previously discussed. Fully 73 percent of black men and 69 percent of black women thought that black men put too little emphasis on education and (with slightly less agreement) too much emphasis on sports and "maintaining a tough image." A full 59 percent of black men blamed themselves; they believe that racism still exists and have experienced discrimination in their lives but, overall, accept responsibility for the less than successful outcomes of their own lives.[53]

The validity of these self-criticisms is impossible to measure. We are discussing more than thirty-five million people, many of whom have not explicitly described their beliefs about victimization, separation, and education. But existing data do underline a persistent theme in contemporary black culture. In their capacity as negative role models, whites still tell many blacks how to think and act in a wide variety of both incidental and crucial (e.g., education) aspects of their lives. For example, over the three years it took to research this book, my own African American students have consistently affirmed that they experience pressure not to "act white," that is, to do well in college.

Fifty years after the civil rights and black power movements began, whites remain such powerful producers of the black agenda that Debra Dickerson compares them to Harry Houdini, who "once famously struggled for hours picking a jail cell lock, only to lean in exhaustion and have the door swing open. It had never been locked at all. All that confined him was in his own head. That's blackness."[54]

It is also whiteness. Neither group will think for itself until there is a liberating sense of surgical separation. So, to repeat, the dichotomy is not crucial in and of itself.

It is crucial because the words *white* and *black* store the cultural knowledge that tells us how to think and act in countless social situations.

It is crucial because one dehumanizing consequence of forty years of significant social change is that whites remain an all-powerful negative role model for millions of African Americans.

It is crucial because the dichotomy deliberately directs us to a cultural drama that seats whites down below, blacks in the balcony, and the rest of humanity in standing-room only. In the disunited states of America, we cannot tell Latinos, Asians, Indians, Arabs, Filipinos, and seven million mixed-race Americans to assimilate into a culture that fails to recognize their humanity in a positive sense.

Being outside the dichotomy *and* nonwhite is to wear a six-pointed star designed by Henry Grady. We reiterate "the fundamental assumptions of white supremacy" as we casually use the sinful word that closed America's doors to Jesus Christ in 1913.

After trying to assimilate into the dichotomy, fusions and none-of-the-above immigrants argue that we need to move on. As the rest of the book proves, the newcomers have already reconfigured American culture; and, in the case of Latinos, those who imagine a "presumed alliance" with blacks are in for a rude awakening. Axioms of contemporary Latino thought supposedly include these beliefs: "Since Latinos are not responsible for the Plight of African Americans," Latinos "come to the table with a clear conscience" and a clean slate. They want to transcend the future, not repeat it.[55]

Murals and Mexicans

———————— ❋ ————————

Chicanos in the United States

Balboa or Diego Rivera

When Mexican Americans enter the United States, they are asked to assimilate into a nation that harbors drastically different interpretations of their place in the history of the Americas. The clash is intense. It is the story of Vasco Nuñez Balboa versus Diego Rivera.

In 1915, the city fathers of San Diego wanted to put their town on the map. They decided to do so by imitating the "White City," the nickname given to the glistening exhibitions at Chicago's 1893 World's Fair. Since this was California, the planners of what came to be titled the Panama-California Exposition proudly favored a "Spanish colonial" style of architecture. Paying their way with gold extracted from Mexico and other Spanish colonies, soldiers of fortune who had succeeded in New Spain returned home. They built mansions but never acquired the social status they craved and expected. Disillusioned, they once again sailed to the New World, where they extracted further riches from the colonies and used them to design buildings based on Mexican imagination. One historian of San Diego's Balboa Park writes, "Many buildings in Mexico were done by men who had only a passing acquaintance with Spanish architecture and its ornate character. Thus the buildings showed a decided Indian influence."[1]

This was Spanish colonial architecture, a style that used Mexican carpenters and stonemasons to erect monuments ornamented with Spanish names and symbols. American architects created the Balboa Park exposition buildings but, following the colonial storyline, made Spain the center of Mexican and San Diego history. On the face of the California Building, they carved a bust of Philip III of Spain, a Spanish coat of arms, and a statue of Sebastián Vizzcaíno, the Spanish explorer who "rediscovered" San Diego Bay after his predecessors lost it. The rear wall of the building contained a bust of Carlos III of Spain, a Mexican coat of arms, and a statue of Juan Rodríguez Cabrillo, the explorer who first discovered (and then apparently lost) San Diego Bay.

Five years in the planning, the exposition's groundbreaking ceremonies (on July 19, 1911) were designed to attract national and international attention. "King Cabrillo" presided over a ten-part historical pageant. Part one of the pageant included a group of Aztec priests sacrificing Indians to the god of war. Balboa then saved the day by taking possession of the Pacific Ocean for the king of Spain, who "presided over the Fall of the Aztec Dynasties and the rise of Christian rule." Eventually, the pageant's promoters raised the American flag over Old Town San Diego, with a quick stop in Rome. "King Neptune presided at the wedding of the Atlantic and Pacific Oceans." Brothers under the skin, Columbus and Balboa discovered the New World, only to see it rediscovered and renamed the United States of America.

The exposition proved to be such a success that the California Building and other buildings remain to this day a central element of San Diego's Balboa Park. Even the greenhouses flourish as part of an outdoor museum that now also contains the Centro Cultura de La Raza. Prominent signs direct visitors to the Centro Building. But, once you arrive, it looks like a water tower. Actually, it *is* a water tower donated to La Raza as a sign of the Mexican influence in Southern California. You enter the metal monster expecting to find murals designed by local youth or at least large prints of the museum work of Rivera, Orozco, and Siqueiros. Instead, there is a large portrait of Marcus Garvey, the Jamaican leader of the back-to-Africa movement in the early twentieth century. Other portraits celebrate Malcolm X; Martin Luther King Jr.; and, with a wall of his own, Che Guevara. Even here the dominant colors are white and black. The Centro Building does offer a newspaper devoted to Native American issues but nothing as magnificent as Diego Rivera's rediscovery of Spanish, American, and Mexican history.

In 1929, Rivera began what is arguably the best-known mural in the Americas. Called "The History of Mexico," the mural is a spectacular portrait of Mexico that mocks U.S. perceptions of men like Columbus and Balboa. At Mexico's National Palace, the New World turns into what Chicanos now call Occupied America. "The History of Mexico" is the lasting alternative to the White City or Balboa Park because it proudly presents all Mexicans with an image of self that defies the white/black dichotomy. Mexicans must be none-of-the-above because the first Mexican was a combination, a fusion of fused ancestries.

To reach the mural, you need to cross the Zocalo (the main plaza) in Mexico City. The plaza is filled with every imaginable temptation— even shamans—but with luck and persistence, you can squeeze yourself into a group of uniformed Mexican students also getting their first glimpse of Diego Rivera's masterpiece. While the massive mural spans three walls, teachers trying to instill a sense of national identity focus on only three figures: the Spaniard Hernán Cortéz, the Indian Malinche, and their child, Martín. Cortéz is proud, rugged, and ruthless, while Malinche stares wistfully into space; she could be dreaming as she comforts the bronze-skinned boy fearfully burying himself in his mother's embrace.

The boy, Martín Cortéz de Malinche, is the first Mexican. Combination is his middle name, mixed with his proud and undeniable ancestry. For Mexican children the mural is a mirror: students see themselves on the wall as teachers use Rivera's colorful image to celebrate the ethnic fusions created by Spanish imperialism as the axis of Mexican national identity. From this perspective, Columbus and Balboa found not a new world but the ancient civilization of the Aztecs. On one wall, Rivera paints that ancient world, including its notorious human sacrifices. The sun shines a bold yellow at the center of the Aztec scene; despite the battles and poisonous serpents, the portrayal is a heartfelt homage to a world destroyed by the Spanish explorers and their Christian missionaries.

No Spaniard escapes blame in Rivera's rediscovery of Mexican history. Soldiers use cannons to destroy the Indians. Even as some priests are baptizing converts, other priests are torturing Indians for daring to worship their own gods. At the top of this center wall, Mexicans are saving Mexico. Heroes and villains of Mexican history appear side by side because, as Desmond Rochfort has written, "the ideological premise of the center wall is that Mexican national history arises out of the conquest."[2]

In 1929 that conquest focused on the Spanish; today it includes the American conquest of the Mexican Southwest. Two diametrically different versions of the past define the status of Mexicans living in the United States. In a world of white and black, Balboa (or Christopher Columbus) discovered the New World for a new race. In the world of Diego Rivera, Mexicans started as a fusion born from colliding civilizations. As the first member of La Raza, Martín Cortéz de Malinche was multicultural before the word even existed.

Mexicans make up 63 percent of the Hispanics in the United States. They have led the list of new immigrants to the United States for more than a decade, and one study estimates that Mexicans now represent the largest immigrant group in thirty of the fifty United States. California boasts more Spanish-language radio stations than all the nations of Central America combined; and in Texas gubernatorial candidates have suggested a televised debate in Spanish.[3] And why not? A visitor walking through San Antonio or Austin hears Spanish almost as often as English.

Mexicans aspire to mainstream status in America, and their fused nature should be an inspiration to anyone seeking to transcend the white/black dichotomy. They could help redefine American national identity. It is a gift if we are willing to begin with a message to the Reagan White House.

On June 25, 1985, Deputy Secretary of Agriculture John R. Norton III wrote a letter to Dr. Ralph Bledsoe, special assistant to the president for policy development. Norton's letter referred to a seasonal worker program that could finally eliminate the millions of Mexicans working illegally in the United States. The Reagan administration wanted to get rid of the Mexican problem that threatened to expose its tacit support of the illegal labor force and give the lie to its law-and-order ideology. Norton understood the president's position but suggested two insuperable obstacles. First, "we have had an implied national policy to encourage our citizens to rise above the necessity to perform agricultural harvest labor as a means of livelihood." Second, "our border states where the preponderance of our fresh fruits and vegetables are produced have depended on labor from south of the border since the very inception of this type of diversified agriculture." Americans expected fresh fruits and vegetables at the supermarket, and that meant that the White House needed to accept "*the total dependence of the (agricultural) industry on Mexican labor during approximately sixty years.*"[4]

As Richard Rodriguez puts it, Mexicans were here when here was there; and U.S. agricultural and business interests relied on Mexican labor in the development of California, Texas, New Mexico, Arizona, and Colorado, among other states. As Charles Teague told readers of the *Saturday Evening Post* on March 10, 1928, "most of the great development work of this area has been accomplished and is maintained by Mexican labor. The great industries of the Southwest—agricultural, horticultural, viticulture, mining, stock raising and so on—are to a very large extent dependent upon the Mexican labor . . . This region's railways were built and their roadways are maintained by Mexicans."[5]

America relied on Mexican labor, but, as Edwin Meese, then attorney general, told President Reagan in a spring 1981 memo, the dependence had extended to more and more industries. Although the persistent stereotype was that undocumented Mexicans worked almost exclusively in agriculture, the reality in 1981 was that, while agriculture did rely on Mexicans, other industries also found them indispensable. The attorney general stressed that "only 15–25% of illegal aliens are now in agriculture; most are in blue collar and service occupations." In hotels and restaurants, on construction sites, and in office clean-up crews, Mexicans were needed by the nation so much that "everyone agrees on increased border enforcement; but no one believes this will solve the problem."[6]

In 2007 America still needs Mexican (and other) immigrants as much as the immigrants need the work. But, instead of trying to face the truth, we seem determined to avoid it. As Congressman Ted Poe (R-Texas) stressed on November 16, 2005, "The Mexican American War started because Mexicans did not recognize the Texas-Mexico border at the time. They ignored the treaty that their dictator, Santa Anna signed, and they invaded the United States in 1846. Sound familiar? It seems to me that a second attempt at invasion and colonization has already begun. Is Mexico trying to retake the Southwest? . . . Only history will reveal the answers to that."[7]

Poe is right, but not in the way he intended. History—accurate history—is the only way to understand Mexican resistance to the white/black dichotomy and the melting pot metaphor. We can never appreciate this aversion unless we also appreciate how Mexican immigrants got to the United States and how they have been treated since their arrival. Mexican reactions to U.S. culture arise under particular economic and political conditions, in a culture that, even as it endlessly relies on Mexicans, simultaneously struggles to define the "racial" designation of the Mexican people.

The Lone Star State

In 1969 Senator Walter Mondale (D-Minnesota) drove to the Texas-Mexican border. As part of his research for congressional hearings, Mondale wanted a firsthand look at border crossings and at the mass of "commuters" who, instead of swimming, walked across an international border without ever presenting a passport. As Mondale watched the workers cross the bridge unhindered, he saw that many waved new crisp baptismal certificates. Curious, Mondale asked immigration officials about the use of documents that were obviously hot off the press. Certainly, no twenty-five-year-old man or woman owned a creaseless baptismal certificate, and, even if they did, what did it prove? That the day workers were Catholic?[8]

To Mondale's surprise—he remarked, "I had never heard of this until I went down to the border myself"—the baptismal certificates "proved" that the Mexicans were American citizens. Fake birth certificates were harder to get and cost more money to buy. Instead, workers went to the back door of a local church or some other location, got the baptismal certificate, and then raced across the border like a power walker. As Mondale explained to his colleagues, "they are coming through there so fast that if they bothered to check one out of every twenty of them, they would have had Mexicans backed up to Mexico City."

Immigration officials echoed the senator's concerns. They emphasized their enforcement efforts: "For the seventh consecutive year there was an increase in the number of claims to false citizenship encountered by the Border Patrol." The statistics might have made them look better, but since all concerned agreed that the baptismal certificates were new, and bogus proof of citizenship at that, why did officials allow the endless line of Mexicans to cross the border each day?

The charade continued because American employers dream the impossible dream: of employees who work for low wages, who labor under miserable conditions, and who conveniently disappear back into Mexico or at least to another part of Texas or the United States. In 1969 the baptismal certificates helped solve a short-term problem that never addressed a long-term need. As one grower told Congress in 1920, "the Mexican in Texas has been there from the time of the Republic and before we were there." Moreover, "our entire industry, beginning, whenever it commenced, back in 1836, is absolutely and unconditionally based upon Mexican labor."9

Taking pictures of remote crossings in Arizona, contemporary critics want us to focus on what Professor Otto Santa Ana, tongue in cheek, calls a brown tide rising. Chicanos might ask that we forget the tide and focus instead on the currents that made Mexicans such an important part of the American way of life.

In the late nineteenth century, land, water, and people became commodities throughout the Southwest and especially in Texas. The small Mexican elite still thought of land as "a family patrimony, as the basis for preserving a traditional way of life." Ranchers—Anglo or otherwise—saw land as raw material for the business of raising and selling cattle. Ranchers needed money to buy the land and more money to pay cowboys to enclose it with barbed wire. In Texas, Scottish bankers helped provide the capital, and Mexicans who failed to become "real" ranchers found themselves eliminated from the land as quickly as pesky prairie dogs. With the fences in places, Mexicans and Americans with cattle but no land discovered that their animals were suddenly deprived of access to water and food. They responded by cutting the fences; but over time traditional rights lost out to legal rights. This displacement of the Mexican landowners produced what David Montejano calls "devastating and irreversible effects"; only the lower classes remained because, except for a few exceptions, the Mexican elite never adapted to the idea of land as a commodity rather than as a sacred end in itself.[10]

As the nineteenth century ended, ranchers who successfully fenced out the competition suddenly discovered that they had competition of their own. With the growth of a railroad network and the evolution of a national market, wealthy capitalists with vision soon moved to turn cattle ranches into commercial farms. In Texas—and in California—crops like cotton and labor-intensive fruits and vegetables offered a new means to more money. Ranchers sold their land to developers who quickly faced an unforeseen problem. Farms needed farmers, and Texas lacked the right kind of people to farm the land.

In response, Texas developers borrowed a page from P. T. Barnum. Distributing thousands of brochures throughout the Midwest and the South, developers promised "an Eden like existence" to anyone interested in a farming paradise. Long before the invention of free trips to investigate a time-share in Hawaii, Texas developers used the first and third Tuesday of every month to underwrite "special excursion trains" that brought midwestern and southern farmers to southern Texas's "Magic Valley." The parched soil needed water, but for those with ambition and access to capital the lure of Eden proved to be irresistible. Montejano stresses that the resulting land rush was one of the most phenomenal land movements in the history of the United States. Commercial, labor-intensive farms multiplied as the nature of the population in Texas and other Southwest states changed dramatically.[11]

Emigrating from the South and Midwest, the newcomers arrived with a white and black worldview. Whites ate here; blacks ate there. These farmers knew what to do under the watchful eye of Jim Crow. Meanwhile, the Mexicans living in Texas, Arizona, New Mexico, and California presented a definitional problem to the new whites. One contemporary observer explained that "society in the Southwest cannot easily adapt itself to the handling of a second racial problem . . . for Mexican immigrants there is no congenial group to welcome them . . . they are not Negroes . . . they are not accepted as white men, and between the two, the white and the black, there seems to be no midway position."[12]

Writing for *Scribner's* magazine, John G. Bourke told a national audience that southern Texas was "the American Congo." Even in Laredo and Brownsville, people of fine breeding existed, but they "exerted about as much influence upon the indigenes as did the Saxon or Danish invaders upon the Celts of Ireland." In fact, the generous Texans who gave Mexicans the right to vote "cast the precious pearl of the ballot before swine." It was time to accept a simple fact: Mexicans "constitute a distinct class resisting all attempts at amalgamation."[13]

Some Mexicans managed to escape the Congo characterization. In California, a more expansive definition of *white* could include people who spent time in the sun because, as a way to compensate for brown skin, European ancestry raised a person's social standing. Even a drop of Spanish blood, "if it be only a quatroon or octaroon, is sufficient to raise them from the ranks of slaves, and entitle them to a suit of clothes, and to call themselves Espanoles, and to hold property if they can get any." In New Mexico, Mexicans in search of creating a midway position called themselves "Hispanos." Celebrating their glorious Spanish ancestry, Hispanos saw nothing wrong with the celebrations in the White City or Balboa Park. On the contrary, they accentuated their links to Spain and to the European roots that might give them social status in the American Southwest.[14]

In Texas whites gave Mexicans little room to maneuver. They decided who got what, and they decided to segregate the Mexicans as a means of resolving a now institutionalized contradiction of American life. As one fellow noted, *"irrigation means Mexicans."* One demanded the other, especially when it involved the "stoop and squat" labor that no white American wanted to do. So, here was the problem: how could the whites "absorb" immigrants they never wanted but always needed? Only 5 percent of the population of southern Texas in 1900, Mexicans increased in numbers as fast as the laws designed to keep them in their place, that is, working on the farms and picking crops—for as long as the farmers needed them.[15]

Ironically, this effort to prevent Mexican assimilation arose during the height of the national movement to Americanize immigrants capable of amalgamation. White Russians got into the melting pot, while Mexicans learned that their nonwhite status meant they were incapable of Americanization. They therefore learned to read forbidding signs denying them entry to everything from eateries to hotels. In 1902 Texas legislators passed the poll tax laws that removed the privilege so carelessly granted. In addition, the few Mexicans who got a chance to go to school found themselves in inferior, segregated facilities. Spanish was the one and only language of instruction there in a society demanding that Europeans learn English as the first step toward becoming full-fledged Americans.

Another irony is that the movement to restrict immigration of Asians and southern Europeans increased the need for Mexicans in the American Southwest and in other parts of the United States, for example, Michigan. With no hint of sarcasm, Congress in 1920 listened to farmers plead for Mexican labor and then titled the hearings "Temporary Admission of Illiterate Mexican Laborers." Six years later an Arizona farmer in search of seasonal workers reminded Congress that it paid for many of the large and small irrigation projects that created demand for Mexicans. Congress needed to reopen the gates because, as the farmer argued, "we feel, gentlemen, that there has been born in the West an infant Empire. We feel that you are its legitimate father, now what shall we do? Shall we let it grow up a dwarf, a hunchback, or shall we develop it to its full stature?"[16]

Congress answered by closing its eyes to two of the earliest controversies concerning Mexicans, the Immigration Service, and the Border Patrol. With Mexicans already accounting for 10 percent of *legal* migration to the United States, immigration officials allowed labor recruiters to place their offices in a prominent location: Recruiters stood right outside the buildings of the Immigration Service. No one policed them nor did anyone bother with illegal Mexicans at the end of a fiscal year.

Testifying in 1928, District Director of Immigration Grover Wilmuth explained that the Border Patrol paid the costs of transporting immigrants back to Mexico. When he ran out of funds toward the end of the year, Wilmuth told Congress he simply allowed his prisoners to "voluntarily return" to Mexico. Congressman Bird J. Vincent could not believe his ears. You mean you "turn him loose in the country?" When Wilmuth said "absolutely," the following exchange took place.

Congressman Vincent: The very fact that you had, say, a dozen Mexicans herded in some place and that you gave them a chance to go back to Mexico and they said they would not go, and then you very politely turned them loose, that would indicate to their mind that there was a screw loose somewhere, would it not?

Grover Wilmuth: Yes sir: that is a natural inference.[17]

The Road to Aztlán

In 1924, 87,648 Mexican immigrants legally entered the United States. The number arriving because of the "screw loose" program is unknown. In 1931, only 2,627 Mexican immigrants entered legally. The Depression crushed agriculture with such force that one estimate from California counted more than two workers for every available job. Somebody needed to go, so the U.S. Department of Labor assured the nation "that work would be provided for unemployed Americans by deportation of employed illegal aliens." In the decade 1930–39, Mexicans accounted for 1 percent of the U.S. population but 46.3 percent of all individuals deported. Estimates vary on the precise number of Mexican immigrants exiled, but an educated approximation is one million men, women, and children. Fully 60 percent of these exiles were U.S. citizens. It was a cruel, unprecedented expulsion of a people, leaving scars so deep that, even in 2006, many of those exiled refuse to talk about it.[18]

In 1942 the U.S. government reopened the Mexican-American border. Starved for labor because of the war effort, Washington looked south, with its new Bracero Program (*brazo* is Spanish for "arm"). Over time, U.S. officials made agricultural and other American employers more dependent on Mexican labor than ever before. It was an unintended transformation, whose ripple effects extend into the twenty-first century.

The Bracero Program was predicated on the notion that, with the Mexican government policing the process, laborers' rights would be protected. Meanwhile, farmers would get the cheap labor they wanted. The first line of the contract signed by laborers said this: "The worker will be employed exclusively in agricultural work."[19]

But what happened if the temporary laborer decided to leave the farm and seek work elsewhere? As a long-term job, stoop and squat labor only appealed to the most desperate; anyone with a chance to leave the farm for a better job elsewhere would probably do so. Especially if nonagricultural employers readily accepted the now illegal workers (e.g., in Chicago), the Bracero Program contained a built-in contradiction: temporary workers left the farms while agriculture's needs remained the same or even increased. Somebody still needed to pick the crops, or, as California agricultural commissioner B. A. Harrison told Congress, "I have lived in Imperial Valley for a good many years. I can say that historically the desert areas have depended entirely on the Mexicans to stand the intense heat in those areas." Unfortunately, people tired; they got too old to do stoop labor, and their children, seeing what happened to their parents, took jobs in the cities. The result was that "about every twenty years . . . we find it necessary to have a new blood transfusion, so to speak, to get a new supply of stoop labor."[20]

Between 1942 and the end of the Bracero Program in 1964, more than four million workers came to the United States as temporary laborers. By definition, the number of illegal immigrants remained hidden in the Texas, Arizona, New Mexico, and California underbrush. The one certainty is that the demand for labor proved to be insatiable. The archives at the Lyndon Baines Johnson Presidential Library in Austin contain a mountain of telegrams to then Senator Johnson. Year after year, one message after another, the pleas remained the same. Keep Washington off our backs and let us have the only workers who will do the work we need. As W. T. Millen, president of the Bailey County Farm Bureau, told Senator Johnson in 1958, "they [Mexicans] will do a type of work such as irrigating and hand labor that the American who is used to high wages will not do . . . so please see if something can be done to right this injustice being imposed on the farmer."[21]

Injustice is in the eye of the beholder. Farmers only thought of themselves, oblivious to charges of economic slavery and, just as important, the rigid segregation of Mexican students throughout the Southwest. Farmers only wanted another generation of stoop and squat labor. Conversely, after World War II, the roughly four million Mexicans living in the United States also sought social justice because they began to analyze seriously their children's prospects in a society that denied them even the tiny openings offered to African Americans. Institutions like Howard University or Tuskegee University allowed at least some African Americans to get a higher education.[22] In contrast, Mexicans encountered a world that offered no openings, only an educational system that systematically condemned their children to a future on the farm, in the mines, or in construction.

In 1946 people who identified as Mexican Americans tried to work within the system. In *Gonzalo Mendez v. Westminster,* a couple and four co-plaintiffs sued four California school districts for segregating their children. Orange County administrators had decided that, allegedly for the children's own good, English-speaking students should attend school in one building, while Spanish-speaking children should go to another. However, students took "no credible language test"; those who looked Anglo went to the school with markedly better facilities and supplies, while those who looked Mexican or had a "Spanish surname" went to the run-down building. In a society that supposedly welcomed the assimilation of its immigrants, the U.S. District Court for the Southern District of California found, in *Mendez v. Westminster,* that "the evidence clearly shows that the Spanish speaking children are clearly retarded in learning English by lack of exposure to its use because of segregation." In addition, "it was also established by the record that the methods of segregation prevalent in the defendant school districts foster antagonisms in the children and suggest inferiority among them where none exists."[23]

When the district court ordered the California school districts to desegregate, it listened with all the attention that farmers and other employers reserved for their workers. De facto, little changed after *Mendez*, as Mexicans in search of a different future argued about tactics and strategy. Throughout the forties and fifties the League of United Latin American Citizens (LULAC) often sought to dissociate itself from African Americans. It agreed that Mexicans suffered from learned prejudice and institutionalized discrimination, but, as a cure, "it promoted the image of Mexican Americans as a white ethnic group." In response, the critics who fathered the Chicano protest movements of the 1960s asked a simple question: Why would we want to assimilate into a society that refuses to teach our children the English language as it systematically prepares them for the low-wage, low-skill jobs that are the "destiny" of the inferior Mexican people?[24]

Asociación Nacional México-Americana (ANMA) offered an alternative. Founded in Denver in 1949, the Spanish-speaking organization represented Mexicans who worked in the mines, mills, and smelters of Arizona, California, Colorado, New Mexico, and Texas. ANMA cited the 1846 Treaty of Guadalupe Hidalgo as a prime example of how the United States made promises but never kept them. Seeking to end Anglos' systematic subjugation of Mexicans throughout the Southwest, ANMA endorsed a radical reaffirmation of traditional Mexican values and beliefs. If the American school and political system taught "inferiority," then Mexicans needed to find a sense of pride and dignity in their past and their culture. Instead of assimilating into white society, Mexicans needed to "never completely integrate themselves into all aspects of the national life of this country." Instead, by speaking Spanish and cultivating ethnic roots, ANMA sought a basis for political organization that felled two Anglos with one stone. Teach people to be proud and they walked with dignity as they now challenged and even defied the society that, since 1846, created "*el pueblo olvidado*" (the forgotten people).[25]

ANMA's message scared many Mexican and Anglo Americans in 1952. The FBI began to investigate the group and, alleging communist infiltration, called ANMA a security threat to the United States. The organization defended itself, but the battle quickly drained its scarce resources. ANMA was effectively defunct by 1954. LULAC and other white-leaning organizations carried the flag of Mexican rights for the next decade as the elimination of the Bracero Program left both countries—not to mention Mexicans and Mexican Americans— with another institutionalized problem.

Mexico now depended on American jobs as much as America depended on the cheap, exploitable Mexican labor. Remittances— money sent home by the workers—were a major source of support in maintaining the unemployed in Mexico. They were only able to stay home because others went north. If the demand for legal workers and the toleration of illegal workers ceased, the United States now faced the prospect of more rather than less migration because Mexicans and the relatives who could no longer depend on remittances would need to find jobs wherever they could.

Fear of a flood of new immigrants was one motive behind the decision by the governments of the United States and Mexico to join forces—in the early 1960s—by creating factories south of the Rio Grande. Mexico changed its laws to permit U.S. factories to establish themselves near the U.S. border and outsource to Mexico the assembly and other low-skilled jobs that saved money for U.S. corporations as they created jobs for the Mexicans, who, with work available, would presumably remain home. In practice, many of the jobs only went to young, tractable women, so the men still needed to find work north of the border. They easily did so because, despite predictions by Secretary of Labor Willard Wirtz, farmers refused to replace stoop and squat labor with the latest technology.

Mechanizing agriculture could replace the need for Mexican labor but only under certain conditions:

- *If* President Johnson and Congress stopped the creation of new provisos that allowed employers to escape responsibility for hiring illegal laborers.

- *If* Congress and the president policed the labor contractors who increasingly provided a legal shield for employers.

- *If* the Border Patrol actually enforced the laws—remember those birth certificates in 1969—against the entry of illegal workers.

When the president and Congress yet again caved into farm interests, the system fed on itself. Workers came, they eventually left the farms, and the demand to replenish the labor supply proved as forceful as the civil rights movement and its offspring, the National Farm Workers Association headed by César Chávez.

ANMA preached cultural solidarity in a decade dominated by politicians like Senator Joseph McCarthy. As the 1950s ended, new Mexican activists worked during one of American history's most inviting decades for radical social change. With different perspectives about the struggle for human and civil rights, Martin Luther King Jr. preached from a pulpit in Alabama while Malcolm X spoke from one in Harlem. On campuses students staged strikes challenging allegedly autocratic administrators, and, with the publication of *The Feminine Mystique,* Betty Friedan helped start the women's movement. Meanwhile, Rachel Carson published *Silent Spring,* the peace movement preached against the war, and in Washington Congress transformed the nation's immigration laws in 1965 because all men and women were created equal.

Even the language changed. Since *Negro* was allegedly a white word for African Americans, *black* suddenly became a positive rather than a negative social identity. Black was beautiful and so too the environment for minority groups seeking to assert their rights and their heritage.

In the Southwest, Mexicans rediscovered not Balboa's Pacific Ocean but their membership in "La Raza Cósmica" (the Cosmic Race). Mexicans became Chicanos, a group whose indigenous roots claimed to be older than the Native Americans.

Joaquín and La Virgen de Guadalupe

In March 1966, César Chávez led a march from Delano to Sacramento, California. He was accompanied by Emiliano Zapata and La Virgen de Guadalupe. In presenting a list of demands called "The Plan of Delano," Chávez openly "borrowed" from the revolutionary "Plan of Ayala" presented by Zapata in 1911. Equally important, when Chávez or one of his associates read (in Spanish and in English) the plan at each stop's evening rally, they proudly and intentionally reaffirmed a Mexican tradition. One commentator correctly noted, "few rhetorical documents have been more powerful for Mexican Americans."[26]

Chavez's other companion, the "dark faced" Virgen de Guadalupe, is the mother of all Mexicans. She appeared to an Indian named Juan Diego in 1531, speaking the commoner's language of Nahuatl and wearing blue-green robes, the color reserved for the Aztec deities who created and unified the universe. She also wore a maternity belt—the symbol of new expectations—and was surrounded by the golden rays that suggested the presence of the sun god, Quetzalcoatl. Cynics say that the Virgen is the sinful creation of a Catholic bishop seeking to convert the heathens. Whatever version one accepts, it was a stroke of religious genius for the Virgen to have given these instructions to Juan Diego: Build a shrine to me on the site brutally destroyed by the Spanish. Build my home on the one that formerly housed Tonanizin, the "gentle" Aztec goddess of earth and corn, whose Nahuatl name means "our mother."

Like Martín Cortéz de Malinche, the Virgen represents an incredible bridge between one world and another. After her appearance, all Mexicans suddenly had someone to listen to their prayers and help them through bad times. By T. R. Fehrenbach's estimate in *Fire and Blood,* in the first fifteen years after her appearance, nine million Amerindians happily accepted their baptism into the Catholic religion.[27]

Four hundred and thirty-five years later, César Chávez used the Virgen to preach pilgrimage, penance, and revolution. Mexican pilgrims marched on Sacramento and demanded, for the descendants of the dark-skinned Virgen, "justice, freedom and respect from a predominantly foreign cultural community in a land where he [the Mexican

American] was first. The revolutions of Mexico were primarily upris-
ings of the poor, fighting for bread and for dignity. The Mexican
American is also a child of the revolution."[28]

Chávez preached revolution, with an assurance that the Virgen
cleared his path. He seemed quite secure in his cultural beliefs, and
he certainly knew his place in the pilgrimage. He was a poor Mexican
American courageously and adamantly demanding bread and dignity
from a foreign cultural community.

In the decade of civil rights, many Mexican Americans wanted to
confront the establishment. But these younger activists wanted far
more than the rights of farmworkers. They argued that, however
important, focusing on farmworkers "reinforced" the stereotypes sug-
gesting that only one type of Mexican existed; and, in sharp contrast
to César Chávez's assured use of traditional Mexican religious beliefs
and symbols, many younger Mexican Americans felt lost in the foreign
cultural community. In a photo taken in 1970, Chávez sits at a table
surrounded by young people wearing brown berets, capes, and masks
that hide as much as they reveal. A huge portrait of the Virgen looks
on as the young people sport symbols derived from the Black Panthers
and Che Guevara. The generations joined in the struggle for justice,
but, for the younger people, a short poem called "Yo Soy Joaquín" (I
Am Joaquín) resonated with the force of a *new* cultural revelation.

Here is a portion of the poem:

I am Joaquín,
lost in a world of confusion,
caught up in the whirl of a
gringo society,
confused by the rules,
scorned by attitudes,
suppressed by manipulation,
and destroyed by modern society.
My fathers
have lost the economic battle
and won
the struggle of cultural survival.

And now!
I must choose
between
the paradox of
victory of the spirit,
despite physical hunger,
or
to exist in the grasp
of American social neurosis,
sterilization of the soul
and a full stomach.[29]

Written in Denver by Rodolfo "Corky" Gonzáles, the poem depicts the experiences of someone who fled the farms for the city. Gonzáles "was the product of an urban environment, a man who spoke to the young because he and they wanted to escape the stifling sense of shame that came with being Mexican American." In another line, the poem reads, "Inferiority is the new load . . . I look at myself and see part of me who rejects my father and my mother and dissolves into the melting pot to disappear in shame."

Written in 1967, the poem spread through the nation not by e-mail but my mimeographs. Copied on school, business, and (I would guess) church machines, the poem found a ready audience among young Mexican Americans who passionately wanted to create a future full of hope. Unfortunately, "I Am Joaquín" asked as many questions as it answered. Joaquín definitely knew what he opposed. Now came the hard part. What did he propose?

With questions literally on everyone's lips, another activist, Luis Valdez, provided a way to radically and imaginatively rethink the past. "Most of us know we are not European simply by looking in the mirror . . . the shape of the eyes, the curve of the nose, the color of skin, the texture of hair; these things belong to another time, another people."[30]

Who were these people? Valdez and his cocreators decided the solution was, as with the change from *Negro* to *black*, to turn a negative into a positive. During the Bracero Program, many Indians had apparently pronounced "Mexicanos" as "Mesheecanos." This was quickly turned into a derogatory term for Mexicans. As the slander had it, these people were so bad they did not even know how to pronounce properly their own name.

With Valdez as an advocate, *Chicano* became a positive word for a new ethnicity, invented in California yet having deep roots in the nonwhite origins of the Mexican American people. Murals appeared on every street corner and freeway pillar as Chicanos rediscovered Deigo Rivera and his mentor, José Vasconcelos. As Mexico's secretary of public education in the 1920s, Vasconcelos commissioned many of Deigo Rivera's early works. He wanted something the people could touch because he believed they represented La Raza Cósmica. Vasconcelos argued, "The days of the pure whites, the conquerors of today, are so numbered that it is as if they were already our predecessors." Whites destroy races; we assimilate them, and "this gives us new rights and expectations of a mission without an historical precedent."[31]

In one passage of his essay "La Raza Cósmica," Vasconcelos talks about America's prejudice toward the Japanese. "The white women of San Francisco actually refuse to dance with members of the Japanese Navy," even though they are as intelligent, refined, and handsome as anyone on earth is. Vasconcelos stresses that, while people are also aware of bloodlines in Latin America, that awareness is "infinitely less," and in the deep divide between north and south of the Rio Grande lies the future of humanity. The cosmic race is, for Vasconcelos, "the definitive race," the race "made with the genius and the blood of all peoples, and, therefore, more capable of true fraternity and a really universal vision."[32]

Embrace of La Raza Cósmica requires that Chicanos make a number of very important decisions. In Spanish the concept of *raza* is rooted in the notion of *mestizaje;* following writers like Cuba's José Marti, Vasconcelos uses the word to underline the ethnic combinations that make us (Latin Americans) different from them (Anglos or North Americans). *Raza* denotes ethnic mixtures that contrast sharply with the white and black world created in the United States. But, would the new race get a color? Or, radically breaking with the past, would the new race affirm ethnic fusions by stressing that physical differences—recall the handsome Japanese officers—are *only* wonderfully diverse manifestations of our underlying and indissoluble unity? From this perspective, *raza* would ignore the physical in favor of the beliefs, values, and practices that defined people by what united them, their membership in the only race that actually existed, the cosmic race.

An answer to these questions came in March 1969. "Yo Soy Joaquín" author "Corky" Gonzáles and his Denver associates hosted a weeklong conclave widely advertised as a "National Chicano Youth Liberation Conference." Worried about the assimilation of Mexican youth into the white world of the gringos, Gonzáles argued that *los vendidos* (the sellouts) would return to *la raza* if Chicanos offered them a meaningful analysis of their identity and future as a nation. "Nationalism exists but until now, it hasn't been formed into an image people can see. Until now it has been a dream . . . nationalism is the key to our people liberating themselves . . . we are an awakening people, and emerging nation, a new breed."[33]

The new group's declaration of independence was published at the end of the weeklong conclave. "El Plan Espiritual de Aztlan" (the Spiritual Plan of Atzlan) was a manifesto that discovered the original homeland of the Mexican, now Chicano, people. In Aztec history, Aztlan indicates the mythical place of the origin of the Aztec peoples. Scholars had long and unsuccessfully searched for the actual location of Atzlan, but now, here it was, incredibly, right before their eyes. In a bold and an imaginative display of cultural creativity—of Fernando Ortiz's transculturation—Chicanos claimed that Aztlan and the American Southwest were different names for the same thing. In this scenario, Chicanos came first, long before La Virgen de Guadalupe and the other symbols of Mexican culture. In fact, instead of the Chicanos being descended from the Aztecs, the Aztecs traced their roots to the Chicanos. Even before Native Americans, the new genealogy claimed, Chicanos peopled Aztlan or what soon became "occupied America."[34]

The plan also declared the independence of their mestizo nation. Following Vasconcelos, Chicanos celebrated their many ethnicities, but, following whites and blacks, they also asserted themselves as a

bronze people, with a bronze culture. To critics this looked like a contradiction. Races were by definition homogeneous groups of people.
How could Chicanos be mixed and pure at the same time? And,
equally important, why measure differences by skin color in the first
place? In announcing their revolution, Chicanos had chosen a criterion to define themselves—skin color—that affirmed the ideology of
the slave traders who replaced *Moor* with *black*. *Chicano* rejected *white*
as it simultaneously set the parameters of the Chicano response.
"According to Chicanos, and many Mexicans today, Mexicans were
racially brown by nature, and contrary beliefs, politics or attitudes
could render one inauthentic but not actually white." The tragedy for
many Mexicans in 1969 revolved around a simple fact: They thought
they were white, and false consciousness moved them to embrace a
society that would never accept them. Like the Syrian Hamas Shadid
in South Carolina, Mexicans were chasing after the impossible.[35]

Focusing on color also produced a negative impact on other
"people of color." In its strongest articulations, *Chicano* redefined
people by what already divided them in a poisonous fashion. Soon
after the plan's publication, attorney Oscar Zeta Acosta announced
that "the black man came here as a slave. He is not of this land. He is
so removed from his ancestry that he has nothing but the white society
to identify with. We have history. We have culture. We had a land."
Chicanos meant to get back what was theirs—the Southwest—but for
all the diversity of their ethnic roots, Acosta said that some counted
more than others did. "Of course there is Spanish and European
blood in us but we don't often talk about it because it is not something
we are proud of. For me, my native ancestry is crucial."[36]

Chicanos wanted to produce a sense of pride so they discarded the
roots they despised and emphasized the roots they relished. This
sleight of hand put symbols like La Virgen de Guadalupe into a secondary category because the link that really mattered derived from
the Chicano's indigenous roots. Acosta stressed that, in contrast to
blacks, "we do feel solidarity with the American Indians because we
are Indians . . . I look upon them as my blood brothers. It is the Indian
aspect of our ancestry that gives meaning to the term 'La Raza.'"[37]

A month after the publication of "the Spiritual Plan of Atzlan," students in Santa Barbara published another important manifesto. It created new and deep divisions within the Mexican American world when it stressed that "Chicanismo involves a crucial distinction in political consciousness between Mexican American [or Hispanic] and a Chicano mentality." By definition, Mexican Americans lacked self-respect and pride; by assimilating into white, gringo society they affirmed the cultures that enslaved them. In contrast, the Chicano identity emphasized a rebirth of the indigenous pride that moved people to become self-determining members of a vibrant community. With training and education, Mexican Americans must see the light; they "must be viewed as potential Chicanos." Meanwhile the best way to let them see the light was to again follow Vasconcelos: "At this moment we do not come to work for the university but to demand that the university work for our people."[38]

To foster the renaissance Chicanos created a nationwide organization that even today maintains active chapters in universities throughout the United States. The slogan of the Moviemiento Estudiantil Chicano de Aztlán (M.E.Ch.A.)—"for those in the race, everything, for those outside the race, nothing"—focused student organizers on two goals: work in the community to arouse and create Chicanos and work in the university to develop the Chicano studies programs that would liberate the Mexican elite, the few who did get a chance to go to college. "Our people must understand not only the strategic importance of the university . . . they must above all perceive the university as being our university."[39]

No one told the professors or the administrators. In a battle that is still raging, Chicanos wanted the university to develop the local communities, to make colleges relevant to the people. In response, professors talked about academic integrity and the search for knowledge. To this day, Chicano and other ethnic studies programs are often accorded less prestige than they deserve because they are viewed as intellectually lightweight. In academic eyes, the presumed link to community development is a stain that never disappears.

Ultimately, however, Chicanos have won battle on university campuses across the United States. Their professors taught their history, and, with the concerted push to use higher education as a crucial source of *raza* consciousness, movement leaders finished the essential design of what they wanted and how they got what they wanted.

Whatever its shortcomings, the Chicano movement did offer Mexicans an appealing alternative to the white/black dichotomy. Internal disputes soon weakened or destroyed specific movement organizations, but thirty-five years later, *Chicano* remains a significant identity for Mexican Americans throughout the United States. Equally important, movement organizers became professors. Especially west of the Mississippi, they established and institutionalized ethnic studies programs that only use this name: Chicano studies. Throughout California, New Mexico, and Texas, many universities may also have a program in Latin American or Caribbean studies, but, in addition, they normally have a separate program of Chicano studies. Since 1970, UCLA's program has proudly published a journal called *Aztlán*. Its spring 2004 issue featured a piece about "Corky" Gonzáles, among other articles, all in Spanish. Meanwhile, the Chicano studies program at the University of New Mexico offered courses in the spring of 2004 that focused on the "impact of Anglo American imperialism on the Mexicans of El Norte (the American Southwest)." And, in an introduction to Chicano studies, students needed to answer this question: "What does it mean to be the descendent of an Aztec princess and a Spanish conquistador?"

Chicanos answered the race question with "none of the above." They celebrated *mestizaje* and the existence of a presumably homogeneous group of brown, sometimes bronze people. That left the white/black dichotomy firmly intact. No one heeded Albert Murray. Whites and blacks talked by one another, he lamented, as Chicanos, defining themselves as nonwhites, reaffirmed, "in one key hyphenated and hyphenating word," all "the fundamental assumptions of white supremacy and segregation."[40]

Ronald Reagan, George Bush, and the Rule of Law

Chapter 8 contains an analysis of the contemporary illegal immigration debate. But that debate—and the accelerating anger of Americans and Mexicans—cannot be understood without first analyzing the actions of a well-intentioned president. In 2006 we are still feeling the consequences of the legislation initiated by the Reagan administration.

From 1965 to 1986, fully 23.4 million undocumented workers made a round trip to Mexico. Coupled with legal migration, the net number of new, permanent residents totaled roughly 5.7 million Mexican Americans. In terms of identity, many would become Chicanos; but, as they made that transition, President Ronald Reagan confronted this fact: More than 80 percent of the new Mexican workers lacked documents.[41] They flaunted the law, and that bothered the president. How could the United States claim to be a nation of laws, when employers and employees throughout the country flagrantly violated one law after another, one generation after another?

The president considered the usual options—a guest worker program, amnesty, more immigration slots. But guest workers needed to have a form of identification that would allow employers to check their status. When someone suggested a national ID card, the president himself spoke to the issue at a cabinet meeting. He argued that ID cards "smacked" of totalitarian states; America would never accept such a system so "we proposed instead a system whereby two or more standard IDs [e.g., birth certificate, driver's license, green card, or even social security card] could be used to insulate an employer against a charge of illegal employment."[42]

No one asked how the rule of law prevailed if you "insulated" employers from punishment when they knowingly broke the law. Employers and lobbyists had skillfully pressured Congress for a "get out of jail free" card. Meanwhile, the president and his staff encountered serious problems with legalization. First, the American people would not swallow three to six million illegal immigrants in one gulp. Second, if the president made it too easy for Mexicans to become legal, he would be rewarding those who broke the law to enter and work in America. Finally, and this was the real problem, by admitting so large a group instantly into the welfare system, not only would the nation incur massive new costs at a time of fiscal restraint, but, equally as important, the president did not want "to run the risk of corrupting people who have for the most part revealed a strong devotion to the work ethic."[43] America would be corrupting the Mexicans whose presence allegedly corrupted the country they had entered illegally. In the end, the White House negotiated and renegotiated with the appropriate House and Senate committees for more than four years.

The Reagan administration did its homework. It knew that undocumented migration meant more Mexicans or, even worse, more Chicanos; year after year, the White House seriously sought to change and enforce the laws. However, for White House staffers, lobbyists were lurking around every corner; the lobbyists were vigorously supported by senators and congressmen, who were themselves financially supported by the lobbyists and their American employers. In memo after memo, the White House tried to give immigration reform some semblance of sanity, but in 1986 the president surrendered. He supported a bill that mocked his intentions as it dramatically increased the number of legal and illegal Mexicans living in the United States of America.

Called the Immigration Reform and Control Act, the legislation offered amnesty to anyone able to prove continuous residence in America as of January 1, 1982. If someone lived in California or Texas before that date, he or she received legal status. That assured the rule of law except for what the White House called the "shadow effect." Staffers expected many more permanent residents than Congress promised because "more persons, including dependants may already be here." In addition, "many persons legalized may seek to *bring in* family members." They would use the family reunification preference provisions of the immigration laws so one person could actually mean three or four new immigrants. And, when those immigrants brought in their relatives, the ripple effects assuredly went into the twenty-first century. For those opposing Mexicans, the new law came with a high price tag, raised again because, in the shadows, the new immigrants showed a relatively high birthrate.[44]

The Reagan documents argue that final effect proved to be the most interesting of all: "many persons may *come* across the border illegally and claim eligibility as an individual or a dependent." When the news got out, people would rush across the border and buy licenses or other IDs that proved residence before January 1982. In a flash, the hot-off-the-press documents "dried them out" as efficiently as the tactics used during the Bracero Program or the baptismal certificates waved to border guards under the watchful eye of Senator Mondale in 1969.

With urban employers assured of workers, farmers deftly secured their interests by including "SAWS" in the new laws. This stood for "special agricultural workers" who had to prove that they labored in agriculture at least ninety days during 1984–86 or at least ninety days during the year ending May 1, 1986. Those who possessed or bought documents that proved agricultural employment could get permanent residence status within a short period. Staff memos indicate that this was a take-it-or-leave-it deal: the SAW "amendment is not considered negotiable in conference." SAWS obviously promised even more "shadow effects," and, as staffers noted, "it was an inequitable, ineffective and costly scheme to provide field harvest labor." Since SAWS need not work in agriculture "once admitted to the U.S.," the program arrived with a built-in need to "replenish" the SAW labor force, and, even more ominously, staffers doubted the estimate of one million SAWS—who became permanent residents—during 1987–91. If only because "aliens may be able to fraudulently claim eligibility for participation," the White House knew that the number of SAWS grew as quickly as the documents streaming out of copy or other machines throughout the Southwest.[45]

The bill did come with an employer verification provision. In capital letters, the White House learned that "EMPLOYERS WILL BE REQUIRED TO REQUEST AND VERIFY EMPLOYEE DOCUMENTS AND REQUIRE EMPLOYEES TO FILL OUT FORM REGARDING STATUS." In regular typescript, staffers said that an affirmative defense "was available to employers who keep records of documents checked to verify employment status."[46]

Once passed, the bill's dual legalization programs "ultimately provided residence documents" to more than 3 million people: 1.7 million legally authorized because they supposedly lived in the United States before 1982 and another 1.3 million of the SAWS who often did produce the fraudulent documents predicted by White House staffers. As Californians complained about the influx of new Mexican and other Latino immigrants, Los Angeles witnessed the legalization of some eight hundred thousand formerly undocumented workers. In six other metropolitan areas, the totals exceeded one hundred thousand permanent residents and the relatives who soon followed in their legalized wake.[47]

In surrendering to Congress, the lobbyists, and their employers, the Reagan administration championed the rule of law as it opened the door to a "Mexicanization" that soon overwhelmed many of the older ethnic enclaves in the Southwest. Chicanos met the "FOBs" (fresh over the border) who in some cases represented 40 percent of the local population.[48] In time, people started to identify themselves as "Chicana-Mexicana" or "Mexicana-Chicana."[49] The Chicano call to arms, "Occupied America," began to take on a very different meaning because the new legislation did nothing to stop what Attorney General William French Smith said was the "primary motivation" for Mexican and other immigrants: "Attractive employment opportunities in this country, particularly when compared to opportunities in the sending countries."[50]

Employers won the battle as the Reagan administration, in the name of law, embraced this irony: It legalized the illegal as it simultaneously allowed other illegals (the SAWS) to become fraudulently legal under the auspices of a bill dedicated to eliminating the illegal.

This history is important because, especially after 1986, many Americans continually complained about the millions of Mexicans invited to the United States by the employers who, with one hand, affirmatively defended their workers' right to work and, with the other hand, pulled the voting lever that eliminated many of the rights and benefits received by illegal workers and their children.

Americans looked for a scapegoat. They blamed Mexicans and other Latinos when, in reality, all they needed to do was check out the contractors who arrived to hire the illegal immigrants "shaping up" each morning at the nation's Home Depots. Or, even more obviously, they could inspect the status and ethnicity of the labor force that, on the Home and Garden Television network, does the stoop and squat labor required by programs like *Curb Appeal* and *Designer's Challenge.*

Mexifornia

In December 1997, the U.S. Government Accounting Office (GAO) reported that more than six hundred thousand undocumented workers were living and working in rural America. Farmers relied so heavily on this illegal labor force that they lived in perpetual fear: If anyone ever enforced America immigration laws, the nation's supermarkets' fruit and vegetable shelves would be empty. Luckily, farmers pleading for yet another version of yet another Bracero Program had no cause for concern. The Immigration and Naturalization Service (INS) only devoted 2 percent of its resources to work-site enforcement, largely in the nation's cities. Meanwhile, the Border Patrol spent billions of dollars trying to make a spectacular show of stopping the "brown tide rising." But, in reality, undocumented immigration increased from 3.9 million in 1992 to 5 million in 1996. Farmers—and meat packers and motel owners—did not need to worry. The undocumented labor pool was larger than ever, and the INS never meant to bother the farmers. "Conducting enforcement operations in agriculture is particularly resource intensive," the GAO explained. In addition, the INS lacked the will, and, given its deployments on the Rio Grande, it had exhausted the resources needed to enforce the laws no employer wanted the INS to enforce.[51]

A decade earlier, the Reagan administration tried to develop a sane response to legal and undocumented Mexican (and other Latino) migration. When it failed, Reagan or any of his successors could have told the truth about the century-long, total dependence of agricultural employers on Mexican stoop and squat labor. He could have explained that, as Mexicans (and other Latinos) moved to the cities, even more Americans relied on Mexican labor as, simultaneously, more farmers needed to replenish the labor force that just left for the city. Finally, he could have explained that, with two societies so dependent on one another, Mexicans sent home close to ten billion dollars a year in remittances. U.S. banks urgently wanted a piece of this action and had developed a system for loaning big money to Mexican banks, which used as collateral for their U.S. loans the remittances that Mexicans would send in the next year.

Instead of telling the truth, one administration after another boasts about the supposed success of border enforcement. Meanwhile, at the border, coyotes (smugglers) charge more than ever. But, as of 2006, financing now comes—quite often—from relatives *already* in the United States. What happens is that a U.S.-based relative finds a coyote, makes a down payment for the newcomer, and pays the remainder when the undocumented immigrant arrives in Chicago, Los Angeles, or Houston. In this manner, "delivery is guaranteed, safety is increased, and migrants and their families achieve some protection against fraud." All the while, one White House after another fails to advertise a simple fact: that coyote money earned in the United States "represents yet another instance of social capital translating directly into U.S. access to build self perpetuating momentum into the migratory process."[52]

The fear of border enforcement, whether real or imagined, does have an effect: many undocumented Mexicans (and other Latinos) simply stay in the United States rather than risk capture. And, to obtain full civil and other rights, many recent immigrants decide to naturalize. Mexico countered that trend with a dual citizenship program, and, as a result, the United States now has more Mexicans than ever, allowing many of those Mexicans to maintain cultural ties to both nations.

In *Mexifornia: A State of Becoming* (published in 2003) Victor Davis Hanson stresses that many of California's most vocal critics of Mexican (and other Latino) immigration lack a "consistent ideology"; however, they are "sometimes *stunningly hypocritical* in simultaneously hiring illegal aliens and advocating immigration reform" (emphasis added). On the street, Americans want the piñata that only they get to punch. Meanwhile, at the White House, our close analysis of policy-making under Ronald Reagan underlines that the truth makes way for absurd backstage deals celebrating law enforcement rooted in fraudulent documents. Consequently, many uninformed—and well-informed—Americans blame the victim with such ferocity that Congress and the states pass laws that harass and punish the undocumented labor continually sought by all American employers. Mexicans (and other Latinos) become the nation's internal enemy of choice as too few people analyze an indisputable fact: More Mexicans now live in the United States than ever before. Seal the border tomorrow and more than twenty-five million men, women, and children remain an integral, imaginative part of American life.

Mexicans are not going home. They are home; and their home is our home.

For his part, Hanson worries about Mexifornia. He agrees that Americans exploit Mexicans, yet he wants Mexicans to assimilate into the American way of life. New immigrants represent 40 percent of California's total Mexican population, and, with programs like Chicano studies and dual citizenship, they can sustain easily their old culture in the new one. California turns into a cultural extension of Mexico as Hanson laments "the destruction of the old assimilationist model that integrated my boyhood Mexican friends into an American outlook and expectation." As he remembers the Bracero era," a sense of humility and balance achieved through comparison with contemporary societies elsewhere, and confidence in our values, measured against a recognition of innate human weakness, framed all such debates about the American experience."[53]

Robert Nisbet wrote that nostalgia functions as the rust of memory. With the best of intentions, Hanson romanticizes the past as ably as a Norman Rockwell illustration; he also stunningly forgets a past that included economic slavery and segregated Spanish-by-design schools.

We cannot go back. In fact, we were never "there" in the first place. As the Bracero Program made clear, Americans never wanted Mexicans to assimilate. Those Mexicans who tried to do so often failed or, even worse, acted like whites by distancing themselves from blacks. We need to "right" history so that we can have a national debate about immigration rooted in fact. Instead of trying to make Mexicans like us, we should examine how they see themselves and then ask what their assessments portend for the United States of America.[54]

The Pew Foundation's 2002 National Survey of Latinos reported that, on the issue of racial identity, "Latinos clearly indicate that they do not see themselves fitting into the five racial categories used by the U.S. Census Bureau and widely utilized elsewhere." Latinos are *not* White, Black, Asian, American Indian, or Native Hawaiian and Other Pacific Islander. Instead, "Latinos were virtually alone in breaking away from the standard racial categories. In Census 2000, Latinos made up 97 percent of the respondents picking the 'Some Other Race' category."[55]

Like the seven million mixed-race Americans (see chap. 7), Latinos reluctantly use the ugly and absurd language of "race" to describe themselves as "some other race." They become members of a Latino or Hispanic ethnic group, loosely define that made-in-America label as a race, and then emphatically refuse to pass as whites, even if they can do so. The Pew Foundation report indicates that only Cubans (55 percent) offer a majority that sees itself as white. Meanwhile, whether young or old, members of the other Latino groups offer little support for the white identity. Among "all central Americans" only 14 percent accept the white label; the figure for Puerto Ricans is 19 percent, for Dominicans it is 12 percent, and for Mexicans it is 17 percent.

Hanson is correct. Mexicans in particular and Latinos in general do not assimilate into white, American society. However, if they did, would that be a success story? Assuming that white Latinos treat blacks like white Anglos, a successful assimilation sanctions the racial and ethnic status quo. Assimilation could even mean that white Latinos treat Asians, Arabs, and Indians as "nonwhites." Perversely, white Latinos could become the victimizers of America's "people of color."

Assimilation is another dead end. It sanctions white supremacy as it neglects transculturation, the reconfiguration of American society spearheaded by Mexicans throughout the Southwest. In *Brown: The Last Discovery of America,* Richard Rodriguez even offers an ideology that moves beyond Chicano. Playing with words, Rodriguez says, "I extol impurity." He writes about race in America in hopes of undermining the notion of race in America.

Rodriguez says that Latinos occupy the passing lane in American demographics because they recognize an obvious fact: Like Cortéz and Malinche, people make love with one another. In 1500 and in 2006, men and women produce children who are ethnic fusions. Indeed, for any Mexican with two eyes, we are all ethnic fusions. "By contrast, white and black discussions of race in America are Victorian; they leave out the obvious part." Forgetting who made love with whom, whites create and blacks sanction pure categories. They both argue that, when Asians and Mexicans make love, they create mixed-race-children. Finally, after denigrating the human norm of ethnic fusions, whites and blacks retreat to their two, and only two, thoroughly sanitized ivory towers.[56]

Rodriguez makes a simple request. Destroy the towers, intermingle, and bless the children who, instead of mixtures, are a continuous and imaginative reconfiguration of the only race that exists, the wonderfully "impure" human race.

While Rodriguez intentionally reconfigures beliefs and values, his Mexican contemporaries reconfigure cities and the spaces within them. Almost unnoticed in the criticism of Mexicans is the army of "anonymous heroes" who resurrected dead neighborhoods throughout Los Angeles. After the Watts riots in 1965, Mexicans (and other Latinos) transformed many of the worst census tracts. Mike Davis notes that tired, sad little homes saw themselves resurrected. People even used tropical colors, so, instead of paying big money for a trip to the Caribbean or Acapulco, tourists could drive through the streets of Florence-Firestone and get a glimpse of the browns, oranges, and aquamarines that vividly bring life to a formerly dead urban landscape.[57]

This is transculturation at its best. Unfortunately, instead of applauding these efforts, traditional authorities often impede them. Urban planners want white houses with white picket fences. They can ingest Mexican food but not Mexican and Caribbean ideas about the use of public space. For example, one of the most wonderful aspects of cities and towns throughout Mexico, Latin America, and the Caribbean is their public plazas. In Los Angeles, a firm called Barrio Planners broadcast a simple slogan: "Let a hundred placitas" bloom." Let the people create public plazas in the middle of one of the world's most congested cities and let's see if Mexicans (and other Latinos) can create beauty and a sense of hospitality out of nothing.

It is already happening, even in underground passages. Walk through the tunnel that leads from old-town Sacramento to the modern section, and you can admire an exquisite Mexican mural. The colors light up a dark that proves that, ultimately, it is a matter of our disposition toward the cultural differences that exist and will continue to exist. We can think of the differences as an incredible banquet of cultures. We happily step up to the table and taste and savor whatever we wish. Or, we can argue that Mexican murals are good enough for the best museums in the world but not good enough for the public spaces of California and the rest of the American Southwest.

The choice is ours, in a society where Chicanos live side by side with Mexicans and Mexican Americans. There is general agreement about race and the color white, but after that the differences among Mexicans (and other Latinos) begin to materialize. Questions of class, education, village, generation, and location in the United States also influence a person's definition of the meaning of Mexican in the United States. We can still create a nationwide sense of community, especially if we use one of the strongest values of Mexican culture, the love of family. We could build on that love by following the Mexicans, who, with Richard Rodriguez, want to recognize "impurity" for what it actually is: a means of welcoming everybody into a great family of civilized human beings.

Four

Asian Americans

———— ✺ ————

Non-European and Nonwhite

Pure Patriots, Perpetual Paradoxes

The luncheon tables were adorned with purple paper stars. At scores of circular tables, each setting included a red, white, or blue napkin, standing at attention at the right side of the plate. The purple stars on the bread plate shined because Hawaiian elementary students had generously decorated each one with bright sparkles, gold stars, and a different, child-scripted comment. Mine said, "God bless America," a fitting way to open a veterans luncheon sponsored by the Japanese American Citizens League (JACL).

The league celebrated its seventy-fifth anniversary in August 2004, and the luncheon offered everyone a perfect opportunity to say thank-you to the "Go for Broke" regiment, a group of Japanese American veterans who had participated in some of the great ground battles of World War II. In one legendary assault, the regiment saved 211 Texans caught behind German lines in the Vosges Mountains. After three days of fighting, with little progress, the Go for Brokers decided to shoot the works. The segregated unit of Japanese American soldiers weathered ferocious, face-to-face combat, suffering more than 800 casualties. As the Defense Department later noted, "For its size and time in combat, less than two years, the 442nd regiment is the most decorated unit in U.S. military history." Its men received no less than eighteen thousand individual awards.[1]

At the luncheon's head table, nine of the Go for Broke veterans—many in their eighties—wore loose-fitting white shirts and button-covered caps from their organization. The other invited guests included Filipino veterans; a member of the Tuskegee Airmen; a group from the Navajo Code Breakers; and, finally, a group of women veterans who had served as Air Force service pilots. The JACL wanted to celebrate, prominently and publicly, the efforts of soldiers who still wore the psychological scars of prejudice and segregation. The Go for Broke veterans recalled storming into Dachau with the very first American contingent. Japanese Americans happily freed the Jewish prisoners waiting to die. However, because the United States was using barbed wire and armed guards to hold more than 110,000 Japanese Americans in relocation camps back home, the military's public relations experts erased the role of Japanese American soldiers. Instead of missing in action, the Go for Broke regiment found itself missing in history.[2]

No one tried to hide these scars at the weeklong convention, JACL national director John Tateishi stressed that "what defines the organization is memory," the memory of prejudice, segregation, relocation camps, and the uncommon valor of men who proudly fought for America even though their parents could never become U.S. citizens.

Yet, despite these ugly memories, the event betrayed no hint of bitterness. The moderator asked that we stand for the march of the flags from the Punahou School Junior ROTC. I thought he meant American flags; instead the young cadets marched in with the flags of the fifty states. Delaware, Pennsylvania, New Jersey, Georgia, and Connecticut: the flags arrived in the order of their state's admission to the Union. With obvious reverence, the youngsters set their banners on the stage until sustained applause greeted Hawaii.

Each of the veterans at the Go for Broke table stood at attention, saluting the flag with pride and passion. Many of the veterans and the audience of roughly five hundred people placed hands over their chests and sang, often with eyes closed, the national anthem. To an outsider, it looked like a Fourth of July celebration sponsored by the Daughters of the American Revolution.

After lunch, Hawaii's senior senator, Daniel Inouye, finally took the stage. The buzz at lunch centered on what he would say and how he would manage emotionally a luncheon that meant as much to him as it did to the nine men at the Go for Broke head table.

Senator Inouye was just about to celebrate his eightieth birthday. He walked slowly, weighed down by age and a chest full of military decorations, including the Congressional Medal of Honor. Inouye had enlisted when he was nineteen and lost an arm in combat. With tears in his eyes, Inouye told the story of returning home to California to see his parents. After the war, he wanted to look his best, so he went for a haircut. When he tried to sit down in the chair, the barber abruptly told the soldier without an arm: "We don't cut Jap hair."

This story was old news. The day before, veteran Mas Hashimoto told us he never gets into a barber's chair without thinking of Senator Inouye. One hateful incident can sear with the impact of a branding iron. It is a memory that never fades. Yet the JACL and its members transcend the obvious pain.

Senator Inouye accentuated the positive. "All men are created equal," he reminded the crowd. If we embraced the human revolution proposed by Jefferson and his colleagues, we would understand America's importance in the world, which moved young men to "shoot the works" for God and country.

In Hawaii, pure patriots celebrated the country they love and the political principles that govern their lives. And yet, after a century of complete assimilation, Japanese Americans are still treated like outsiders. Conversations with a wide cross-section of the JACL membership revealed that they often had to endure questions like, "Your English is so good, what nationality are you?"[3]

Why were so many Americans surprised that Hiro Nishikawa, Mas Hashimoto, or John Tateishi speak perfect English? Through the schedule of JACL workshops and luncheons, the strongest accent I heard was my own, from Brooklyn. Everybody spoke effortless English, and, when an Arab speaker used Japanese during a presentation, he joked that no one understood what he had just said. These all-Americans generally speak only one language: it is English. And they artfully use it to underline their terrible predicament. In everyday interactions, Asian faces often make other Americans act like customs officers in an airport. It is as if they are being asked, "Your passport please. Tourism or business? And how long will you be staying in the United States?"

Japanese Americans—like millions of Chinese, Korean, Vietnamese, or Cambodian Americans—are perpetual foreigners, because American culture still teaches its children to underline race rather than character, to see an allegedly "exotic" face rather than another human being. During a workshop, Tateishi pointed out that when ice skater Sarah Hughes defeated Michelle Kwan in the Olympics, the headlines in some U.S. newspapers read: "American Beats Kwan in the Olympics." The born-in-California Chinese woman suddenly lost her citizenship in another everyday manifestation of making Asians America's perpetual foreigners.

As one reaction to their treatment, Asians have begun to regard themselves as people of color because rejection by the mainstream has fostered their identification with other minorities. In interviews and conversations during the conference, I asked if this was not a self-defeating tactic. To embrace the identity "person of color" is to accept white as the hidden dictator of racial standards, and, just as ominously, our society poisonously divides itself into us versus them, the victims versus the victimizers.

I consistently got the same response: What is the alternative? Where is the language and set of attached beliefs that will finally allow fourth- and fifth-generation Japanese to be 100 percent Americans? To many members of the JACL, talk of a cultural revolution seemed like dreaming, while, in the real world, Japanese Americans were still regarded as citizens with a foreign passport. In response, they embraced the identity "people of color" and stood up for anyone who reminded them of themselves.

In a forum entitled "Issues Facing the JACL," speakers noted that, after years of struggle, the JACL finally received a prominent, public apology for the internment of Japanese Americans during World War

II. They even received a small amount in reparations; but what came next? How was the Japanese experience relevant in the twenty-first century?

The answer was 9/11. The day after the hideous attacks on the World Trade Center towers, the JACL formally offered its assistance to Arab Americans throughout the United States. Arguing that "We know what it feels like to be the object of hatred," the JACL extended the open hand of solidarity to all Arab Americans in the event that, once again, an entire ethnic group should become a candidate for abuse or incarceration. Ironically, just days before the JACL conference began, Michelle Malkin published *In Defense of Internment,* a forceful justification for the incarceration of 112,000 Japanese Americans in World War II. Malkin posited Japanese internment as a template for what a nation needs to do when, as on 9/11, it is under assault.

With incarceration even a remote possibility panelists stressed a painful point: "Our genealogy should scream, 'pay attention'." Accept "the discomfort of witness" and assist Arab Americans by endorsing the values and beliefs celebrated at the veterans luncheon. One after another, panelists told the audience that the U.S. Constitution is a wonderful blueprint for political behavior because it guarantees the civil rights of all its citizens. They wanted to make sure that all Americans get and retain those rights and offer special support to Arab Americans because no one should repeat their history in U.S. history.

The JACL stood behind Arab Americans. When it was time to say good-bye, the organization spotlighted them at the "Sayonara Banquet": the meals were blessed by an Arab cleric, in English, Arabic, and Japanese; and the JACL proudly presented its Edison Uno Civil Rights Award to Ismael Ahmed. The Brooklyn-born cleric heads an ethnic organization devoted to "combating intolerance toward Arab Americans throughout the United States."

As I left the banquet, I recalled Samuel Huntington's *Who Are We: The Challenges to America's National Identity.* To Huntington, America's significance as a civilization revolves around the "American Creed" and "Anglo-Protestant culture." Lose either one and you sacrifice the values and beliefs that make the United States a role model for the entire world.

It is an interesting argument, especially for Japanese Americans, who after a spectacularly successful assimilation endorsed the American political creed with unrivaled passion and commitment. Yet Anglo Protestant culture created the racial prejudices that exclude Japanese Americans—and all Asian Americans—from full acceptance into American society. A white/black world leaves no room for Asians. Too many still recall the words of Congressman John Miller (D-Washington) in 1923. In justifying the exclusion of all Asians from American life, Miller said, "a Japanese frequently wants to marry a white woman . . . and 'a half caste' is a failure in most cases . . . the half-caste Indian is a failure; the half-caste black man is very likely to be a failure; but the half-caste oriental is worse. He seems in the majority of cases to inherit the vices of both races and the virtues of neither. It makes, as a general rule, a bad product."[4]

Miller not only wore his prejudices on his sleeve but forgot why Japanese men often married white women. Since the United States forbade the immigration of Japanese women, white women were one of the few available marriage candidates. This history is a terrible legacy of mainstream Anglo Protestant culture, and the legacy lingers every time someone asks an Asian why she or he speaks good English.

Here are just a few of the peculiar paradoxes confronted by Asian Americans:

- Stalwarts like Samuel Huntington want Asians to embrace an Anglo Protestant culture that, into the twenty-first century, often refuses to embrace them.
- Asian Americans perceive the profound inadequacy of the white/black dichotomy but, lacking any alternatives, often identify as people of color. They define themselves as victims of a nation for which their family and friends fought and died.
- Asians marry outside their ethnic group with increasing frequency. In 1923 Congressman Miller called the children of these unions "half-breeds," the "bad product" of a match made in the streets. We still call them halves (or hapas), and the absence of progress is as obvious as the children's and our confusion.

Because Asians confront these all-American paradoxes on an every-day basis, many seek to transcend the categories imposed by Anglo Protestant culture. They struggle to liberate themselves from a dichotomy that relegates them to the nonwhite margins, as it simultaneously reaffirms white superiority. In plain, JACL English, millions of America's most patriotic citizens are asking the rest of us to rethink the meaning of Asia and something called Asian Americans.

Asia as a European Fiction

Consider two examples.

On the west side of Amsterdam's seventeenth-century Royal Palace, Atlas carries a huge globe; his bulging muscles work to hold, literally, the world in his hands. Just below Atlas's statue, the city maiden of Amsterdam relaxes. Wearing a crown and a smile, she lounges on her throne, arms graciously open to the four continents of the world. From either side of her throne, masters and slaves rush in, offering everything from elephant tusks to gold; the world exists to satisfy the maiden's whims, needs, and fancies.

On the frontispiece of an eighteenth-century English book, the city maiden of London lounges on her throne, a small globe at her side. The globe is surrounded by gross caricatures of Africans, Americans, and Asians; the page caption reads in part, "She rules Asia's fertile Shores, Wears her brightest Gems, and gains her richest Store." An Asian slave is poised by her side with a fan and a wooden umbrella. It looks exactly like the miniature umbrellas served with drinks in thousands of America's Chinese restaurants.[5]

These examples demonstrate ethnocentrism at its worst. Europe is the world's axis; indeed, in its contemporary meaning the word *Asia* did not even exist until Europeans decided that, as the most civilized people on earth, they deserved to rule the world. As one scholar stresses, "there is no equivalent word in any Asian language nor such a concept in the domain of geographical knowledge, though expressions such as the 'Sea of China' or the 'Sea of Hind' held certain analogous meaning in Arabic and some of the Indian languages."[6]

Asia is a European invention. It may trace its earliest origins to the

Assyrian *asu,* meaning "east," or it could have had its deepest roots in local names that, over time, grew to encompass a group of incredibly diverse cultures and geographical regions. Whatever the case, the word very effectively separates us from them, Europe and the land mass to *our* east. As David Theo Goldberg stressed in 2006, "the long historical presumption of Europe" is that it "assumes whiteness and Christianity"; everyone else "is not of Europe, not European, doesn't (properly or fully) ever belong."[7]

The Asia concept homogenizes cultures as different as China and India, Korea and Afghanistan, Iran and Japan; the word deliberately ignores reality because its only aim is to create a series of exclusions. First is Europe and then everything that is "not Europe." You begin with a positive, and, as if using a racial hierarchy, you descend the continents that, as inferiors, rush into the embrace of the city maiden of Amsterdam.[8]

Asia only exists in relation to Europe, so adopt the terminology and you willingly or unwillingly adopt the firmly attached prejudices: Europe is superior. And Asians are yellow, exotic, mysterious, inscrutable, underdeveloped, docile pagans who, for much of U.S. history, only existed in the imagination of European writers and the occasional traveler. Iris Chang writes that, as late as 1848, less than fifty Chinese people lived in the continental United States. Small numbers of Japanese university students first arrived in 1868, followed by laborers who initially flocked to the sugar plantations of a remote island called Hawaii. Recruited by labor "body shops," Koreans and Filipinos trailed the other ethnic groups as agricultural interests sought, as with Mexicans today, a cheap and expendable labor force.[9]

Well into the late nineteenth century, actual experiences with Chinese or other "far east Asian" cultures were in very short supply; so, before and after the American Revolution, even independent Yankees rooted their thinking in European models. Henry David Thoreau advised his fellow citizens, in 1849, to "behold the difference between the Oriental and the Occidental; the former has nothing to do in this world; the latter is full of activity. The one looks in the sun until his eyes are put out; the others follow him prone in his westward course."[10]

Over time, New England's inhabitants laid a fresh layer of their own conceits over the European foundations they had inherited. America may have lacked the maidens of London and Amsterdam, but it did have a "city on a hill." Think of Woodrow Wilson and his unquestioned, fundamental axiom, "What America touches she makes holy." It is a twentieth-century example of an eighteenth-century proclamation. America was the redeemer nation; "and American 'exceptionalism' began in the conviction that God created only one truly free and democratic nation on earth and that it was in the best interests of all other nations to study America and learn from her."[11]

Here is an important insight, credited to Samuel Huntington. America is and is not a nation of immigrants. The first immigrants *settled* the United States. Over two hundred years, they established a set of beliefs and practices, and when other immigrants arrived after the American Revolution they did or did not fit into the cultural rules and recipes created by those who, after they killed many of the continent's first inhabitants, then settled the New World.[12]

From Massachusetts to Georgia, Anglo Protestant culture adopted Europe's attitude toward the place called Asia and added to it the notion that only free white people could be citizens of the United States. When large numbers of Chinese and Japanese immigrants came to the U.S. mainland in the middle and late nineteenth century, they entered a nation that, by definition, saw them as non-European foreigners. They were peculiar, backward, and exotic. But, at least initially, no one knew if they were white or capable of assimilation into the New World created by the first settlers.

In the South, the few Chinese who crossed the continent found themselves in the same predicament faced by the JACL veterans fifty years later. Given the scarcity of Chinese women, Chinese men who wanted to establish families in the New World often married white women. In the South at least, those marriages generally escaped the opprobrium reserved for marriages between whites and blacks. After all, many Chinese sported lighter skin than whites. It took time to classify these foreigners, and early Chinese immigrants sneaked through the cracks. They were almost Americans because they were almost white.

Congress finally resolved the ambiguity in 1869, when Senator

Charles Sumner of Massachusetts asked his Senate colleagues to stop using color as a basis for a person's chance to vote or to hold office. Sumner's colleagues leaped into action but not as Sumner had intended. Senator James R. Doolittle of Wisconsin summed up the opposition: let Sumner continue with his "sledge hammer blows against the terrible word white" and he would immediately jump from voting rights to citizenship. When Sumner replied that he had just such a bill locked in a Senate committee, Doolittle and his colleagues first paused for laughter and then moved into action.[13]

Senator John Conness of California said that, if courts applied the citizenship laws in an even-handed fashion, Sumner's ideal meant the possible inclusion of Chinese citizens, admitted because unscrupulous politicians wanted to get votes by any means possible. However, Conness and all Americans "acquainted with the Chinese character and population knew that not one in ten thousand of them has any capacity whatever for American citizenship." So, he continued, "I wish to continue the word 'white' in the naturalization laws because it excludes no one that may not properly be excluded unless perchance a man in ten thousand of Chinese origin."

Senator Oliver P. Morton of Indiana agreed. The Chinese "belonged to another civilization, one that can never unite or assimilate with ours. They can never become Americans in heart and feelings. They can never fuse with us. They have a civilization that holds them from us and will do so as long as we shall live; and I doubt whether their children born in this country can or will assimilate with our civilization."

The senator also worried about justice. For example, from 1852 to 1870 the "foreign miner's tax" collected from primarily Chinese miners totaled five million dollars; that sum equaled 25 to 50 percent of California's state revenues during the eighteen-year period.[14] Senator Morton agreed that "in California and everywhere on the Pacific Coast" Americans treated the Chinese "most cruelly"; they have "suffered cruelties and indignities and outrages that, as we are informed, would shock humanity itself." So what would happen if the Chinese increased in numbers; quickly "outnumbered the white people on that coast"; and, with no exclusion clause in place, decided to become

Americans citizens? Eventually they might seek redress of their grievances. Senator Morton said, "Who could blame them?" However, the
Senate still needed to exclude the Chinese because the United States
needed to protect against the "catastrophe" of population growth coupled with a demand for equal rights and opportunities. Remember,
"They can never mingle with us. They can never be a part of the American people. They will have a civilization that will stand like a wall of
iron over them and us, between their children and ours."

White stayed in the naturalization laws, and this debate helped
transform the Chinese into an Asian archetype against which Japanese, Korean, Indian, and Filipino immigrants would soon be judged.
Greed and selfishness as well as economic and political interests certainly played a part in the brutal reception granted to the Chinese
immigrants. Throughout the nation, labor unions fell back on a common hatred of the Chinese as a way to create solidarity among their
members. Samuel Gompers began his organizing career by launching
a boycott of Chinese cigar makers, demanding that consumers only
buy boxes stamped "Made by White Men."[15]

The Asian newcomers fit into none of the approved racial categories. After the Civil War, people of African descent were reluctantly
granted the right to citizenship, while Asians found themselves on the
docks, ready for deportation to their country of origin. As Samuel
Huntington rightly stresses, "American national identity and unity
derived from the ability and willingness of an Anglo elite to stamp its
image on other people coming into this country."[16] In the case of the
Chinese, the stamp said, "Rejected." The Anglo Protestant elite
resolved its immigration problems by establishing a new assumption
of American culture: After 1870, and especially after the Chinese
Exclusion Act of 1882, "far east" immigrants represented a triple negative—not European, not white, and not capable of assimilation.

The last of these negative epithets is especially important because
the persistent myth of the American melting pot ignores the nineteenth-century exclusion of Chinese and other Asian immigrants.
Asians were, by definition, a forbidden ingredient, forever incapable
of adding something positive to the American mix.

One cruel contradiction of American history is that, despite the institutionalized disdain (after 1882) of mainstream American culture for people of Asian descent, many Americans continued to recruit the Asians, who could never assimilate even if they imitated the behavior of Boston Brahmins. Asians endured the contradiction as American policymakers created another. The nation that venerated its Declaration of Independence also established, after 1898, a new colony in the Philippines. In 2006 close to two million Filipinos live in the United States. After the Chinese, they are the second largest Asian American ethnicity. Yet, until very recently, Filipinos received treatment similar to the Japanese American Go for Broke soldiers at Dachau. Filipinos were missing in American domestic history because they were lumped into a category that only contains negatives. And, just as important, Filipinos recall a history that few Americans wish to remember.

Our Little Brown Brothers

What Americans call the Spanish-American War is known in Havana as the Cuban War for Independence. Move to the mainland and the Cubans take a backseat to the great powers who decided destinies in the Caribbean and in the Pacific. As President William McKinley put it in a note to himself, "While we are conducting war and until its conclusion, we must keep all we can get. When the war is over, we must keep what we want."[17] As it turned out, we wanted Puerto Rico, the Philippines, and Guam. But, once we owned them, what would we do with them?

The Philippines presented a peculiar problem. As Senator Horace Chilton of Texas told his colleagues when they debated, on February 4, 1899, the treaty that ceded the island nation to the United States, "there is no homogeneity among those people. Some have never been under the actual sovereignty of Spain. The natives represent all grades of society from rank savages to the semi civilized children of Spanish and Chinese fathers and Malay mothers." Chilton understood the "vastly exaggerated" economic possibilities but wondered, "Why are we asked to run the risk of admitting large numbers of Chinese and crossbreeds of Chinese and Malays into the Republic, to say nothing of the vast Malay millions that stand behind them. In the Philippine Islands today are more than 500,000 Chinese and descendants of Chinese."[18] Senator Albert Beveridge of Indiana echoed these concerns. "What alchemy will change the oriental quality of their blood and set the self governing currents of the American pouring through their Malay veins?"[19]

No alchemy could accomplish this goal because, as William Howard Taft, the first American governor of the Philippines, assured his colleagues, our "little brown brothers" needed at least fifty or hundred years just to understand the concept of "Anglo Saxon liberty." However, despite the roadblocks erected by biology, destiny called. Senator Edward Wolcott of Colorado championed "Anglo Saxon restlessness." He argued that the "blood of the race beats" with the need "to plant our standard in that far-off archipelago which inevitable destiny has entrusted to our hands."[20]

We needed to be there. Unfortunately, locals proved so "abysmally backward" that the American administrators were compelled to bar them from joining the Elks Club and, except as servants, from even entering the army or navy clubs.[21]

Faced with backwardness, Congress decided to create something new, declaring Puerto Rico, the Philippines, and Guam the first *unincorporated* territories in U.S. history. From the Louisiana Purchase to Hawaii, all territories received the promise of eventual statehood. Puerto Rico, the Philippines, and Guam were different, however, because no one wanted to promise statehood to territories with populations as incompatible with Anglo Saxon liberty as the Chinese and the Malay. And, since Article IV, Section 3 of the U.S. Constitution gave Congress the right to make "all needful rules and regulations" for U.S. territories, the islands became a part and *not* a part of the United States. The Constitution would and would not be applicable, but no one knew for sure because this was groundbreaking colonialism. For example, it took more than twenty years for the Supreme Court to decide that colonial subjects did not have the right to a trial by a jury of their peers.

By creating the legal hybrid of an unincorporated territory, Congress squared the circle, achieving the desired economic and military advantages without according citizenship to the Chinese and Malay masses. In 1902 Filipinos became "citizens of the Philippine Islands" and, simultaneously, "nationals" of the United States of America. They theoretically received freedom of entry to the United States. But, when it came to citizenship, Congress followed the advice of Senator Orville Platt of Connecticut: the new noncitizens had whatever rights "Congress pleases to give them."[22]

Philippine nationals never received a right to U.S. citizenship. In Hawaii, Alaska, and California, Congress—and the agricultural and cannery interests—slowly let Filipino immigrants become a powerful Asian force in American life, but, as nationals instead of aliens, Filipinos led a precarious existence. The Senate and House could revoke their peculiar status at any time, knocking them right back into the alien category.

Filipinos received only one guarantee: that they would receive the same treatment as other Asians. In the 1930s, Filipino men, like their Chinese and Japanese American predecessors, dated white women in the absence of Filipino alternatives. In the city of Watsonville, California "racial mixing" generated such animosity that vigilante groups attacked Filipinos for five days. The riots scared the nation and stimulated a congressional desire for territorial changes. Congress passed the Philippine Independence Act in 1935; the idea was to give the Filipinos sovereignty and then subject them to the same restrictions as Chinese, Japanese, and Koreans. As a sovereign nation, the Philippines got a maximum quota of fifty new immigrants a year.[23]

It is hard history to accept yet essential for any understanding of the roots of Filipino migration to the United States. They became "almost Americans"[24] because the expressed will of Congress accurately reflected the expressed will of the American people or, perhaps more accurately, the imposed will of the Anglo elite.

A Sociological Obsession

Congress closed America's doors in 1924. For the next forty years, newcomers from England, Ireland, and Germany made up roughly two-thirds of all desired immigrants. The old-seed immigrants were deliberately used to replenish America's contaminated genetic stock while the Asians who remained in the United States tried to survive as not European, not white, and not capable of assimilation. The last issue bothered a discipline out to prove that sociology deserved recognition as a hard science, as a body of knowledge proffering truths as reliable as any mathematical or chemical theorem.[25]

American sociologists consistently focused on immigration and assimilation. Fascinating in their own right, these topics also acted as hot-button public issues for more than a generation.[26] America excluded new immigrants, but millions of old ones remained, and sociologists thought they knew *exactly* what would happen.

Robert Park called it "the assimilation or Americanization cycle."[27] Using the same language employed by missionaries and by politicians as different as Theodore Roosevelt and Woodrow Wilson, Park and his University of Chicago colleagues argued that, as scientific truth, immigrants and Americans always engaged in the same cycle of four quite predictable stages. The groups competed; they experienced conflict; they accommodated one another; and, finally, the immigrants always assimilated into the host culture.[28]

Park convinced so many colleagues to follow his lead that his text received the nickname "The Green Bible." Assimilation became the only or principal object of inquiry for American sociologists studying immigration and its consequences. Because the discipline knew what would always happen, the focus on assimilation acted like blinders on a horse. In Cuba (see chap. 1), the anthropologist Fernando Ortiz proved that interacting cultures often produce social change rather than accommodation and assimilation. But American sociology stubbornly focused on assimilation. Immigrants became Americans, and those who did not—for example, the Asians or Orientals—were regarded as the exceptions that caught the eye of inquiring sociologists.

For Asian Americans the single-minded focus on assimilation acted—and acts—like a boomerang. Since Asians could not assimilate—recall the assurances provided by Senator Conness in 1869 and Senator Chilton in 1899—they became the "oriental problem." Sociologists tried to understand their inability to complete the Americanization cycle, and, as Asians yet again became a sociological dilemma to be resolved, scholars laid a new layer of exoticness onto the already marginalized group. Chinese, Filipino, and Japanese Americans were already despised in everyday life; however unintentionally, sociology stamped this marginalization with the imprimatur of science: Asians were the outsiders who never fit in.

Since sociological theory demanded assimilation, sociologists naturally wanted to solve the oriental problem. Tragically, the discipline never questioned the merits of the civilization to which Asians were expected to assimilate. Given the hatred and animosity expressed toward them by the Anglo elite, why would any sane person of Asian descent willingly embrace a society that preached hatred of self and hatred of his or her backward, Asian heritage?

In *Growing Up Nisei* (*Nisei* means second-generation Japanese American), author David Yoo remembers how, during the thirties and forties, many well-intentioned European Americans advised him and his friends: Separate yourself from the blacks and you stood a good chance "to advance and attain the title of honorary Aryans."[29] If that was the pot of gold at the end of the assimilation rainbow, who wanted it? Perhaps the real problem was the beliefs and values enshrined in mainstream Anglo Protestant culture.

Sociology rarely if ever asked these questions. Instead, it accepted U.S. culture and, with it, the white/black dichotomy that helped make Asian Americans perpetual outsiders. On a city map showing the "distribution of racial groups," the sociologists put a black spot for Negroes; a white spot for Caucasians; and a half-white, half-black spot for Orientals. Even when they recognized difference, the supposedly objective sociologists taught generations of their students to think only in white, black, and the polka-dot exceptions.

Those exceptions could make progress. When, in 1926, Robert Park met a woman who talked and acted like the Americans I met at the JACL, he made this comment: "I found myself watching her expectantly for some slight accent, some gesture or intonation that would betray her racial origin. When I was not able, by the slightest expression, to detect the Oriental mentality behind the Oriental mask, I was still not able to escape the impression that I was listening to an American women in a Japanese disguise." To Park this validated the sociological view of the world. Despite her features, this woman had become "the embodiment of successful assimilation at its extreme, a perfectly normal American wearing an exotic Halloween mask." With his eyes closed, Park saw a woman as American as the disdain for Asians. With his eyes open, Park suddenly saw the Japanese disguise, and the woman who was once the same as anyone else became as foreign as her origins.

Park, literally, could not believe his own eyes, nor could he question the unstated assumptions that guided—and still guide—many sociological studies. Park wanted his former students—many of whom were now professors at universities throughout the United States—to examine the intermarriages of white and Asian people. Unfortunately, the very idea of intermarriage depended on the unstated assumption that homogeneous racial groups existed. You could, after all, only have inter- or mixed marriages if you first assumed that definable races—that is, Caucasians—existed and that those wholes created "mixed breeds" when someone married outside the race.

Instead of questioning the racial system that caused so many problems for Asian Americans, Park and his colleagues reaffirmed it. They saw a white and black world, and they taught at least two generations of the best students in the best American universities that Asians represented the "ultimate symbol of exotic difference."[30]

Of course, if you managed to close your eyes, the differences disappeared.

Chinatown, Prejudice, and Ethnic Extremes

For Asian Americans one continuing tragedy is that, instead of Anglo Protestant America making the admittedly hard commitment to challenge the past, recent history only repeats and reinforces the poison that is already there. This was especially true from 1924 to 1965 because the Asian population concentrated itself in very few locations and, when European Americans did actually encounter an Asian person, they did it in places like Chinatown, a word that connotes, in the United States, an exotic enclave where "they" live.

In 1940 Rose Hum Lee found that twenty-eight American cities contained the Chinatowns that provided most Americans with their only image of Chinese people and culture.[31] In Washington and Honolulu, prominent signs still direct tourists to Chinatown. But, once you arrive, Chinatown is more memory than reality. "They" once lived here, but that was years ago. In the nation's capital, the signs above the storefronts are in Chinese script, but down below it is Fuddruckers, Chili's, or Burger King.

In San Francisco or New York, Chinatown remains a magnet for tourists. In Manhattan, they eat at one of the 450 restaurants that provide jobs for more than fifteen thousand people.[32] But, never go to the traps reserved for the tourists. Instead, make contact with a sophisticated New Yorker and the insider whispers the location of a place that serves "real" Chinese food, a touch of Beijing reserved for those who know how to bypass the hayseeds looking for egg rolls and fried rice.

San Francisco also remains a haven for the exotic, but it is a sanitized version of what awaited travelers during the Depression. Businesses lacked customers, so "they redoubled their efforts to draw tourist revenue, no matter what the means: Make tourists WANT to come; and when they come, let us have something to SHOW them."[33]

Tourists in the thirties and forties saw a labyrinth labeled "the wicked city." Insider guides took tourists to "the world under Chinatown, a world filled with narcotics, gambling halls, and brothels, where beautiful slaves, both Chinese and white, were kept in bondage." As a bonus, the wide-mouthed voyeurs also visited "fake opium dens and fake leper colonies."

In Los Angeles, youngsters pulled rickshaws for the "white sightseers." In New York, they cautioned visitors to hold hands; criminals lurked behind every door, waiting to snatch anyone stupid enough to walk the streets alone. Chinese merchants even paid awful actors "to stage elaborate street dramas, including knife fights between opium-crazed men over possession of a prostitute."

Locals protested. Watching the ridiculous, if popular, Charlie Chan movies was bad enough; but, given the ugliness in front of their doors, residents like Lung Chin first seethed and then acted. He fought with the guides because they nurtured and sustained the prejudices that existed. On many occasions, he shouted, "that's a lie" and then "hit them."

To survive during the Depression Chinese merchants seconded the prejudices displayed in Congress. As Iris Chang rightly emphasizes, "the guides cultivated fear and suspicion among white tourists, whose brief glimpses of Chinatown may have been their only contact with Chinese Americans during the exclusion era." No one "knows how many people walked away certain that the Chinese could never assimilate." Nor does anyone know "how many Chinese Americans endured racial discrimination and a hostile job market in the United States as a direct consequence of the myths fostered by Chinese tourism and spread through white communities by tourists who 'saw it all' firsthand."

What we do know is that, even in 2006, Chinatown offers many Americans their only easy opportunity to see it like it is. Here are just some of the states where Asian Americans represent less than 1 percent of the total population: Maine, Kentucky, Indiana, Arkansas, Alabama, North Dakota, South Carolina, Vermont, and Wyoming. Here are states where they represent 1–1.5 percent of the population: Idaho, Iowa, Michigan, Oklahoma, Ohio, New Mexico, New Hampshire, Nebraska, Missouri, and Wisconsin. Corresponding figures for other states look like this: In Hawaii, 63 percent of the people are Asian or Pacific Islander. In California, it is 12 percent. No other state is in double digits. The figure for New York is 5 percent.[34]

As with whites and blacks (see chap. 2) America represents for Asian Americans a nation of geographic and ethnic extremes. "They" are out there; meanwhile the rest of us rarely or never see "them." And, when we do, too many of us still expect a performance like the one given by Rose Hum Lee in the forties and fifties. Speaking "perfectly fluent, flawless English," she first gave a seriously informed lecture titled "The Chinese in America" or "The Nationalist Party." She then went backstage, changed her clothes, and wearing a traditional *cheong sam* (long silk dress) sold Chinese souvenirs to an audience who thrived on knowledge of the exotic.[35]

Chinatowns are but one symbol of American exclusion. After Pearl Harbor, hatred of the Japanese became so fervid that other Asian

Americans took to wearing distinguishing buttons. Knowing that "we all look alike" to European Americans, Koreans announced, "I Hate the Japs More Than You Do"; Chinese placed signs in their stores that read, "This is a Chinese shop," and they wore pins that said, "I am Chinese."

The Nisei lacked any shields as they tried to protect themselves from a fourth negative imposed by the federal government. In addition to being non-European, nonwhite, and incapable of assimilation, Nisei were now designated as "nonaliens." It was a peculiar term, even in a world at war. Technically, only their parents, ineligible for citizenship, expected to be pariahs, but, once the war began, Nisei found that, as "nonaliens," all generations received the same treatment. Everyone took a train ride to the relocation camps while, yet again, Europeans immigrants received different treatment than they.

Two ethnic groups occupy the top spots on the federal government's summary list of immigration to the United States: Germany and Italy. In 1941 the United States also declared war against fascist Germany and Italy. And, in addition to maintaining strong ethnic ties, many German and Italian Americans imitated the Nisei: They were second-generation Americans. For example, from 1891 to 1900, 505,000 immigrants arrived from Germany and 650,000 from Italy. The figure for Japan was 26,000. In the decade 1901–10, 341,000 immigrants came from Germany and more than two million came from Italy. The figure for Japan was 130,000.[36]

Why were Japanese Americans shuttled off to prisons while their first- and second-generation German and Italian contemporaries remained free? As knowledge of the German genocide of millions of Jewish people spread, why were German Americans not tarred with the same brush used to paint the Japanese? Why were Americans so inconsistent in assigning an ethnicity the collective guilt for the sins of its country of origin? To be sure, the genocide occurred in Europe, while Pearl Harbor was a direct attack on Americans. Nevertheless, how many barbers said to a German American, "We don't cut 'Kraut' hair"?

In *Yellow*, Professor Frank Wu writes "that more than any other episode, the internment of Japanese Americans during World War II

confirmed that Asians Americans are not accepted." When it was suggested to FDR that Italian Americans be interred like their Japanese
American contemporaries, Roosevelt laughed it off: "They were a
bunch of opera singers." Moreover, if Italians were interned, that
meant that Joe DiMaggio wore a different kind of striped uniform. He
could play ball in Arizona while his father, who settled in San Francisco in 1915, watched from the sidelines.[37]

The second-generation Yankee Clipper epitomized the myth of the
melting pot. He is the quintessential all-American, yet his second-generation background is very similar to that of the Nisei. In explaining
the different treatment, those who defend internment argue that,
"because so many Americans had German or Italian ancestry," any
effort "to evacuate all ethnic Germans or ethnic Italians away from
coastal areas would have done more harm than good to the war
effort."[38] So, if this argument is followed to its logical conclusion, the
federal government knowingly allowed millions of potential German
and Italian spies and saboteurs to remain in positions of authority and
opportunity, while the much smaller number of Japanese required an
unprecedented incarceration.

The situation in Hawaii is even more baffling. Michelle Malkin
begins *In Defense of Internment* with a Hawaiian example of Japanese
American support for the Japanese enemy. She wants to show us that
the military necessity argument was valid but neglects an obvious fact:
No one interned the Japanese in the very place Japanese Americans
were theoretically most dangerous. Instead, because Hawaii was home
to many Japanese, the United States used the same argument for them
that it had employed with German and Italian Americans: It was
impractical to put them in camps because, if we did so, the island's
economy might collapse.[39]

Pearl Harbor certainly played a role in the differential treatment of
the Japanese. The brutal attack enraged a nation. But the rage took
root in nearly a century of Anglo Protestant antipathy toward Japanese, Chinese, Filipino, and other Asian people. Separate the rage
from the years of congressional and everyday diatribes against the "yellow menace," and you ignore the differences that made Joe DiMaggio
such a suitable spouse for Marilyn Monroe. Even in one generation, a

European American with especially appealing skills could assimilate with alacrity. FOB (fresh off the boat) became a positive attribute when mythmakers extolled the wonders of the European American melting pot.

In sharp contrast, the Japanese could never assimilate; the only thing they fit into was the camps that forced Mas Hasimoto's father to make a decision never required of a first-generation German or Italian. Asked to swear loyalty to the United States and "forswear any allegiance or obedience to the Japanese emperor," the Issei (first-generation Japanese American) faced an impossible choice. If they renounced the emperor, they disavowed the only citizenship to which they were entitled. If they swore allegiance to the United States, they became stateless, since, by definition, they could not be American citizens.

After the war ended the lasting reservoir of prejudice against the Japanese in particular and Asians in general offered the only available template for assigning the role of Asians in American life. As late as 1964, only 1.5 percent of all immigration slots went to immigrants from Asian and Pacific countries. Even with President Kennedy's white knights of Camelot in charge, half the world's population received virtually no right to enter the United States.

Representing the JACL, Mike Masoka told Congress in 1964 that it was finally time to end the racist system that assigned immigration spots based on national origin. Instead of being labeled "an unwanted and inferior people," Asians desired full and enthusiastic acceptance into American life. Congress could never erase the indignity, the hurt, and the humiliation caused by the exclusionary laws; but, as a new beginning, Congress could abolish the institutionalized hatreds that had lasted through two world wars.

Congress agreed. It opened America's doors to the world in 1965, but with no expectation and absolutely no desire for significant numbers of Asian immigrants to America. As we know, the change was intended to benefit Europeans in general and Greeks and Italians in particular. That was Lyndon Johnson's private promise to a reluctant Congress. He never meant to open the floodgates to millions of Asian immigrants; and he certainly never meant to lose the war in Vietnam, which brought millions more Asians to the shores of a nation already embroiled in a struggle between whites and blacks.

Model Minorities and New Whites

It is a historical paradox: after 1965 the civil rights movement makes the color of your skin more important than ever before. By 1970 or so, *black* replaces *Negro* as a positive identity; and, in 1976, the federal government begins to require that all Americans check an appropriate box—white, black, or other—on the census forms. Race formally receives recognition as a cornerstone of American national identity at the very time that the United States admits immigrants whose previous exclusion rested on a triple negative: Asians were non-European, non-white, and not capable of assimilation.

Over forty years the United States *forever* changed the ethnic composition of the American people. Chinese, Korean, Indian, Vietnamese, Cambodian, Hmong, Amerasian, and especially Filipino immigrants arrived in large numbers, only to learn that, in addition to the traditional American prejudices, Asians lacked any way of easily adjusting to the dominating dichotomy. As a second-generation Vietnamese youngster put it in an article entitled "Splitting Things in Half Is So White," "this is a phenomenon that a lot of people go through where you know you are conscious of the fact that you are different and that you are who you are, except there is no name for it."[40]

Anglo Protestant culture lacked a basic vocabulary to describe the newcomers as something other than racial afterthoughts, the "others" of American life. So, the Census Bureau created new, made-in-America races. After white, black, and Native American, the bureau turned a long list of ethnic groups—Chinese, Filipino, Korean, Guamanian, and Samoan—into races. While that made the "racial" categories more bizarre than ever, old and new Asian Americans nevertheless struggled to make sense of the confusing categories. And yet, even as they tried to fit in, to their surprise and amazement, many white Americans said they fit in better than anyone else did. Asian Americans were now the model minority, a success story that made America look better than ever before.

It started in the late sixties and has reached such a crescendo that one activist at the JACL conference in Hawaii told the audience that, in California, Chicanos sometimes call her "master." As a sarcastic sign of respect to the "new whites," Chicanos sometimes bow down before her.

The model minority myth rests on a very shaky foundation—the idea that immigrants' economic success is the consequence of their cultural background. In his book *Money,* Andrew Hacker compares "median household income" to "region of ancestry." As with our analysis (in chap. 6) of Cuban success in Miami, the unstated assumption is that ancestry equals success. "Culture is taken at face value and treated as self explaining."[41] No one asks why, if Asian culture is such a powerful positive force, poverty still exists in Korea, China, or India. Is the culture only activated when immigrants arrive in the United States? And even if that were so, the cultural explanation of immigrant success neglects a crucial fact: immigrants rarely offer a representative sample of their culture of origin. Coming from a Buddhist nation, many Korean immigrants are Christians. And one in nine Indian men in the United States is a physician, who arrives speaking perfect English. Can we explain the success of these immigrants based on their *continent* of origin, or do we need to spotlight their extraordinarily levels of education, linked to language skills and job openings throughout the United States?[42]

A variety of variables always affects the economic success or failure of particular immigrant groups.[43]

- What is the attitude of the federal government? Does it offer the massive assistance offered to Cubans or the temporary assistance offered to Amerasians who, as a negative "bonus," arrive in the United States with no language skills and very little education?

- What is the nature of the job market? As with master's degree computer specialists coming from China and India, does the economy desperately want what the immigrants offer, or, if your immigrant cohort boasts fewer skills, do you find yourself doing twelve- and fourteen-hour shifts driving a cab in New York or Washington, D.C.?

- Finally, do immigrants find an already existing and thriving immigrant community? Koreans, for example, not only received substantial support from their governments, but, over time, they created the Koreatowns that, like Little Havana in Miami, make it much easier for new immigrants to succeed.[44]

To accept a continent or a culture as an explanation of immigrant success is to grossly oversimplify a very complex topic. For Chinese, Japanese, or Filipino immigrants, the praise of Asian cultures seems like a trip to the fun house. In the twenties, their cultural origins entitled them to exclusion from the United States. Now, after 1965, those same cultural origins are the source of Asians supposed amazing success in the United States. For an aged Asian, the laugh is at the expense of Anglo Protestant culture. In a relocation camp in the forties, the same Japanese American now comes from one of the world's premier cultures. Over only one lifetime, a man like Mas Hashimoto finds himself transformed; formerly a "nonwhite," he is now a "new white."

When we ignore the many factors contributing to immigrant success or failure, we also ignore the millions of Asians who barely survive on the lowest rungs of the U.S. ladder. Asian scholars like Sucheng Chan stress that, as early as 1970, "fully 25% of all gainfully employed Chinese men in the United States were cooks, waiters, busboys, dishwashers and janitors." They also stress that to cite family income as an indicator of success is to forget the real reasons why so many Asian women are in the labor force. Boosters of America suggest that the high number of Asian women who work is a sign of their ready acceptance by employers. The truth is "that more Asian American women are compelled to work because the male members of their families earn such low wages."[45]

Finally, in *Forbidden Workers*, Peter Kwong reminds us that the allegedly great Asian cultures produce people who eagerly and exhaustively exploit their own. In New York, agencies around East Broadway advertise jobs up and down the East Coast. Good ones pay one thousand dollars a month; those provided for the illegal Asian immigrants offer wages that can net as much as two or three dollars an hour.[46]

Yet, despite the absence of substantial theoretical or practical support for the myth, it persists. Why? Henry Yu offers this awfully accurate answer: "Thinking about Orientals has always been thinking about what it means to be American."[47] Asians turn into a model minority because—what irony!—they can *assimilate* into the United States, while blacks and Latinos never behave as admirably as the new Japanese, Chinese, Filipino, Korean, Vietnamese, and Cambodian immigrants do.

Perversely, the reappraisal of Asians occurs because white Americans remain the axis around which all ethnicities revolve. Following the process laid out by Robert Park in the twenties, today's Asians supposedly prove that anyone—even Asians—can assimilate and succeed in the United States. Just close your eyes, and you can see the fulfilled promise of the American Dream as plainly as the sun shining over that city on the hill.

While the rest of America embraces the myth, Asians struggle to debunk it. In addition to underlining the poverty of millions of Asian immigrants, critics stress that the model minority myth conceals an "invidious" assessment of African Americans. The successes of Asians apparently prove that any failures of African Americans stem from their own cultural deficiencies. Asians who want to be people of color find that, instead, they have been designated "honorary Aryans," whose purported success feeds into existing resentments of many African Americans. As early as 1970, Albert Murray suggested that the last thing he wanted to hear was a new arrival complaining about the "lack of initiative, self-help and self-pride" among black people.

In truth, Asians rarely make those accusations. Whites make them for Asian Americans when they employ the model minority myth. Whites then go home and leave Chinese or Filipino activists exposed to the heat from comparisons they neither made nor endorsed.

But the good qualities with which Asian Americans have been saddled can become a liability. As Frank Wu writes, "Every attractive trait matches up neatly to its repulsive complement." If Asians become more successful than whites, suddenly "intelligent" becomes "calculating and too clever" for your our own good. Superb in science? You must be mechanical and not creative. Polite? No way. Instead, you are "submissive and inscrutable." Even economic success can make you "deviously aggressive and economically intimidating."[48]

This is a classic no-win situation that utterly ignores three continuing facts of Asian American life. Asian Americans do hit a glass ceiling; they do experience continuing and significant prejudice; and, in a world of whites and blacks, they remain none-of-the-above. For example, as of August 2004, no Asian American was the CEO of a Fortune 500 company. And, Hollywood produces television shows about Hawaii—a state where 63 percent of the population is Asian or Pacific Islander—that have no Asian characters, not even Filipino or Chinese servants.

Asian Americans know what they oppose. But, when it comes to actually creating that new "synthesis" beyond white and black, as Eric Liu argues, "What's missing from Asian American Culture is culture."[49]

Asian American Panethnicity

Liu is both right and wrong. In the sense that Japanese, Korean, Filipino, or Vietnamese ethnicities each represent a particular language and history, Asian Americans lack a single, collective culture. No one set of beliefs, values, and practices even remotely links the six most populous of these groups: Chinese (2.3 million), Filipino (1.8 million), Asian Indian (1.7 million), Vietnamese (1.1 million), Korean (1.1 million), and Japanese (796,000). Turning to the smaller groups—Cambodians (172,000), Hmong (169,000), Taiwanese (118,000), and Thais (113,000)—the differences multiply as the possibility of a unifying culture diminishes.

But Liu is wrong because, for example, the very words used to define the groups are both negative and all-American. In the Census Bureau's affirmation of Anglo Protestant culture, Asia includes India but not Afghanistan or Iran. The divisions are arbitrary, reflecting a set of beliefs and values shared by Americans and Asians for nearly 150 years.

Here are four contemporary examples of a shared Asian American culture. In the summer of 1968, a group of Sansei (third-generation

Japanese American) organized a college conference called "Are You Yellow?" In an attempt to reach out to the many ethnicities encompassed by the Asian American terminology, the group changed its name after the conference to "Oriental Concern." A year later, recognizing that "Oriental" conjured up images of Charlie Chan and his children, the group changed its name to "Asian American."[50] All three labels—especially the use of color—reflect American beliefs about Asian people. But, in addressing their concerns, the students shared the language: it was American English in the era of civil rights. Like the Mexicans who became brown (see chap. 3), the Asian youngsters embraced yellow against a backdrop of white and black.

In the summer of 2004, Bill Parcells, head coach of the Dallas Cowboys, explained football strategy to a group of reporters. "You've got to keep an eye on these two, because they're going to try to get the upper hand. Mike wants the defense to do well, and Sean, he's going to have a few . . . no disrespect for the Orientals, but what we call Jap plays. OK, surprise things." At the conclusion of the press conference, Parcells repeated himself: "No disrespect to anyone."

In response, a Texan named George Hirasaki made this comment: "Parcells probably was not realizing that he was being a racist by using a word that he thought was acceptable."[51] As long as he says, "no offense," the slur disappears; furthermore, in using the word *Oriental,* Parcells casually employed the loaded language that dates back to the earliest years of raw prejudice against Chinese and other Asian immigrants. America is still "rough on rats." Meanwhile, in responding to the prejudice, George Hirasaki used perfect American English to refer to "racism." He agreed that Japanese people are a race and therefore locked himself into the Anglo Protestant thinking that also dates from the mid-nineteenth century.

In 1999, Thomas Kuwahara, a Japanese American helicopter pilot from Hawaii, driving through Fannett, Texas, came across a street labeled "Jap Lane." How could such a slur exist on a public road? Kuwahara subsequently discovered that a broad coalition of people of color had been fighting to change the name since the mid-nineties. He joined their battle, and in July 2004 the local county commissioners finally agreed to erase Jap Lane. Pressured by negative publicity in the *New York Times* and a letter from Senator Daniel Inouye, Jap Lane became Boondocks Road, "despite the vocal and universal opposition of the Lane's residents." Apparently, residents saw nothing wrong with the word *Jap*. It was just another example of outsiders imposing "politically correct" speech and, in the process, trying to rewrite Texan and American history.[52]

Meggy Wang was born in Michigan and raised in northern California. She attended Los Gatos High School in California. Meggy speaks some Chinese, but her accent is from California, and her Chinese vocabulary is limited. When she and her brother got lost during a visit to China with their mother, she told two uniformed train officials, "we're from America, you see, so we don't really know what we are doing." His interest piqued, one official asked, "what state?" Meggy had no idea how to say California in Chinese so, stuttering her way through the encounter, she managed to blurt out, "we're from San Francisco, which literally translates to 'Old Golden Mountain' in Chinese."

Both officials laughed. Meggy was a Chinese joke. "You don't know how to say California in Mandarin?" Caught with no appropriate words to use, Meggy's pride sank. She simply said, "No I don't," provoking more laughter from the officials. The encounter in China also brought another negative memory to Meggy's mind. When she and her family visited the botanical gardens in Seattle some time earlier, they asked an elderly man to take a family photo. He happily agreed and, as he was about to click the camera, asked, "so are you visiting the country?" Meggy wanted to cry because "it was there in the train station in Tainan that I realized that I was a foreigner everywhere I went, no matter how fluent I was in English or how un-American my facial features were. I could be mistaken for an Asian tourist as certainly as I could be laughed at for being an ill spoken A.B.C. (American Born Chinese)."[53]

Meggy Wang is an all-American Asian American. A prisoner of American history, she is a foreigner in her country of birth, and she also possesses the kind of "un-American" face that moves so many young Asian Americans to use glue or tape to create "white eyes." The kids fold the tape into their eyelids, and, with luck, they stay white until they return to their Asian American homes.

Meggy's predicament symbolizes the tragic side of Asian American culture, in which one absorbs the beliefs and values of the Anglo elite and then makes a response that somehow offers a sense of self-esteem and *ethnic* worth in a society that says you come from an inferior race.

Asian Americans respond with short- and long-term strategies and solutions. As they did with Jap Lane or Chink's Peak (formerly in Pocatello, Idaho), a variety of Asian American organizations fight prejudice wherever it exists. Meanwhile, on the Internet, *Asian Week* is a cheeky publication that takes no prisoners. In a September 2004 Arizona Republican primary between David Schweikert and Garry Ong, Schweikert sent out invitations to a barbecue fund-raiser with this advisory: "No Tofu Dogs allowed." Ong filed a complaint with the Anti-Defamation League; *Asian Week* instantly cited "Big Trouble in Arizona," as it took their case and Schweikert's response to the nation. He offered no apology. After all, "it was just for the fun of it."[54]

Seeking an apology or a street name change is the necessary and admirable pursuit of reform. Seeking a transformation of Anglo Protestant culture is to storm the city on the hill, to cultivate change that utterly rejects the language and the attached beliefs internalized by Asian and "all" Americans.

Like the teenagers using tape and glue, Eric Liu always sought to defy stereotypes about Chinese people. "If Asians were alien, I'd be ardently patriotic. If Asians were shy and retiring, I'd try to be exuberant and jocular . . . If they were perpetual outsiders, I'd join every establishment outfit I could and show that I, too, could run with the swift." Ultimately, Liu concluded that he had locked himself in a "do it yourself" prison: "The irony is that working so duteously to defy stereotype, I became a slave to it. For to act self-consciously against Asian 'tendencies' is not to break loose from the cage of myth and legend; it is to turn the key that locks you inside."

What a great line! As with black anti-intellectualism, whites still rule the day whenever a Chinese person strives to prove "them" wrong. Whites never need to threaten or use force because once you padlock your mind you live in a cell with no need for guards. You guard yourself, all the while working to sustain whites and their Anglo Protestant culture.

As one of a bevy of Asian American activists, Eric Liu calls for a new synthesis, a "made in the U.S.A." model for looking at self in a manner that transcends the white/black dichotomy. From this perspective, "Asian American is but a cocoon, something useful, something to outgrow." But when? Liu and his colleagues are part of a generational change. The most recent Chinese immigrants not only resist assimilation; they actively engage in a "reverse re-segregation process." Instead of defining success as a move to the suburbs, they favor the same three cities pioneered by their ancestors: San Francisco, Los Angeles, and New York. Fully 70 percent of the two million Chinese Americans live in five states: California, New York, Texas, New Jersey, and Connecticut.[55]

These culturally creative newcomers live between past and future; and, like the rest of us, they need to answer two crucial questions. How do we all break out of our cocoons? And how can we offer all Americans an equal opportunity for self-respect and ethnic pride in a world with just one human race?

Liu wants to rely on his children and his children's children. That is an option if they begin life as Asian Americans. In Hawaii, the leadership of the JACL also emphasized that the organization's future rested in the hands of its youth. But, during one of the breakout workshops, an aged veteran posed an important question: What ethnicity were the youth? All of his children had married outside of their ethnic group. They were fusions of Japanese and, in many instances, European ethnicities. Conceivably, they would choose to identify with their Japanese roots. But, defying stereotypes, the aged veteran suggested a new name for the JACL. Perhaps the organization needed to rethink its identity in the twenty-first century.

His suggestion fell on deaf ears. It made little sense to a group of people who seemed to know more about what they opposed than what they proposed. Radical change can only occur when we each unlock our own mind.

Five

The Other Others

——— ✦ ———

Indians and Arabs

Arabs: The Invisible Americans

Assimilation Equals Whiter than White

In 1909 Cincinnati's U.S. Circuit Court was asked to determine the fate of a Syrian man born in Turkey. Were Turks Caucasians? If so, the man had the right to become an American citizen. If not, he would be deported.

The issue seemed so important to the *New York Times* that, on September 30, 1909, the newspaper ran an editorial—"Is the Turk a White Man?—that sought to define the racial status of Turkish people. The editorial's arguments still resonate in the contemporary Arab communities of Dearborn and Los Angeles.

The *Times* said that the Turks had started out as "the yellow or Mongol race." They quickly established an empire in India and then "swept down into Persia, overran Arabia and Egypt, and invaded Europe to Vienna." As they marched west, the Turks "freely intermingled with the Caucasian races whom they subjugated." They intermingled with so many people that the *Times* identified the following components in their collective ancestry: Arab, Kurd, Slav, Albanian, Greek, and foreign slave girls of more mixed ancestry. Assuming the "foreign slave girls" claimed roots in Africa, Turks also possessed black blood, a contaminant stressed by the *Times*. "A trace of Negro blood, if only enough to stain the fingers about the nails will bar a person from white society."

And yet the *Times* claimed the Turks as white Europeans. Even though "their mind does not work as ours" and "they are a cruel and massacring people who have lost none of their ancient proclivities," the Turks were Europeans "as much as the Huns, Finns and Cossacks." They deserved recognition as the formerly yellow people who, after intermingling with the Caucasians, became the white, European children of, among others, Albanians, Greeks, and African slaves of more mixed ancestry.[1]

Two days after the *Times* editorial, a Lebanese-born journalist, Salloum Mokarzel, wrote a response to the newspaper. Why did the United States focus on race? "The main point at issue in this question . . . is not the practicality of considering the Turk a white man, but the possibility of considering every Turkish subject a Turk, eliminating in this general classification all distinction of race, language and religion."[2]

Mokarzel's letter defined the battle between American and Arab perceptions of social identities. The *Times* focused on race and skin color, while, as Arab scholars stress, people from the more than twenty nations under the Arab banner tended to identify more closely with nationality than with "racial" groupings. For people actually born on the southern slopes of the Caucasus Mountains, race was a peculiar concept, which only assumed importance when Arabs came to America and suddenly discovered that they fit in as well as a fig in an apple pie.

Remember our earlier discussion of Faras Shahid and Jesus Christ. In 1913 Shahid and Jesus were both deemed ineligible for naturalization because they were not members of the white race. George Dow, "a Syrian of Asiatic birth," also received a no in 1914, but, instead of sheepishly accepting the verdict, Dow argued that he and his ancestors were whiter than white. In his appeal to the Federal District Court of South Carolina, Dow rejected the Salloum Mokarzel line of argument in favor of American racial categories. He stressed that, if the federal courts wanted to talk about race, then Syrians were Arabs, "the purest type of the Semitic race and therefore Syrians had a better claim upon the White Race than that of the modern nations of Europe."[3]

Dow won his appeal. He got to be white, but Syrian immigrants continued to face the same legal struggles as late as 1923. The "walnut colored" Arabs clearly confused Americans, so, as a reaction to that confusion, the early Arab (mostly Christian) immigrants from Syria and Lebanon expanded Dow's arguments and said that no one should be excluded because of their heritage. Instead, Americans mistakenly lumped Arabs (who were white) with inferior races. Thus, as they worked to clear up the perceptual errors, "the external classification issues imposed in America did not alienate or even deter their civic loyalties to their new homeland." On the contrary, "the outcome of the yellow race crisis no doubt strengthened the immigrants' resolve to value and cherish their exonerated racial status as whites."[4]

The Syrians and Lebanese won an acquittal. They were not black, yellow, or red, but whiter than white. While this imaginative reconfiguration of American culture proved temporarily successful in the courts, it forcefully sustained the dichotomy and its negative judgments of "nonwhite people." Whatever the protestations of Syrians or Lebanese, the "walnut" skin color of many Arabs forever made them a problem to their host culture and even to themselves. As Anne J. M. Mammary writes, growing up as an Arab in mid-twentieth-century Detroit, she received an "internalized hatred of Arab peoples along with the racist 'relief' that we are not, in my grandfather's words, 'as dark as black people.'"

For twentieth-century Arab immigrants, becoming American often included a learned hatred of blacks; a learned hatred of yourself; and, simultaneously, a positive identity rooted in the ultimate negative. "Our (Arab) self definition often came by denying and running from variously deep shades of olive skin and at the same time clinging to the power in the United States that comes from having a sense of self delineation as being 'not someone else—here not someone darker.'"[5]

Arabs learned to build an identity around the happy conclusion that they were not black. It is a revealing commentary on the traditional meaning of assimilation for America's "other others" and a pointed reminder that the century-old *New York Times* debate is anything but ancient history.

As in 1909, Americans today remain so confused by Arabs that, according to the Census Bureau, Arabs are the white people who attacked America on 9/11. However, because of the variables cited in chapter 1, the contemporary Arab American reaction to U.S. culture now includes a number of new responses. One subgroup refuses to act like George Dow and his whiter-than-white contemporaries. Today, these mostly younger Arab immigrants assimilate by becoming "people of color" and, simultaneously, a minority group who argue that they are invisible, not one of the groups recognized when Americans discuss race, color, ethnicity, and the need for social and economic justice.

The irony, of course, is that whether white or of color, the dichotomy *still dominates* because the people of color contingent assimilates by defining itself in relation to the labels, beliefs, and values established by the very worst representatives of American culture. It is such a dilemma that a second subgroup of Arab Americans attempts to defy the dichotomy by emphasizing their religion over their race, becoming "Muslim first" in the Christian civilization that refused citizenship to Jesus Christ. It is a dizzying transformation that often begins in the Michigan cities of Dearborn and Detroit.

Warren and Schaefer

In Dearborn, the intersection of Warren and Schaefer Avenues is the spot. The easy convergence of these streets signals the beginning of what many people call (with some exaggeration) the largest Arab city outside the Arab world. Population estimates vary widely; some say two hundred thousand people of Arab descent live here; others say three hundred thousand, but all agree that the "Arab" population includes Syrians and Lebanese (the majority), Palestinians and Yemenis, Iraqi Chaldeans and Coptic Christians from Egypt.

Approaching Warren and Schaefer from the west, you drive by the

Henry Ford Museum; past an upscale food, cheese, and wine market; and along a wide thoroughfare that includes the steel and glass executive offices of the Ford Motor Company. As you pass down Michigan Avenue toward Schaefer, the Arabic signs begin to appear. Right next to a large Thai restaurant, banners promise the opening of a huge restaurant offering "Mediterranean cuisine." The equal prominence of Arabic and English text suggests that "Mediterranean" is a code word used to attract a mixed clientele. Arabs eat here, but everyone is welcome.

Make a turn, drive to Warren, and, as one recent immigrant put it, "I thought I was still in the Arab world." Everything is in Arabic and English; by my odometer estimates, the community easily extends for a couple of miles on either side of the Warren and Schaefer axis. At the Arabian town center, you can buy coffee beans and cardamom. Figs are sold in five- and eleven-pound boxes. At the back of the market, a line of plastic containers house every grain imaginable. Neatly showcased on top of a counter stands a large selection of glass hookahs for a smoker's morning, afternoon, or evening pleasure.

Most of the town center's women customers wear the *hijab*. For believers it is a lovely way to feel God's presence. Like Hasidic Jews in Brooklyn, the Muslim women of Detroit make shopping a religious experience. From one end of the community to the other, butcher stores prominently advertise that they only sell halal (lawful) meat. As Allah stressed in the Quran, halal is an injunction to eat only "wholesome" foods. Signs therefore announce "Halal Pizza" and "Halal Famous Hamburgers." The "All Country Buffet" not only offers Halal meats but, in addition, assures its clients that it uses no "jello gelatin" (usually of pig origin), no lard, and no soy sauce, which contains, after fermentation, 2 percent alcohol.

Doctors and dentists offer their services in functional, brown brick buildings; I see nothing resembling the tree-lined, manicured "Class AAA" medical offices found in high-end Detroit suburbs like Grosse Point. Patients who want to supplement their Western-style care can walk to the "Chinese Herbs and Cosmetic Center." Oddly, its signs appear in Arabic and English but not Chinese. Attorney Joumana Kayrouz's huge billboards portray her with long flowing blonde hair and plenty of lipstick. She offers to answer any of your legal questions—in Arabic—on AM 690.

Entering Dearborn from the east, you cross the railroad tracks, pass through a tiny community of Mexicans, and enter an industrial zone contaminated enough to satisfy anyone interested in an early death. Wading through the smoke and litter, signs eventually welcome you to a safer zone, an Arab community dominated by immigrants from Yemen. They announce that fact in English (and Arabic) as I seek to find a museum founded by the Arab Community Center for Economic and Social Services (ACCESS). Founded in 1971, ACCESS is "a human service organization committed to the development of the Arab Americans community in all aspects of its economic and cultural life." When urban renewal strategies threatened to bulldoze the community into oblivion, Arabs united and created an organization to defend their interests and their space. Located across the street from the Romanian Pentecostal Church, ACCESS now claims to serve more than 119,000 people. Its staff is predominantly female, some wearing a *hijab*, some as stylishly dressed as attorney Joumana Kayrouz.

The museum is actually a work in progress. In May 2005, when I visited, ACCESS was still preparing to help open its huge, modern facility on Michigan Avenue. Staffers proudly pointed out that this would be the first museum in the United States dedicated to Arabs and Arab American culture. But that spring the museum was still housed in the hallway of the ACCESS community service building. A visitor could learn about coffee, architecture, jewelry, music, education, calligraphy, and tent and village life. Small dolls, the men in traditional garb with huge moustaches, slept in an exhibit that stressed the importance of local identity to Arab culture. Many of Detroit's Arab immigrants came from the same village and, like Mexicans in California, recreated the old world in the new.

The religion exhibit spotlighted one of the elements that allegedly made Arab Americans unique among their fellow citizens; as members of Islam, they revere Allah. The showcase labeled the "Three Great Religions" conceded that both Judaism and Christianity deserved equal recognition as great religions; but Islam abandoned the legalism and ethnic separatism of Judaism and the Christian doctrine of original sin, the crucifixion, and the resurrection. Islam, the last and best of the three religions, "put a practical emphasis on the oneness of God and the necessity of serving God through good deeds and pious living."

Since more than 60 percent of Arab Americans claim a form of Christianity as their faith of choice, the Islamic bias surprised me. In truth, the assertion of Islamic superiority accurately reflects traditional beliefs and cultures. Moreover, roughly 90 percent of Arabs do at least nominally embrace a version of Islam, while the other 10 percent—the majority of Arab Americans—are Christian Maronites, Copts, Assyrians, or Chaldeans. For an American, it is like reading the Bible in ignorance; you need a glossary just to understand the differences among these types of Christianity.

Suad Joseph argues that the Islamic link among Arab peoples is one tool that Americans use to mask significant linguistic, cultural, and historical diversity. As the appendix at the end of this chapter suggests, Arabs come from more than twenty nations, including Morocco, Egypt, Libya, Tunisia, Lebanon, Syria, Palestine, and Kuwait. In his essay "Against the Grain of the Nation—The Arab," Joseph argues that Americans make Arabs comprehensible by creating a homogeneity that utterly denies the significant differences.[6] Americans compress twenty nations into one and say that everybody who lives in this mythical Arab nation—the Middle East—is an Arab. We conflate the Turkish and Iranian nations and the significant differences among and between Turks and Iranians, not to mention all the other nations in the region. Finally, we equate Arabs and Middle Easterners with Islam, despite overwhelming evidence to the contrary. Only 20 percent of the world's one billion Muslims are Arab. Islam certainly originated in what Americans call the Middle East, but, in reality, Arabs are a small minority in a religion that, in American eyes, they allegedly monopolize.

This paradox has enormous consequences. Especially in relation to religious preference, the Arabs in the United States do not reflect majority preferences in western Asia and North Africa. Notwithstanding this fact, Joseph points out that "the erasure of difference among Arabs and Arabs in America serves the creation of another difference:

the difference between the free white, male American citizen and this constructed Arab."

The problem for Arab Americans is that they need to define themselves in relation to America's "peculiar fixation on race"[7] and in relation to a concept of "Arab American" that falsely and negatively homogenizes a very diverse population. In the extreme, Americans even manage to make Islam a racial issue. Mary Ramadan argues that "to be white has been understood historically to mean being of European extraction." Additionally, white has meant Christian. So, even if they are Christian, others perceive Arabs as Muslims, which, in Ramadan's eyes, makes Islam "a religion of color."[8]

The suggestion that we can have both people and religions of color testifies to America's maddening fixation on race. It is no wonder that Arab Americans simultaneously call themselves a minority, ambiguous insiders, and invisible. We preach nonsense and then ask them to demystify the babble. It is an impossible task, but many of Arab America's best minds nonetheless try to do the impossible.

An Invisible Minority

It has become cliché to say that Detroit's worst neighborhoods look like a war zone. And yet the rubble has been cleared from some areas of the city. Near the museums, you see a few burned-out or collapsed buildings, but the overwhelming impression is that somebody cleaned up the debris and left nothing in its place. In the shadow of the General Motors skyscrapers and the Greek Town Casino, a visitor sees block after block of vacant land. It waits, along with Detroit inhabitants, for a future that includes more than three casinos within a two-mile range.

This is a big, vacant city in the middle of a battle between blacks and the immigrants who some allege were responsible for its deterioration. One of the most telling salvos in that battle was the 2004 "PowerNomics Economic Development Plan for Detroit's Under-Served Majority Population," that is, African Americans. In the fall of that year, the Detroit City Council tried to create an Africa Town by using the casino tax revenues "to create an economic development fund for the sole use of African Americans." Arab Americans would presumably receive none of the funds because they were part of the problem, not the solution. Arab immigrants took away jobs, and that dynamic "does not coincide with what is in the best interest of Detroit or its MUP (majority underserved population)."

When Mayor Kwame Kilpatrick vetoed the council's recommendation, council members quickly overrode the mayor's veto by a vote of seven to two. That moved Kay Everett, one of the dissenting members, to write this to the *Detroit Free Press:* "The madness of scapegoating immigrants and others who are not of African descent must stop. Non-black immigrants are wrongfully blamed in the PowerNomics report for ripping off community resources and taking jobs from blacks. So the Detroit City Council passed two racist resolutions that will divide our beloved city as much as the deadly race riots of 1967 and 1943."9

In short, the Detroit City Council leaders wanted to create an Africa Town and exclude people who come from Africa. It is strange at best because Professor Ali Mazrui notes that the word *Africa* originally began in North Africa, Tunisia to be more specific. It probably derives from the Berber language, and it originally only referred to North Africa. In time, it expanded to the entire continent and then contracted to Africa below the Sahara when European colonists decided that Africa meant "black" Africans. Americans of all colors have sheepishly accepted Europe's prejudiced position, so, as with the one-drop rule, in Detroit African Americans use the thinking of the worst Europeans to fence out people who originated the word *Africa* and come from Africa, only to discover that they are not African in the United States.

Detroit's problem is the nation's dilemma. The white/black dichotomy mercilessly divides us into victims and victimizers. However, the motor city victims who blame Arab Americans for ripping off resources and opportunities echo a complaint made by Albert Murray in 1970. "Not even the most degenerate rituals of the South are more infuriating to multigenerational U.S. Negroes than the pompous impertinence of those European refugees who were admitted to the

U.S. on preferential quotas, who benefit by preferential treatment because of the color system and who then presume to make condescending insinuations about the lack of initiative, self-help, and self-pride among Negroes."[10]

Murray understandably spoke with anger about white Europeans. Meanwhile, in Detroit, many Arab Americans trying to make sense of our racial operating system see themselves as people of color, harshly treated by the same society that oppresses African Americans. Equally important, just like the Mexicans who warned African Americans about the issue of responsibility for injustice and inequality, Anan Ameri told the *Detroit Free Press* that "the racism in this country and the legacy of slavery is not the doing of immigrants, who often are subject to racism and stereotyping themselves."

According to one study, Detroit's most recent Arab immigrants are "largely poor and unskilled, have limited English proficiency, and are often illiterate even in Arabic." They also experience prejudice that runs from "sand nigger" to "camel jockey."[11] Arab Americans have serious economic problems, and they experience "racial" prejudice in a system that, especially after the civil rights movements, makes skin color and ethnicity as important a variable as it was when the *New York Times* published its editorial in 1909.

The difference is the variables (cited in chap. 1) that today foster a reconfiguration of American culture rather than a reaffirmation of its traditional beliefs and values. When Arab Americans enter the United States, they may just as easily encounter a decided bias *against* European and American culture and significant support from groups who want to "right" American history. In Detroit or elsewhere, Arabs may regard white as a negative identity, yet, when they try to make sense of our operating system, this is what many Arab Americans discover.

As argued at the Unity Conference for Minority Journalists, "there are four basic food groups of people of color, you know, there is African American, there is Indigenous, there is Latino, there is Asian. So, there is no space in that for Arab women. *For me it is problematic to assume that Arabs just do not fall into any category.* It is also problematic to assume that Arabs are white because we are not European and because the Arab world was colonized, first by the West—specifically by Europe and carried on by North America—and it is still colonized and most people do not understand that" (emphasis added).[12]

This in-between status moves some analysts to think of themselves as not quite white or, even worse, invisible. Arabs have no category of their own in a society that mocks their cultures and the religion—Islam—that is a primary axis of identity for 90 percent of the most recent immigrants to Detroit, Los Angeles, or San Francisco. Nadine Naber notes that American print and broadcast media makes Arab Americans "incomprehensible." Following the rest of the culture, the media first homogenizes twenty nations into one and then portrays Arab men as "irrational and violent, particularly towards women." Meanwhile, the women learn that they are "a supra-oppressed group of women in comparison to white American women, who are idealized to represent equality, democracy and justice."

Note the comparisons. To participate effectively in America, Arabs need to see themselves against the backdrop of the white/black dichotomy. They may decide they are neither, but when they seek to redress their grievances, they find themselves arguing with blacks about being African and with a media that makes "white women" the supposed role model for the docile and oppressed Arab female. Theoretically, the women's movement is about choice; however, if an Arab woman makes the following comment she has problems. In the words of Shams Alwujude, "my recognition of my Yemeni history helps me to know which way I should be heading in my life. I choose to dress like a Muslim so that I may honor my religious beliefs and my identity."[13]

In response to so many competing pressures, Arab Americans have at least three general options. One, the route chosen by George Dow in 1914, is to identify as white. Avoid the American insanity by embracing it. This can work for light-skinned Arabs, who pass as assimilated Americans in suburbs across the United States. However, this attitude produces an assimilation laden with racial judgments. As a young Arab in San Francisco put it when discussing the women who might be acceptable to his parents, "Asian is the worst. Black . . . they would think you were joking. It is not even an option. They would never get over it. You would be the topic of discussion for the next . . . I do not know how long."[14]

A second general response is to demand, with the mixed-race population, a separate (minority) category for Arab Americans. If rights and privileges are granted in America according to racial and ethnic categories, then Arabs need to step out of the white shadows and achieve prominent visibility by becoming a fifth "people of color" food group. Throughout the 1990s, Arab Americans were forced by the Census Bureau to contemplate the incredible disconnect between the "white" label proffered by Washington and the "sand nigger" realities experienced by Arab Americans. The Census Bureau had listened to Arab American complaints and seemed on the verge of offering a solution when the demands of the mixed-race groups overshadowed those of Arab Americans. In the race to secure redress of grievances, mixed race Americans won the day, while Washington opted to postpone consideration of the Arab American proposals indefinitely.

The third and final option is to continue the search for a new identity in what amounts to a racial and ethnic never-never land. Arabs are legally white but not white, visible (as negative stereotypes) but invisible. As one young man succinctly summed up his position, "I cannot be a white Anglo Protestant but I have to be something. Everyone has an identity. People keep asking: 'What are you? What do you believe? Why does Islam oppress women? Why do you marry four wives? Why does your religion teach violence?' Suddenly you begin to realize that you do not know what a Muslim is and you begin to search for yourself."[15]

This young man thought of himself as a Muslim, not white, black, a person of color, or even an Arab. Religion is a recurring identifier in this and other cultural reconfigurations occurring in the Arab community. Instead of assimilating, Arabs are behaving like Ortiz's Cubans, offering a culturally creative response to the dominance of the new host culture.

As Nadine Naber writes, Arab Americans are "talking back," in a simultaneous rejection and acceptance of American culture.[16] The focus on Islam signals a reconfiguration of U.S. culture as provocative as the one developed by Mexicans when, as ethnic combinations, they cleverly created the identity Chicano.

Muslim First

In her detailed analysis of the San Francisco Arab American community, Nadine Naber writes about "Arab cultural re-authenticity," a worldview that resists assimilation by labeling Arab culture morally superior and good and Anglo Protestant as morally inferior and bad. This stark new dichotomy is a reaction to America's involvement in the political affairs of Israel, Palestine, Egypt, and Jordan. Especially after the 1967 Arab-Israeli War, Arabs in the United States perceived a significant rise in the level and type of hostility directed against them. Trying to influence the political process seemed "futile," so organizations like the Arab American University Graduates (AAUG) worked to counter the stereotypes through education and community efforts. Simultaneously, Arab Americans began to reconfigure, on their own terms, the meaning of the "Arab" label. This struggle for reauthenticity never emerged, as with the Puerto Ricans or the Chicanos, into a struggle for national liberation or an attempt to create a separate Arab American nation. Instead, as Naber points out, it persisted as an ongoing response to transnational migration and the pressures of assimilation and integration within the United States.

Some Arab Americans "reinvent" themselves by reacting negatively to demands for assimilation *and* to demands for multiculturalism. The former wants to create 100 percent Americans; the latter erases cultural differences by claiming that all cultures are equal. Instead, they assert the presence in the United States of a "true Arab culture," whose unifying core is an affirmation of the Arab world, focusing on the singular importance of the Arab family. As one young woman put it, "in high school there was tremendous anxiety and tension between my wish to have a normal high school experience and my parents', mostly my mother's deep anxiety that *she would lose me to the Amerikan*. That was the famous line over and over and over again."[17]

A foundation stone of any good Arab family—indeed in the dichotomous American system or any good family at all—is the need to control who marries whom. Both men and women experience significant pressure to marry within the parameters set by their parents. An Arab man can date a "white woman," but marriage to an

Amerikan, white, or Anglo[18] is a betrayal of true Arab culture and one's family. In this context, the word *betrayal* connotes everything from the loose morals of white women to a lack of respect for one's parents to a willingness to exchange a good and pure culture for a contaminated one.

The negative reaction toward American things is crucial, but, paradoxically, that reaction allows for a sliding scale of acceptable mates, many unacceptable to the very Americans who are the negative role model. Marrying a white man or women represents betrayal of the Arab ideal; but marrying a black, Mexican, or Asian is often even worse, because it presumably leads to a loss of status and respect both in Arab *and* American circles.

To reinvent themselves, some Arab Americans behave like members of nativist organizations, despising other minority groups. Naber underlines this paradoxical result of cultural creativity. "When he forbids his daughter from marrying a nigger," she writes, "he [the father] not only regulates her sexuality, but he participates in the production of the 'American Dream' by differentiating himself, his family, and the entire Arab people from the uncivilized racialized Other."[19]

This learned hatred of minorities occurs in Detroit as well as in San Francisco. One immigrant from Iraq describes this experience in and around Warren and Schaefer Avenues, when his cousin offered to show him around the area. A black man in another car cut the cousin off. In response, his cousin screamed, "You fucking nigger." The immigrant knew no English at the time, but the sentiment required no translation. In Iraq, this man and his cousin enjoyed many happy interactions with dark-skinned Iraqis. What was different about America? His cousin responded in this manner: "I don't know. Everyone does it here."[20]

Arab immigrants come with their own prejudices. The homegrown division between Christian and Muslim reappears when they reinvent themselves in America. Both groups want to preserve true Arab culture, for example, but their definitions of what this is inevitably part ways when it comes to religion. One Lebanese Christian describes her father's reaction to her relationship with a man named Mohammed Abdel Rahman Ahmed Abdel Rahman. Even for Muslims, "it doesn't get any more Muslim than that," she joked. Her father demanded that she stop seeing Mohammed, and she wanted to know why. After all, despite Lebanese beliefs about their ethnic superiority, her father's sisters married Palestinians. If they could do it, why not her?

The difference was Muslim. This young woman's parents wanted to preserve traditional Arab culture, but, being Lebanese, they wanted to do so in a Westernized, Christian fashion. Her father's friends in the United States and Lebanon gossiped about his daughter's betrayal. "He is embarrassed because it is the worst thing if your daughter marries a Muslim and it is the worst thing if your daughter does not listen to you"—especially in the contaminated states of America.[21]

The daughter pointed out that her mother was from Armenia and that both of her parents claimed to be atheists, but it was no use. Muslim was as bad as black, Mexican, or Asian in this Lebanese/Christian/atheist family. For Naber, this desire to control one's children is a "reactionary and conservative" response to life in America. Parents create a romantic ideal of something called "true Arab culture," and they then use a combination of traditional and learned-in-America beliefs to guide their sons and daughters down the proper path. It is a typical first- and second-generation battle, phrased in prejudices that once again underline the negative consequences of assimilating to the dichotomy and the prejudices it espouses.

But another form of Arab American reinvention also points to the nationwide mutiny against white/black thinking. Many young Arabs have turned to religion in their efforts to challenge and reconfigure Anglo Protestant culture. This second-generation response is seen primarily among young men and women who understand what it means to be invisible or not quite white. Along with the political situation in Israel and Palestine, those labels already generated a need for a new, positive identity. But, in addition, these young people saw the meaning of assimilation in their true Arab families. Their parents often blame minorities for creating and perpetuating their social and economic problems. In essence, the parents talk back to America by talking like Americans, and their children talk back to them by reminding them—and Anglo Americans—of the Quran. "The only perfect person is Allah. We are all human, and our skin has nothing to do with the treatment we deserve. A lot of sheiks are preaching, *when a lot of the people are immigrants,* that, in Islam, we do not see color and we should not treat a black person differently than a white person."[22]

Parents say one thing. Allah says another. And for young adults who believe in Islam, no contest exists. "Parents cannot get away with it." The kids listen to the clerics and read the Quran. They then practice what Allah preaches and use the words of God to critique modern Arab culture. Allah wants a color-free society even if their parents and their parents' friends do not. In a society that includes Chicano, Caribbean, Asian, and mixed-race challenges to the dichotomy, second-generation Arab Americans "find fertile ground for reconfiguring the 1990's neo-liberal racial politics [read American-style multiculturalism] on their own terms." They retreat from the peculiar fixation on race, they support universalism, and they reject racial categories as a way to define and treat members of the Muslim community.[23]

They fill this tall order by deliberately defining themselves as "Muslim first, Arab second." This represents a clear, conscious, and even revolutionary attempt to use language "as a vehicle for self-invention." As with any word, the identity "Muslim first" is only important because of the beliefs and values contained within it. A "Muslim first" uses the identity as a clarion call of defiance because, "by reconfiguring the myth of a secular nation state," these young adults and their successors "contest the hegemony of American popular culture as it casts everything that is Muslim in opposition to everything that is American."[24]

With 9/11 and the intifada right before their and America's eyes, these young people repeat the call of African Americans like Albert Murray. Instead of judging Arabs against white norms and ideals, judge yourself against the backdrop of the Declaration of Independence and the American creed. Anglo Protestant culture comes up short. And if anybody wants to know why, just ask the youngsters who have declared themselves "Muslim first."

The definitions of Arab American are quite fluid. This is a work in progress, and the two themes of "Muslim first" and "true Arab culture" by no means exhaust the many possibilities that exist when we examine a panethnic label—Arab American—that includes more than twenty ethnic communities, innumerable religions sects, and class and educational differences. Arabs respond in many ways, but for anyone interested in emancipation from the white/black dichotomy, the choice is clear. True Arab culture is contaminated with American prejudices, whereas "Muslim first" denies skin color as an axis of identity and tries to "right" American history, according to the Jeffersonian ideal that all people are created equal.

Instead of excluding nonbelievers, "Muslim first" opens itself to the world. Indeed, as hard as it might be for a post-9/11 American to take advice from a Muslim, the new identity talks back by underlining the problems that open-minded immigrants encounter when they try to understand themselves *and their parents* by using the concept of race and the white/black dichotomy.

Indians: Brown-Skinned Whites

Takao Ozawa, Bhagat Singh Thind, and the Aryan Revival

In 1923 Supreme Court justice George Sutherland, a naturalized immigrant from England, spoke for the Court's majority when he delivered citizenship opinions that *still* determine American beliefs and attitudes toward immigrants from South Asia. The two cases appeared within three months of one another and reflect Justice Sutherland's and the Court's sincere, considered beliefs. "Naturalization was a privilege to be given, qualified, or withheld as Congress may determine, and which the alien may claim as of right only upon compliance with the terms which Congress imposes."[25]

A justice's job was to determine the will of Congress. In cases that revolved around race, Congress had set a supposedly simple standard: The provisions of the naturalization law applied "to aliens, being free white persons, and to aliens of African nativity and to persons of African descent." It seemed easy enough, but, as Harvard professor Thomas Reed Powell fondly told his students, "Just because Mr. Justice Sutherland writes clearly, you must not suppose that he thinks clearly."

In *Takao Ozawa v. United States,* Justice Sutherland refused to rely on skin color as a test of race. He stressed that "the test afforded by the mere color of the skin of each individual is impracticable as that differs greatly among persons of the same race, even Anglo Saxons." Presumably, Sutherland's own English relatives may have ranged from "the fair blond to the swarthy brunette," while no one would call a light-skinned Japanese man like Ozawa an Anglo Saxon. Dropping color, Sutherland relied on the work of men like Friedrich Blumenbach. In American jurisprudence, "the words white person were meant to indicate only a person of what is popularly known as the Caucasian race." Sutherland stressed that, since the two words were "synonymous," understanding the will of Congress became easier. Of course, "the effect of the conclusion that the words 'white person' mean a Caucasian is not to establish a sharp line of demarcation between those who are entitled to naturalization." Debatable aliens always came before the Court, but Takao Ozawa posed no problem for anyone with two good eyes and sound racial reasoning. He was "clearly of a race which is not Caucasian," and Justice Sutherland confidently excluded him from consideration for citizenship.[26]

Twelve weeks later Justice Sutherland again spoke for the Court in the case of Bhagat Singh Thind. The Supreme Court was only willing to consider Thind's case because the plaintiff was "of high caste Hindu stock, born in Punjab, one of the extreme northwestern districts of India, and classified by certain scientific authorities as of the Caucasian or Aryan race."

Based on Ozawa, Thind presented no problems. As a Caucasian, Thind clearly deserved to walk the red carpet to citizenship. Unfortunately, as Sutherland noted, "mere ability on the part of an applicant for naturalization to establish a line of descent from a Caucasian ancestor will not *ipso facto* and necessarily conclude the inquiry." When it came to a man of high-class Hindu stock, Sutherland now replaced science with popular prejudice. Keep the Harvard professor's admonition in mind when you read this line: "Caucasian is a conventional word of much flexibility as a study of the literature dealing with racial questions will disclose, and while it and the words 'white persons' are treated as synonymous for the purposes of that case, they are not of identical meaning."[27]

In other words, Sutherland was falling back on vague claims about the difference between the popular and scientific meanings of "Caucasian." When used on Main Street or at the local barbershop, the meaning of "Caucasian" narrowed considerably. Sutherland's job was to appreciate the meaning of that difference and enumerate its implications for an Indian who, despite being Caucasian, might not be white.

According to Sutherland, "the term 'race' is one which, for the practical purposes of the statute, must be applied to a group of persons *now* possesing in common the requisite characteristics." Indians admittedly claimed distant Aryan ancestors, but, "while it may be true that the blond Scandinavian and the brown Hindu have a common ancestor in the dim reaches of antiquity, the average man knows perfectly well that there are unmistakable differences between them today." Aryan signaled linguistic rather than physical characteristics, and Thind's Aryan boasts meant nothing to the judge because different races living in close proximity might speak the same language yet be as different as a white and a black man. Sutherland reminded his audience "that our own history has witnessed the adoption of the English tongue by millions of Negroes, whose descendants can never be classified racially with the descendants of white persons notwithstanding both may speak a common language."

Synonymous only meant the popular meaning attached to the Caucasian by real Americans. Whatever ethnologists had to say, the average American simply would not think that Thind was a white man. "It is a matter of familiar observation and knowledge that the physical group characteristics of the Hindus render them readily distinguishable from the various groups of persons in the country commonly recognized as white." Only a dolt confused a Hindu with a white person; and, just as important, only a dolt assumed that any Indian could assimilate into the United States. Once again, the melting pot myth encountered the popular will of the American people. English, French, German, and Scandinavian children "quickly merge into the mass of our population and lose the distinctive hallmarks of their European origin," but, despite Thind's alleged Aryan roots, "it cannot be doubted that the children born in this country of Hindu parents would retain indefinitely the clear evidence of their ancestry."

Brown today, Thind's children would be brown tomorrow. He could not erase the colorful distinction that, according to Sutherland, implied no judgment of inferiority or superiority. Instead, it was a question of Americans being repelled. "What we suggest is racial difference, and it is of such character and extent that the great body of our people instinctively recognize it and reject the thought of assimilation."

Bhagat Singh Thind was a Caucasian or, in today's popular parlance, a brown-skinned white. Sadly, Judge Sutherland's opinions still exclude Indians who, however hard they try, are being prevented from fully assimilating into American life.

Little India accurately boasts that it is the largest circulated Indian periodical in the United States. In October 2004 the magazine featured a long article entitled "The Nowhere Man" by Shekhar Deshpande. Deshpande wrote that, despite wealth, education, and political clout, Indians could never rub out their racial identity in race-conscious America. Doctor, lawyer, or CEO of a Silicon Valley giant, an Indian always discovers that race "shapes their external social identity in the United States." Indians live between the white and black poles, and "the degree of tolerance [they experience] is often shaped by one's place on that continuum."[28]

In 2006, as in 1923, Indians find it impossible to assimilate into a society that still judges them by the color of their skin. One of the most interesting reactions to this exclusion is a resurgence of Hinduism among Indian Americans. In a provocative example of cultural reconfiguration, these new or revived Hindus behave like Arab Americans: they use religion as an axis of identity because "the racism faced by many young South Asians leads to a turn inwards for the reconstruction of one's identity."[29] Defying Sutherland's still potent decisions, many contemporary Indian Americans behave like the Syrian George Dow in the 1920s: They are better than American whites. Thus, Indians openly and proudly assert that their Aryan roots make them superior to other Americans. In temples and summer camps from New Jersey to California, Indians react to racism by celebrating the Aryan roots that make them Caucasian but not white, legal (after 1965) but still incapable of assimilation into Justice Sutherland's popular American culture.

No wonder Indians are "nowhere men." They left their homeland only to discover that the land of milk and honey still considers them confusing and none-of-the-above. Desis (the word implies a fellow Indian) seek a comfortable social space, but, as in 1923, it is still nowhere to be found.

India: A Highly Developed Society

Many Desis have a great sense of humor. They need one to answer the questions they get from everyday Americans. The following examples are from the Web page Desi Humor.com.

Q: What does that red dot on a woman's forehead mean?

A: Well, in ancient times, Indian men used to practice archery skills by aiming at their wife's red dot. In fact that is one of the reasons they had many wives. You see, once they mastered the art of archery and hit the target . . .

Q: I saw on TV that people there walk on burning coals. Why do they do that?

A: We don't have shoes. So we burn the bottom of our feet to make them hard so that we can walk.

Q: Does India have cars?

A: No. We ride elephants to work. The government is trying to encourage ride-sharing schemes.

Humor helps, but the seriously uninformed questions never stop, even after Indians try to challenge some of the stereotypes they encounter. The developed/underdeveloped continuum is a Western invention that arrogantly measures progress according to levels of industrial and technological development: the number of cell phones, automobiles, televisions, highways, and shopping malls. Using a different measurement, India's 5,000-year-old culture includes thirty-five languages, approximately twenty-two thousand dialects, major world religions, and magnificent architectural structures. The United States is 225 years old. Who is the adult? Who is the underdeveloped child?

One of the great moral achievements of contemporary Indian society has been its continuing attempt to "right" history by eliminating thousands of years of cultural contempt for the Untouchables. Historically, Indian culture sanctioned (and, in some cases, still sanctions) the most inhuman behavior against millions of human cast offs, roughly 22 percent of the population. By some standards, Untouchables needed to shout a warning before they entered a street, so that way "decent" could safely avoid them. Untouchables need to walk with a mental measuring device at all times; social norms actually stipulated that they remain thirty-three feet away from the lowest castes; sixty-six feet from those in the middle; and from Brahmins, Untouchables needed a space of at least ninety-nine feet.

English added the word *pariah* to the language by using the Parayans of Kerala as a terrible symbol of human indifference to another person's pain. In 1948 India's pariahs presented seemingly insurmountable problems to a new nation but not to the figures who dominated the constitutional convention. With Jim Crow firmly in the saddle in the United States and talk of affirmative action more than twenty years in the future, Pandit Thakur Das Bhargava stressed in 1948 that special provisions for the Untouchables were "the soul of the Constitution." In a sense, all Indians took a public and solemn "oath" to open the nation's doors to the Untouchables "as a means for expiating our past sins. If any community continues in backwardness, socially, culturally, or educationally, then it should not be a question of ten years, or fifteen years, but up to the time that they are brought up to normal standards, facilities should be given and continued for them."

Indians heroically and honestly confronted the consequences of institutionalized prejudice by trying to inject instant life into a very young democracy. Given thousands of years of barriers to educational and political power, Untouchables obviously lacked the resources needed to gain power in the new nation. So, the Indian Constitution of 1948 reserved 22.5 percent of legislative seats for the Untouchables in both national and state assemblies. All Indians could vote for these seats, but only Untouchables could hold them. This quota-based system was but one solution to a problem that plagues any republic with historical inequities. How can you talk about representative democracy if some groups go unrepresented?

In the expectation that these preferences would end in ten years, Indians also established meaningful educational opportunities and quotas for the Untouchables and mandated that 22 percent of all public employment posts went to the Untouchables. But Indian leaders soon discovered that established beliefs and practices undermine the best intentions. It was difficult to find Untouchables to take these new jobs because most lacked the education and experience needed to carry out the jobs. Meanwhile, the old prejudices thrived. At the 2001 United Nations conference on racism and public policy, India's Untouchables were still handing out buttons that said: "Caste is Discrimination on the Basis of Work and Descent. Equality for All. Free and Uplift Dalits!"

History handed the new nation of India monumental problems, and its leaders courageously faced those problems by accepting moral responsibility. India "failed" for the same reasons America has. Which comes first, the institutional change or the transformation of beliefs and values? Quotas and affirmative action or the cultural revolution that is the theme of this book? In an ideal world, both occur simultaneously; in real life, we stumble along. But when Indians in the United States are asked absurd questions about levels of national development, Americans need to remember that millions of Indians honestly tried "to expiate their sins" while we wallowed in our own.

The first Indian immigrants came from the Punjab region at the turn of the twentieth century. Although most were Sikh, Americans nevertheless called them Hindus. In addition, the popular press called them "inassimilable and possessed of immodest and filthy habits." Even before Chinese and Japanese, Indians proved to be "the most undesirable of all the eastern Asiatic races." As early as 1907, the Indian presence provoked a race riot in Bellingham, Washington, and if members of the Asiatic Exclusion League celebrated the melting pot at Sunday church services, they sought the exclusion of Indians during the other six days of the week.[30]

The league succeeded. With seven hundred Indians in the United States at the turn of the twentieth century, the number only rose to seven thousand when Justice Sutherland told Indians the popular meaning of Caucasian in 1923. As late as 1965, the Indian American population included no more than ten thousand people.[31]

In 2005 the Indian population in the United States officially numbered 1.7 million men, women, and children. The actual figure is much higher because, as among the Mexicans, Jamaicans, and Filipinos, many Indians merit an undocumented status. For example, Indians work by the thousands in New York's restaurant industry, where one educated guess is that 35 percent of the workers lack legitimate documents.[32]

In the 1970s many immigrants from India arrived with educational qualifications that made them exceptional in the United States as well as in India. Today fully 11 percent of Indian male immigrants to the United States possess a medical degree; the figure for Indian women is 7 percent. It therefore comes as no surprise that "the median family income of Indian households is 25 percent higher than for all U.S. households." In California, roughly three hundred thousand generally well-educated Indians work in Silicon Valley's technology firms, representing 15 percent of the high-tech start-ups in the region. One educated estimate puts their median annual income at two hundred thousand dollars a year. Indians now own 30 percent of the nation's hotels and motels. Their success is so great that their white competitors often counter with provocative signs like this "welcome" billboard in Springfield, Massachusetts: "This motel is American owned and operated."[33]

Some Indian Americans do very well indeed. Others work in the most unexpected places. No less than twenty-five hundred of New York's sixty-five thousand Metropolitan Transportation Authority workers claim to be of Indian origin, arguably "the largest number in any single enterprise on the East Coast."[34] Some Indians work the toll booths while others are engineers, but these underground Indians never live in the McMansions built by the doctors and other professionals along the tree-lined streets of posh suburbs like Englewood Cliffs, New Jersey.

Indians Americans' median family income figure is so high because analysts add the income of very rich people to the income of very poor people. A recent community profile prepared by the Asian American Federation of New York indicates that 20 percent of Indians in the city live below the poverty line. More than one-quarter of Indian American adults in New York never graduated from high school, and 13 percent never completed ninth grade. In the restaurant industry, one Indian exploits another because 16 percent of the Indian workers receive less than minimum wage, many never receive pay for long hours of overtime, and 75 percent of the restaurant workers lack health insurance.[35]

Even those with master's degrees walk a tightrope. Here my reference point is the large number of well-educated Indians who arrive via H-IB visas. High-technology firms like General Electric, Microsoft, and Hewlett Packard claim that the nation is desperately short of qualified computer software and hardware technicians. They outsource to (especially) India and China by using body shops that often treat the workers as badly as any Texas farmer treats Mexicans or other disposable workers. The Indian employees of these shops are on visas that normally last for three years, with the possibility of an extension to six years and then permanent residence in the United States. The trick is to have a firm sponsor your permanent status; and to do that these permanent/temporary workers often sacrifice competitive salaries and decent working conditions. At times, workers who want to change jobs need the permission of their present employer, permission from the federal government, and a guarantee from their new employer. It is a lovely contradiction: As they energetically champion global capitalism, American corporations simultaneously limit the geographic opportunities of, in this case, their very well-educated Indian workers.

In this snapshot of the Indian American community, we need to add one more group. In the 2000 census, almost 12 percent of Indian

Americans—221,000 individuals—identified themselves as "mixed race." They and other South Asians (Bangladeshis, Pakistanis, Nepalese) tend not to marry "out" with the frequency of Chinese or Japanese Americans, but the rate is sufficiently high to provoke discussion within the Indian community. When Achal Mehra congratulated a friend on his daughter's impending marriage, he got this "sheepish" response: "It's not like that, she is marrying a white guy." His friend feared ethnic fusions, while other Indians see fusions as a natural consequence of the multiple opportunities and responses Indians make to the United States and its white/black dichotomy. Mehra suggests that "the face of the new Indian American is to be found in the thriving Indian cultures of Malaysia, Singapore, Trinidad and Fiji, where Indians migrated almost a century earlier and forged a multiplicity of blended identities."[36]

One thing is certain. Indian Americans exhibit significant diversity across educational level, class, caste, generation, and "race." These factors alternately aid or impede adjustment to life in the United States. But no matter how an Indian responds, the white/black dichotomy always boxes them in. ABCDs (American Born Confused Desis) are a joke in the literature, but the confusion is real.

None of President Kennedy's "best and brightest" men expected the Indians to arrive. The numbers increased from ten thousand to almost two million in less than forty years. Yet our only frame of reference was the thinking of men like Justice Sutherland. The coincidence of mass immigration with the civil rights movement and multiculturalism meant that skin color became more important as a means to rights and privileges and, theoretically, less important for those who tried to be color-blind. Ultimately, Indians and other Americans share a common bond: Americans do not know what to make of Indians, and, just as often, Indians do not know what to make of Anglo Protestant culture—and of Indians in it.

The Literate and the Articulate

Many Indian Americans share this story. God offered the man a choice between heaven and hell. Heaven seemed nice enough—"soft music, serene angels, and an atmosphere of peace"—but hell boasted wine, women, and song. The man chose hell, only to be placed on his arrival in a cauldron of hot oil. The poor fellow asked God why. He answered: "Last time you were on a tourist visa, now you are on an immigrant visa."[37]

Immigrants, all immigrants, need to adjust to a society very different from their own. When my grandfather came from Spain in 1916, he stayed for a year, decided he hated the United States, and returned to Spain. More than half of the four million Italians who came between 1899 and 1924 returned home because they disliked America as much as America disliked them.[38]

Indians stay for a variety of reasons, and many have no opportunity to ponder the meaning of life in the United States. Driving a cab or working a fourteen-hour day in a restaurant allows no time for the big questions. The goal is to get through the day. Identity questions are a luxury of what Deshpande calls the literate and the articulate.

An Indian colleague teaches physics at my university. One day he scribbled some formulas on the board, only to hear laughter from his students. Since there was not much to laugh at in the formulas, he asked what was so funny. Reluctantly, two African American students answered that, while he obviously had darker skin than they did, no one called him black. This was funny to the kids and to my colleague. Desis know they are not white, and they know they are not black. Yet, since there is no in-between, Desis need to make some intelligent response to a ridiculous question.

In the best of all worlds, Desis, two million strong, might actively question the sanity of their fellow Americans. With his dark skin and super straight hair, my colleague explodes the categories invented by the Europeans, who defined Africa as the land mass below the Sahara, *not* including the light-skinned Khoisans from the deep south. Unfortunately, in a prejudiced society, people are generally reluctant to embrace the most despised category. Indians might agree to be "people of color," but black is a leap most are unwilling to make. White also presents problems, so here are four Indian American responses to the dilemmas posed by the question of color. No one precludes the others; in real life Indians mix and match their responses based on everything from personal experience to a desire to break with Indian cultural traditions.

One response to America is to walk through life using a rearview mirror. Historically this was hard to do, but today it is a cinch. You can sit in a Starbucks in Englewood Cliffs; sip the latest, very expensive mocha concoction; and converse with your grandmother via e-mail or cell phone. She lives in a remote part of India, yet, as Lavina Melwani writes, "in this new world you have to give up nothing to become something else."

In the process of becoming, traditional Indian culture always remains in the background, especially after "the long awaited new year's gift." In 2004, after a long debate, the Indian government offered all Desis the possibility of dual citizenship. Among other things, the Indian government wanted their money. In exchange, Indians realized a dream. As the editors of *Little India* wrote, "Most of us yearned for it as much for emotional reasons as for its economic advantages. As the legal status acknowledges the everyday reality of our lives, this dual citizenship will only bring us closer to India, and we can think of it as our own again. There is now reason and opportunity for real involvement and real effort."

Dual citizens do not make good candidates for assimilation. On the contrary, the opportunity for dual citizenship reinforces this response to the United States: "Home is over there; the United States is just an unpleasant place in which to work."[39] As Andy Iyengar, the head of a twelve-million-dollar telecommunications company, put it, "while I used to think of myself as an 'all-American Indian,' these days I feel different. I feel that India is my motherland and America is my fatherland."[40]

Mr. Iyengar makes his living in the fatherland, while he finds spiritual solace in the motherland. This common strategy leaves many Indians feeling like none-of-the-aboves in nowhere land. These Indians therefore spilt the world in two: "The world of the workplace is a world that must be exploited as much as possible"; and the inside world, the one that contains other Indians, "is a world of culture that must be protected and cherished."[41]

Some of the Indians living this dual life play into the prejudices of the white/black dichotomy. As early as the 1920s, some Indians were using their alleged Aryan roots to distance themselves from African Americans. Today, with the advent of affirmative action, you can be severely, mildly, or even not prejudiced against African Americans yet claim "person of color" status in the affirmative action system. An astute Indian quickly grasps the hypocrisy of affirmative action in action. Many employers resist hiring a black, but they have discovered that one can meet government mandates by choosing darker Indians, "who are considered less troublesome, sometimes more competent, and no doubt socially advantaged."[42] West Indians and Arabs also play this role, and, as they and Indian Americans do so, affirmative action becomes another way to keep African Americans in their place.

A second response to America is to accept a forever-foreign identity. The critic and scholar Vijay Prashad abhors the prejudices of U.S. society, embraces the label "person of color," and denounces a government that preserves "anti-democratic forces like the Saudi royal family." As he sees it, "the distinction between the immigrant to America and the American who was an immigrant is in the cleaning of the toilet." Brought up with someone else doing the dirty work, a Desi *never* cleans his own bowl. An American goes out, buys a cleaner emblazoned with a white caricature named Mr. Clean, and scrubs for all he is worth.

Since Prashad cleans his own bowl, cooks his own food, and repairs his own home, he embraces the progressive desire to do many of life's most tiresome chores. For the past few years, he writes, "I have felt neither Indian nor American but always foreign." He is a stranger in a home with two or three full baths, and he thinks about this "mostly while I am cleaning my (I assume American Standard) toilet." It is a joke with a very serious punch line. No matter how much of a commitment they make, Prashad and many other Indians believe that Americans see them as "forever immigrants." Like recent arrivals from China or Japan, Indians are tolerable but not quite white. Even when they speak perfect, accentless English they get the same question posed to East Asians: Where did you learn to speak English so well?

They are asked this because, among others, Justice Sutherland taught us to see Indians as foreigners, and they know it.

A third Indian response to America is Hindutva (literally, Hinduness), arguably the most fascinating and (from the point of view of social change) most counterproductive response to the white/black dichotomy. Like the Arab Americans who embrace Islam, Indian immigrants simply ignore or disregard the issues of race and skin color in favor of a religious identity. As Arvind Rajagopal notes, "religious identity becomes a way of evading racial marginality and of appearing to side-step that great chain of being that has whites above and blacks beneath."[43] Religion becomes a shield that provides social esteem through an imaginative reconfiguring of Indian, European, and American culture. It is transculturation with a heavy dose of jingoism, all in the name of God.

European scholars and cultural theorists in the early nineteenth century sought the ultimate origin of the European genius in general and the Aryan race in particular. Greece obviously provided a crucial foundation for the continent's cultural splendor, but, eager to distance themselves from the Mediterranean roots of Greek achievements, Aryan writers turned north. To minimize the influence of the Mediterranean, they needed a civilization "wholly independent" of Semitic and African influences, and they ultimately found their racial Rosetta stone in India. Using ancient languages as an alleged source of biological links, French writers like Jules Michelet soon wrote that India was the starting point of European civilization; India was "the birthplace of races and religions, the womb of the world."[44]

In a spectacular leap of faith, India became the original mother of everyone because "the Aryan model of Indian history served to establish the ancient origin of the Aryans peoples (or race) in Central Asia, their migrations first into Iran and India and subsequently into Europe." Indians eventually became Caucasians, and this proved so appealing that, in 1877, Keshab Chandra Sen told a Calcutta audience that English imperialism implied a divine meeting of the minds: "In the advent of the English nation in India we see a reunion of parted cousins, *descendants of two different families of the ancient Aryan race*" (emphasis in original).[45]

Myths developed in Europe gave "great civilization" status to Indians, who accepted their role so readily that, as one recent Indian school text teaches, "the history of India is regarded as the history of the Aryans in India. Their occupation is the most interesting as well as the most momentous event in Indian history."[46] While Indians obviously react to these Aryan assertions with varying degrees of acceptance, the myth persists. When asked what race they belonged to, Indian immigrants to the United States often chose "Aryan." That label never appeared on the census forms, especially after the Holocaust, yet it—and "Caucasian"—remained a touchstone of racial identity when Indians staked their ancient claim to be a womb of the world.

Initially the Aryan claim to greatness lay unused. However, a "lucky" conjunction of events occurred. As Indian nationalism gained strength in the homeland, a need for social esteem and Indian values arose in the United States. One fed on the other, especially as the first generation of Indian Americans began to raise their children. Parents wanted alternatives to existing, ossified racial categories. Labels such as "nonwhite Caucasian" or "ambiguous nonwhite" offered little satisfaction. So, for Indians of all social classes (but especially the advantaged) "the dominant response to the jarring experiences of racism has been to reiterate a national-cultural identity that would give them 'respect' and a claim to a unique cultural heritage."[47]

Indians become Hindus in search of dharma. In the United States, Hindu subsumes the Aryan identity under what Sucheta Mazumdar calls "the essential of nationality." Hindu is "universalized to embrace both the exclusive ethnic identity of the original peoples of India and the authentic cultural essence of the nation."[48] Meanwhile, one translation of the word *dharma* is "protection," while another is "that which holds together" or "sustains a being." Using either definition, one important institutional arm of the search for authenticity is the Vishwa Hindu Parishad of America, Inc. (VHPA). Maintaining close links to the Indian nationalist movement, the VHPA in the United States focuses on promoting unity through a network of Parishad chapters that help sponsor everything from summer camps to the 2000 Global Dharma Conference. Noted swamis offer campers spiritual support—what the VHPA calls succor and support—to families that are searching for ways to impart Hindu values to their growing children.

On college campuses, the increasingly nationwide Hindu Students Council distributes a pamphlet called "Samskar, It's All about Dharma." Students learn to use Hindu as an axis of identity; and in multicultural America, Trisha Pasricha uses the white/black dichotomy to explain her reaction to a sixth-grade history class focusing on world religions. "The majority of the people, including the teacher are white. One African American, two Orientals, and myself, a second generation Indian girl make up the rest of the class." Through grade school, Trisha constantly heard, "Do you speak Indian?" and, when she saw Hinduism presented in the school's texts, she saw "some sort of drag-queen in make-up doing an obscene peacock dance. Out of all the dazzling pictures of Indian culture, *that* is the one they have to stick in?"[49]

Tricia is understandably angry. She embraces her identity as an American Hindu and seeks dharma because "every day, young Desi children and teenagers are understandably tormented because of our perceived background. The school textbooks are half the cause. The average American does not know squat about India, and with the help of poorly researched textbooks, they learn nonsense. *The sheer embarrassment of the situation is enough to make Desi students everywhere wish we could have been 'normal' by American standards*" (emphasis added).[50]

Since normal is out of the question for "brown-skinned whites," Tricia and many other Indian Americans seek protection in Hindutva and dharma. They affirm their Hinduness, turning away from a society that only offers a drag-queen representation of a culture that, as the swamis stress, remains a spiritual womb of the universe.

Hindutva moves Indian Americans to postpone or disregard the dichotomy that is a principal cause of the search for dharma. A fourth possibility for Indian Americans is to transcend the racial nonsense and begin a revolution in cultural thinking. Deepika Bahri cites the need for a "kaleidoscopic and futuristic vision" in which we "undo the categories" against which Indians and Hindus measure themselves and their magnificent and problem-filled heritage.[51]

Few Indians choose this revolutionary path. But it is a promise of hope, the dream of overcoming the variables that move so many Indian Americans to reject accommodation, not to mention assimilation into American society.

APPENDIX:

NUMBER OF ARABS IN THE UNITED STATES

The numbers below represent Census Bureau estimates for the Arab American community. As of March 2005, the bureau estimated 1.2 million Arabs. Other estimates reach to 3.5 million. Given variables that run from undocumented immigrants to the Census Bureau's manner of classifying Americans, it is very difficult to make an accurate estimate.

I provide census numbers for the top ten ethnic categories. The actual numbers are certainly higher; the mystery is how much higher.

Lebanese: 440,279

Syrian: 142, 897

Egyptian: 142,832

Palestinian: 72,112

Jordanian: 39,734

Moroccan: 38,923

Iraqi: 37,714

Yemeni: 11,683

Algerian: 8,752

Saudi Arabian: 7,419

These numbers are hotly contested. Arab organizations generally estimate 3 million or more Arab Americans. They criticize the Census Bureau for not including people who are recognized members of the

Arab League, for example, people from Mauritania, Somalia, Djibouti, Sudan, and the Comoros. Arab American organizations also include—I believe correctly—people of Arab ancestry.

Source: Angela Brittingham and G. Patricia de la Cruz, "We the People of Arab Ancestry in the United States," Census 2000 Special Reports, U.S. Census Bureau, March 2005, 1, http://www.census .gov/prod/2005pubs/censr-21.pdf; see also Randa A. Kayyali, "The People Perceived as a Threat to Security: Arab Americans since September 11," *Migration Information Source,* July 1, 2006, http://www .migrationinformation.com/Feature/display.cfm? id=409. The estimate of 3 million comes from the *Detroit Free Press;* see "100 Questions and Answers about Arab Americans," www.freep.com.

Six

The Caribbean

———— ✸ ————

Puerto Ricans, West Indians, Cubans

Civilization and Pride

Jésus was our guide. The six-hundred-mile trip carried us over roads that often predate the Cuban Revolution. We and our student group stopped at all the big and small cities along the way—Camaquey, Trinidad, Santa Clara—but one immensely impressive aspect of Cuban life never called for any commentary from Jésus. Communities seemed to compete fiercely for recognition. Floral arrangements often signaled the entry to a new town or village. Sometimes citizens draped the arrangements around artful combinations of rocks; in other instances, they used flowers and king palm plantings to spell out the names of their home. People often used machetes to cut the grass near the roads for hundreds of miles; and, compared to the trash-dotted mountains and valleys of Puerto Rico, Jamaica, or Trinidad, Cuba is almost free of litter. It offers an exquisite, spotless landscape in the middle of grinding poverty where farmers plow with oxen and use tractors to pull passengers stacked in an accompanying cart.

I finally asked Jésus about the landscape. How did Cubans achieve such beauty in the face of seemingly insurmountable economic and political problems? Jésus, a man with a very ready wit, seemed baffled by my question at first. He took the landscape for granted, whereas I came from Connecticut, a land of flashing neon signs, malls, and litter. Jésus finally said that Cuba enjoyed a distinct advantage over other Caribbean nations. Since they had no access to soda cans and plastic-wrapped junk food, Cubans had little to discard even if they wanted to litter. It was a good point, but I argued that communities who maintained themselves with so much attention to beauty must have great pride.

Jésus smiled. "Pride! That is all we have left."

With only the subtlest allusion to the punishing U.S. embargo, Jésus expressed his immense pride in being Cuban. We saw it everywhere because, despite poverty, pride in culture and nationality marks one Caribbean nation after another. Puerto Ricans joke that if you get one of them started on *la isla* (the island) they will never shut up. Jamaicans literally light up when they talk about the island, and in Trinidad, Barbados, or Grenada people also light up when speaking about their greatest possession: their country, their home.

Nationality is the axis of social identity for the vast majority of Caribbean people. In Hartford alone, the West Indian community boasts at last count more than ten social clubs. The clubs subdivide by island so that a person from tiny St. Lucia can boast with as much passion as a Cuban or a Puerto Rican.

Consider the problems Caribbean people face in the United States. American Anglo Protestant culture emphasizes the color of their generally darker skins, while they focus on culture, nationality, extraordinary beaches, magnificent landscapes, and everyday civility. It truly angers many Caribbean immigrants that we expect them to assign as much meaning to skin color as we do. When they refuse, many Americans, among them African Americans, accuse them of lying. It often sounds like this: Black faces rarely appear among the Cuban leadership, and Puerto Rican politicians continually boast light or lighter skins. Thus, the Caribbean is just as bad as the United States; you people just refuse to admit it.

Rex Nettleford, the vice chancellor of the University of the West Indies, points out that, because the Caribbean is the crossroads of the

Americas, all Caribbean nations experience an endless process of cre-olisation. Trinidad contains a population with a substantial contribu-tion from India; Jamaica has welcomed thousands of Chinese and Indian immigrants; and, with the Spanish supposedly in command, 60 percent of Havana's population (circa 1600) claimed Portuguese roots. The Caribbean has always experienced such an endless fusion of heritages that Nettleford describes Caribbean people as "part-African, part European, part-Asian, and totally Caribbean."

Since the word *Caribbean* comes from the Carib Indians, we should also include indigenous contributions in the mix. Caribbean people, like Mexicans, learn that they are the product of many heritages; to a Caribbean person, pure, homogenous groups seem as absurd as snow in the streets of Kingston. That does not mean that Caribbean people totally disregard skin color; nations that were colonized by England, Spain, and the United States obviously—and forcefully—learned that skin color played a significant role in who got what and when. The dif-ference is that Caribbean people got control of their cultures and, in the process, made skin color a generally peripheral consideration in everyday life in the popular cultures of Caribbean people.

Americans want Jamaicans or Puerto Ricans to think (and act) in black and white. Qualifications never exist; you see skin color or you do not. When Caribbean people try to explain that their world is much more complicated, we too often write them off as hypocrites and miss one of the most remarkable features of life in many Caribbean nations: When it comes to race and ethnicity, they are among the most civilized people on earth.

With quiet pride and a sure sense of self, Rex Nettleford explains that "the Caribbean has produced fewer monumental material edifices but it has created innate structures of civilized social interac-tion in 'crossroads' communities of differing races, cultures and world views." Walk through the streets of Trinidad's Port of Spain and you see fusions of virtually every possible variety. Everybody is intermin-gled, and, in general, their children seem quite comfortable with one another's dazzling array of physical characteristics. According to Net-tleford, because class or religion counts for much more than biology, "it is the pluralist dimension of Caribbean reality and the corresponding perceptions of life and living that remain among the greatest of the region's attributes."[1]

During our three student trips to Cuba, we made every academic effort to understand the African roots of Cuban culture. But I think our African American students learned far more on the streets than in the classrooms. Walking in Havana or Bayamo, they told us that it was the first time in their lives that they had ever felt comfortable. Skin color was so unimportant that Cubans ignored it, and, after a while, so did some of our students.

That sense of comfort is what Caribbean leaders mean when they talk about civilization in the region. The inhabitants of the crossroads of the Americas achieved a magnificent—if never total—victory over the colonial heritage. Their victory could be a tool for our social change. Unfortunately, we not only ignore the Caribbean model but actually demand that they behave like us. In late October 2004, the Census Bureau announced that it planned to eliminate the "some other race" category from the nation's list of options. Because more than fifteen million Latinos (many of them from the Caribbean) regularly checked this box, the Census Bureau had a problem. It had to give these people a race even though they did not want one. As Preston Jay Waite, associate director of the Census Bureau, explained, "*We are making up the race* for fifteen million people. We would prefer not to do it. It doesn't seem wise to me that we would put at risk the racial statistics of the nation in order to answer an interesting sociological question"[2] (emphasis added).

What kind of nation makes up the race of fifteen million people, none of whom want the race you "need" to give them? As Kathia Mendez, an immigrant from the Dominican Republic, told the *New York Times* when they questioned her about the Census Bureau's intentions, "I am not black and I am not white. We don't define ourselves that way."[3] If the Census Bureau is successful, American culture will force you into one of our two categories, by denying you the box you actually want. We will ignore your self-determined identity and teach you to be as uncomfortable with one another as we are. You will behave like an American and neglect the benefits of five hundred years of cultural creation in the crossroads of the Americas.

The request or demand to relinquish Caribbean civilization runs through the experiences of millions of Cuban, Puerto Rican, and West Indian Americans. They respond in a variety of ways, all saying as much about our civilization as they do about theirs.

Puerto Ricans: Los Boricuas

Puerto Rico is unique. As the oldest colony on earth and, simultaneously, an "unincorporated" territory of the United States, Puerto Rico poses a problem. How do we count Puerto Ricans? Do we discuss only the three million who live on the U.S. mainland? Or, do we also include the four million who live on the island? The latter are U.S. citizens but cannot vote—in Puerto Rico—in a presidential election. Those same U.S. citizens can vote in a presidential election if they live in New York or Maine. They are subject to the draft but have no voting representation in Congress and cannot vote for any of the federal officials who control their destiny.

When Congress and President McKinley seized the island in 1898, they endlessly debated what to do with their new possession. No one wanted a Puerto Rican state, and no wanted to grant the island independence. So Congress got creative and established something unprecedented in U.S. constitutional history, the unincorporated territory of Puerto Rico. Congress retains plenary or absolute power over the island, but it generally lets its residents (in the Caribbean) manage their own affairs, except when it comes to a resolution of the status issue. In the new millennium, Puerto Ricans still wait for a decision, but we cannot. Therefore, I will move back and forth between the mainland and the island because all seven million Puerto Ricans are U.S. citizens and because analysts often forget that Congress made a greater effort to assimilate the Puerto Ricans in San Juan and Ponce than they did the Puerto Ricans in Manhattan and the Bronx.

In response to the new "host" culture, Puerto Ricans reconfigured their world at home and abroad, in the colony and away from it. Scholars like Carlos Torre, Hugo Vecchini, and William Burgos even argue that Puerto Rico is the "commuter nation": its U.S. citizens live in the air, traveling back and forth with such frequency that the Caribbean continually influences the mainland and vice versa. There are Puerto Ricans and Nuyoricans (slang for the mainland Puerto Rican); they are the same thing, yet different.[4]

Borinquen

Going to the airport in San Juan and in Hartford exemplifies one significant, tangible difference between Puerto Rican and Anglo Protestant culture. For us, picking up a relative at the airport is a chore; we may do our wife or son "a favor" by going along for the ride, but if we can stay home and let someone else do it, we will. After all, no one wants to miss the latest episode of *Survivor* or *Lost*. But for many Puerto Ricans a trip to the airport is an anticipated, loving family experience. Six or eight family members crowd into a car bound for the airport and wait eagerly at the gate for an arriving spouse, son, or daughter. In San Juan, the crush of relatives is an everyday phenomenon. Some wait on the glass walkway, spot the relative, throw excited kisses, and then rush to the gate to embrace the relative who is already kissing the other family members. Anglos accentuate the individual and disparage the waste of time. Puerto Ricans key on the family, and for the family they have all the time in the world.

The focus on family dates back to Columbus. Spanish colonists erased the indigenous name of the island—Borinquen—and changed it to San Juan; then, with the discovery of gold, San Juan became Puerto Rico, or "rich port." Within fifty years, the Spanish reduced the indigenous Taino Indian population to less than a thousand people, and that slaughter generated a controversy that still simmers. In his book *El País de Cuatro Pisos* (The Four Storeyed Country) José Luis González argues that the first floor of Puerto Rican culture is African. The Spanish killed the Indians and brought thousands of African slaves and very few of their own. By default, Africans provided the vital foundation for a Puerto Rican identity, and then European and other influences added other floors to the one built by Africans.[5]

Puerto Rican culture is a rich mixture of indigenous, African, European, and North American influences. That culture developed with great independence because the Spanish neglected Puerto Rico for almost two centuries. Between 1651 and 1662, not a single Spanish boat came to Puerto Rico. No one seemed to care, so islanders created a new culture with the amalgam of available ingredients.[6]

The islanders soon began to distinguish between San Juan and *la isla*. The mammoth, concrete fort called El Morro represented Spanish power based in San Juan. Leave San Juan and you entered *la isla,* the place where real Puerto Rican culture was found.[7] In 2006 Ponce still offers tourists a passport that symbolizes local pride: I am a Ponceño and a Puerto Rican. This localized loyalty developed because escaped slaves and soldiers, Taino Indians, buccaneers, and others passing through the crossroads of the Americas discovered the island's superb geographical barriers to intrusion. Travel agents sell the beaches; but many Puerto Ricans still live in the mountains, so high that Puerto Ricans jokingly say that, if you fall over the side, it takes six months for your soul to reach God.

Puerto Rican culture has at least four essential elements: family, language, and the concepts of *dignidad* and *respeto.* Some critics call these latter concepts "slave" values, but in a society ruled by the sword, people developed codes that allowed them to protect their self-respect, even if the powers in San Juan and Madrid objected. Whatever their social-psychological roots, most Puerto Ricans have an inherent dignity and are owed respect. North American managers coming to the island often have to learn how to deal with these aspects of island culture. Raising one's voice indicates a lack of respect that simultaneously tramples on the person's inherent dignity. Outsiders complain that they walk on eggshells in interactions, but the insistence on *respeto* and *dignidad* lends everyday contacts in Puerto Rico (and in New York or Philadelphia) a basic and laudable decency.

Spain so neglected Puerto Rico that, as of 1765, the island was home to only forty-four thousand inhabitants. El Morro crumbled in the sun, and the island's new "indigenous" culture thrived. So, it came as a shock when Spain decided to reinvigorate its Caribbean colonies by substantially increasing the number of slaves and slave owners. Offering everything from land incentives to positions in colonial government, Spain dramatically increased the island's population and the opportunities for conflict between newcomers and criollos, "natives" of the island. The population in 1854 was 492,452, a more than elevenfold increase in eighty-nine years. The number of slaves jumped to 46,918 in 1854, from 5,000 in 1765. However, as a percentage of the total population, slaves dropped from 11.2 percent to 9.5 percent. Puerto Rico never experienced the increase in slaves—or African influence—that became a hallmark of Cuban culture.[8]

Spain sent more reales to Cuba, and that produced labor problems in Puerto Rico. Spaniards eager to milk their colonial, Caribbean opportunities created, in the middle of the nineteenth century, a system of forced labor that alienated the lower classes; simultaneously, the imperial reservation of privileges to Spaniards alienated ambitious criollos who were more attuned to nationality than skin color. These early Puerto Ricans recognized that, like all Caribbean people, they were ethnic combinations. But while skin color may have been a peripheral consideration in the mountains, it assumed more significance for the Spanish authorities based in San Juan.

In 1868 Puerto Ricans launched "El Grito de Lares" (the shout of Lares), a revolutionary effort that failed within a matter of days. The shout of Lares—a town very high in the Puerto Rican mountains—signaled the maturity of Puerto Rican, as opposed to Spanish, culture. Revolutionary leaders like Eugenio Hostos and Ramón Betances affirmed values and beliefs that embraced all Puerto Ricans; skin color was unimportant for these heroes, who are still revered by Puerto Ricans of all political persuasions.

The United States took control of the island on July 25, 1898, in the aftermath of what U.S. historians call the Spanish-American War. General Miles promised freedom and then initiated instead an almost two-year stretch of martial law. Finally, in April 1900, Congress passed the Foraker Act, which assigned virtually all political, economic, and cultural power to Washington. The president would appoint the Puerto Rican governor, who ruled over an Executive Council that combined executive and legislative powers in a single body; the council made the crucial decisions, and it always included a majority of U.S. representatives. Puerto Ricans could vote for members of the House of Delegates, whose only real power, as one of the architects of the colonial administration noted, was the ability to vote yes or no on the island's annual budget. The colonial administration "to a large extent took the whole control over the manner in which the actual administration of affairs shall be exercised out of the hands of the people of the island itself."[9]

Our special interest is the attempt to Americanize the Puerto Rican people. Focusing *first* on assimilation when Puerto Ricans migrated to the mainland in large numbers—during the 1950s—misses a half century of resistance to U.S. culture *long before* millions of Puerto Ricans settled in the Bronx or Tampa. In many ways, Puerto Rican culture was stronger than ever when the "immigrants" finally arrived because all political parties agreed with a statement made by the head of the statehood party, Carlos Romero Barcelo. In his book *Statehood Is for the Poor,* Romero said that, here is "something we all know to be true with our hearts and with every fiber of our beings: namely that to be Puerto Rican is something very special and that we who *are* Puerto Rican are not about to give up our identity for anybody. When it comes to the future of Puerto Rico, our language and our culture are *not* negotiable."[10]

The earliest U.S. administrators had total authority over Puerto Rico and its people, and the island became a U.S. colony at the onset of the movement to Americanize the immigrant. Since General Miles spelled the name of the colony "Porto Rico," for example, islanders learned to misspell the name of their own country, a convention that persisted in federal documents to 1932. Schools were assigned new names—Washington, Lincoln, and Jefferson—that signified nothing to the Puerto Rican people. In the classrooms, U.S. administrators mandated the use of English. Puerto Rican teachers who did not speak English were to teach students who did not understand the English their teachers could not speak. As late as 1937, Franklin Roosevelt reinforced the focus on English, with as much success as his predecessors. In practice, teachers did as they pleased.

The assault on native culture was driven by American economic interests. Coffee was king when the United States took over. In a decade sugar and tobacco reigned supreme, and the island's economy was inextricably linked to that of the United States. In 1897, 15 percent of Puerto Rican exports went to the United States; that figure rose to 86 percent by 1915. Twenty-one percent of Puerto Rican imports came from the United States in 1897; by 1915 the figure was an incredible 91 percent and rising. However important, the numbers do little to capture the nature of colonial economic development. For example, the island could grow sugar but not process it. Processing jobs stayed in the United States, leaving Puerto Rico's agricultural labor force without work for significant periods. Everything depended on the United States: islanders soon joked that, when the North American economy caught a cold, the island got pneumonia.

But not everyone found the new arrangement amusing. Led by a Harvard-educated lawyer named Pedro Albizu Campos, the Puerto Rican nationalists tried everything from creating their own army to assassinating the American head of San Juan's police in 1937. Documents at the Roosevelt Presidential Library show that FDR was rightfully worried about the success of this independence movement. However, Albizu never fully tapped into the culture created in the countryside. He tried to generate a sense of pride by focusing on Spain, the "mother country," the cultural taproot of Puerto Rican greatness. This message never generated mass enthusiasm because, like the Mexicans, Puerto Ricans often regarded their Spanish heritage with disfavor. Memories of oppression overwhelmed the pride that Albizu tried to draw from Puerto Rico's first "mother country."

As another response to U.S. colonial control, Antonio S. Pedreira's *Insularismo* (1934) reeks with pessimism about the miserable state of Puerto Rico's economy and also its culture. Puerto Ricans, Pedreira claims, actually share a learned sense of inferiority. A small island, lacking in natural resources, produces small minds. "It is our honest belief that a Puerto Rican soul does exist though it be disintegrated, disperse, latent, still in thousands of tiny pieces like a painfully difficult jigsaw puzzle which has never been successfully assembled." According to Pedreira, Puerto Ricans had surrendered under the oppressive weight of colonial history and geography.

Pedreira wrote this elegy as the armed nationalists literally were challenging U.S. control from one end of the island to the other. Albizu pointed to Spain, Pedreira raised his arms in desperation, and Luis Muñoz Marin produced a stirring affirmation of the island's culture just before large numbers of Puerto Ricans migrated to the United States. Through the Popular Democratic Party (established in 1938), Luis Muñoz Marin sought to ignore the status issue. He wanted to focus on economic development but to attract the masses to his new political party. He chose popular culture, deftly using symbols that produced both great pride and many votes. The party's newspaper, *El Batey,* was named after the sacred, ceremonial ball fields of the Taino Indians that had been destroyed by the Spanish. Muñoz's slogan was what the people wanted: "Bread, Land, and Liberty." And its inspirational roots were not in Spain but in the Puerto Rican countryside. Muñoz's supporters wore straw hats, the pava that championed *el jibaro,* the peasant who stoically worked in sugar and tobacco to provide love and food for the vital center of Puerto Rican culture, the family.

Evidence of the enormous pride in popular culture that Muñoz resurrected is still seen throughout the island, not to mention in Chicago, New York, Hartford, and Los Angeles. Along the thruway that leads from San Juan to Ponce rises a huge statue, a national shrine to el jibaro. Wearing the pava, he stands with his wife and children as a living testimony to heroism in the face of poverty and colonialism. Opponents called el jibaro a hick, but, among other things, Muñoz's use of cultural pride enabled him to dominate Puerto Rican politics from 1940 to 1964.

Muñoz also made a deal with the devil called economic development via tax breaks. Billing the jibaro as the "Showcase of the Caribbean," Muñoz and his colleagues championed the peasant as they allowed agriculture to languish. Drive the southern end of the island and you still see vast tracts of unused land. Drive the northern route and you see the polluted results of development that used a fishing net approach to industrialization. Offering federal, state, and local tax exemptions, Muñoz pulled in whoever wanted to make a fast buck on the island. He hoped to produce self-sustaining economic development but found, by 1959, that businesses left when their exemptions disappeared or, even worse, businesses blackmailed the Puerto Rican government by demanding continued or new exemptions to stay. Official unemployment was 12.9 percent in 1950; and, after thirteen years of the industrialization "miracle," official unemployment was 12.8 percent.[11]

On the mainland, the jíbaro was a hero no one wanted, but he was nevertheless coming to the United States. Industrialization had made San Juan one of the most densely inhabited cities on earth, and people in search of work received help from the colonial and the native government if they left for the mainland. Muñoz and Washington helped hide the economic failure of Operation Bootstrap by sending roughly 25 percent of the Puerto Rican people to cities like New York and Chicago. Unable to say no to U.S. citizens, the United States received the possible benefits of cheap labor when its thoroughly decaying cities offered few jobs for the Puerto Ricans who came with little education and few marketable skills. Adding insult to injury, the Puerto Ricans arrived in the middle of a civil rights struggle that made skin color more important than ever.

Author and scholar Juan Flores argues that Puerto Ricans responded to the United States in a series of three stages. First was "the state of abandon." Moving from the tropical Caribbean, Puerto Ricans found themselves in frozen Chicago or New York. Oscar Lopez, the Puerto Rican revolutionary, notes that his uncle took him to a ballgame in the late fifties to see the famous Puerto Rican player Victor Pellot. When fifteen-year-old Oscar searched the program, Pellot's name was nowhere to be found. Instead, there was a Vic Power. To Lopez, the name change represented a betrayal. Why would any Puerto Rican turn his back on island pride? The answer was prejudice. Pellot's dark skin produced problems, so he changed his name, and kids like Oscar Lopez felt abandoned in the Windy City and in the Big Apple.

After abandonment comes enchantment, "an almost dream-like trance at the striking contrast between the cultural barrenness of New York and the *imagined luxuriance* of the island culture."[12] Again, in Chicago, you can find innumerable stores named Borinquen, battles to rename U.S. schools for Puerto Rican heroes, and cars with Puerto Rican flags tied to the windshield wipers. The flags go back and forth as a fictional Andrés fixes his hat in *They Have to Be Puerto Ricans.*

"Andrés also bought . . . a multi-color cap with the colors of the Puerto Rican flag—red, blue and white . . . Andrés walks to the mirror; he puts his cap on, takes a close look from his forehead up, thinks about Puerto Rico and he feels good. Andrés washes his cap, rinses his cap, smells his cap, and feels good."[13]

Like perfume from an island flower, you smilingly admire what you left, you long for your "isla heritage," and you try to resurrect it in the United States. Instead of assimilation, Juan Flores stresses that the main content of this second moment "*is the recovered African and indigenous foundation of Puerto Rican culture.*"[14] While the Chicanos discover "La Raza Cósmica" in Los Angeles, the Puerto Ricans happily embrace their combined ethnicities in New York and Chicago. Again we witness the transculturation envisioned by Fernando Ortiz. With great passion, the Puerto Rican "reenters" American life (this is the third moment of the process) by emphasizing the difference between them and us. As a U.S. citizen he is also one of them, but as a Puerto Rican he suffuses his everyday conversation with remarks about *los Norteamericanos*. After a century of U.S. influence, this distinction remains a constant of life in the Caribbean and the United States. The difference is that, on the mainland, the encounter with prejudice produces an even stronger affirmation of being Puerto Rican because "they" are everywhere and they often treat me like dirt because of my accent, my skin color, and my inability to fit into the world of *los fríos* (the cold ones).

Rooted in the Taino and Afro Caribbean world, the Puerto Rican reenters U.S. culture and then reenters Puerto Rico culture. In Hartford, a relatively small city, a jet leaves seven mornings a week for the island; seven nights a week another plane returns. This aerial byway offers Nuyoricans a chance to refresh and reinvigorate their ties to the homeland; the required response to landing in San Juan is a loud burst of applause from Puerto Rican fliers. They are delighted to be home. But the trip is not always easy. Nuyoricans are no longer the real thing. Someone might criticize their accent or ridicule their less than perfect Spanish. An upbringing in the Bronx is not the same as growing up in the mountains near Jayuua.

But in the bosom of the family, all Puerto Ricans again come together as one. It is not unknown for more than one hundred relatives to attend family celebrations. And with digital photography and the Internet, an aunt or an uncle can hit "return" and broadcast the news. Puerto Rico is a culture that creates a deep, lasting sense of family, on the island and in the coldest streets of Chicago.

But it is difficult to forget the status issue. Puerto Rico is a thriving *Latin American* culture, a de facto nation that is also a colony and a commonwealth. Congress claims plenary or absolute power, so Puerto Ricans of all political persuasions must see themselves against the background of American rule. The status issue continually breathes new life into the Puerto Rican identity because it is another manifestation of "them" and "us." On the island, all political parties agree that Puerto Rico is a colony. Embarrassment over that fact produces many different suggestions for change; but when they come before Congress one thing is always clear. The North Americans are up there, behind the desks; we, the Puerto Ricans, are down here, at the witness table. And whatever other differences we have, we again reiterate the point you always force us to make. Our language and our culture are not negotiable.

Interestingly, Puerto Ricans, who made up 80 percent of New York's Latino population in 1960, now account for only 50 percent, and that number is dropping. Large-scale immigration by Dominicans, Chicanos, Colombians, Peruvians, and other Latin American groups in recent years has produced a new cultural mix. Puerto Ricans are learning that they are also Latinos, a new identity that generates both cooperation and competition. As a Puerto Rican, I positively identity with the larger Latino family; yet I also worry that my most important cultural identity risks being subsumed by all these Latinos. In response, there have been calls to form new cultural advocacy groups that focus *only* on Puerto Ricans. It often comes down to claims about who was here (on the East Coast) first and whether the new groups sometimes overshadow the more established ones. Yet again, it is a question of them and us; and, yet again, the Puerto Rican raises his red, white, and blue flag and waves it with passion.

West Indians

Dance Hall, *1993*

The painting's name is *Dance Hall;* the artist is Joshua Higgins, a Jamaican and a West Indian. I first saw *Dance Hall* at the home of Rex Nettleford, the founder of the National Dance Theater Company of Jamaica as well as the vice chancellor of the University of the West Indies. Rex hangs copy number one of *Dance Hall* in the most prominent spot in his dining room. It is a racy painting by most standards; churches and schools would never display the lavish love of life so colorfully depicted by Higgins.

The largest figure in the picture, a Jamaican man, stands near the center of the image. He sports a beret; a loud green, checkered shirt; and white gloves. His eyes make it clear that he is having a hell of a good time. Just below the man is the derriere of a woman dressed in pink; her head is below one fellow's belt buckle while, to her left, another woman with a dazzling smile holds on to her most sensitive parts. Other couples embrace in various suggestive postures while, at the very center of the portrait, a dark-skinned man with straight hair and distinctly Far Eastern features peeks through the crowd. He represents the Chinese influence in Jamaican culture; he is the exclamation point who emphasizes "out of many, one people."

I immediately fell in love with Higgins's painting. It represents the tremendous energy and love of life that run through so many sides of Jamaican society. Problems arose when, as director of my school's Center of Caribbean and Latin American Studies, I brought a copy of *Dance Hall* to the campus. My West Indian students liked the picture. It reminded them of home. But, when I showed it to an African American friend, he became visibly upset. *Dance Hall* represented a stereotypical portrayal of black people; it echoed the negative thinking of whites and so offended my friend that I removed the painting from school and brought it home. When I later mentioned the incident to Rex, he indifferently made this comment: "It *is* a dance hall. What *is* their problem?"

Their problem is people who, because of the one-drop rule, look like black Americans but are in reality an ocean and a culture apart. Many Jamaicans, Trinidadians, and Bayans are darker than most African Americans, yet they wear their ethnicity with as much self-assurance as the flamboyant star of *Dance Hall*. A problem arises when West Indians visit American churches, universities, or dance halls and are expected to worry about the stereotypes of white people. The West Indian, and certainly the Jamaican, generally responds with something like this: "You must be kidding. If white people pay the cover charge, they can dance with us or they can watch us. But I am not going to worry about white people or about African Americans who worry about white people." As a friend from Trinidad put it, "African Americans need to get over it [slavery] and get on with life. Take it easy, but take it."

My friend's flippant and less than empathetic response is a sign of the friction that can arise when West Indians come to the United States. Whites want to treat them as the "good" black people, while blacks want them to admit that color is all-important. West Indians react to all this with a variety of insights about the consequences of cultural reconfiguration and cultural assimilation.

Afro-Creole

After living in the United States for twelve years, a Jamaican teacher made this remark: "They are just now trying to overcome many of the discriminations and what the whites have been doing to them over the period. You see, we West Indians came here with the idea that nobody was better than we are. It was not a matter of color in the Caribbean, it was a matter of haves and have-nots. You came here; it was definitely a matter of black and white. We really haven't ever been discriminated against in Jamaica."[15]

Nobody is better than we are. This statement is a perfect encapsulation of the West Indian sense of self. But how, given the harsh prejudices of British colonialism, did the Jamaicans manage to cultivate a positive sense of themselves and their island culture? The Puerto Ricans talk about *insularismo* and the inherent limitations of being a small island without natural resources. The West Indian responds: *We are the best natural resource in the world.*

In the discussion that follows I focus, for the sake of space, on Jamaica. From the outset, Jamaica was home to extraordinary cultural diversity. In 1673 the island contained roughly eight thousand whites and ninety-five hundred blacks. The whites included planters but also soldiers, officials, farmers, convicts, buccaneers, and prostitutes. Scots, Irish, and Welsh seconded the English presence; the historian Richard D. E. Burton also describes communities of Portuguese-speaking Sephardic Jews who had arrived from Brazil via Surinam and groups of Romanian-speaking gypsies brought by the British to labor alongside Africans on farms and in the sugar cane fields.

The so-called black population included three groups of more or less Spanish-speaking Maroons. They united with the remnants of the indigenous Sarawak Indians and resisted British authority as much as they had resisted the Spanish who brought them to Jamaica. The other "blacks," who, by 1739, outnumbered the whites by a ratio of ten to one, were characterized by a variety of African influences and languages. On the plantations, the ratio often reached one in twenty, offering so much room for cultural creativity that Creole became the spoken language of the slaves, as well as many of their masters. Britain maintained such loose control over everyday life that Burton found villages to be "comparatively free to develop according to their own logic; and that logic, during the first half of the eighteenth century, appears to have been preponderantly African."[16]

Jamaicans proudly championed transculturation hundreds of years before Fernando Ortiz devised the concept. However, Jamaica also experienced a push to reduce the Creole component of its popular culture. In 1834 Jamaica's "Free Coloured" easily outnumbered whites by a factor of two to one; ironically, "the most physically creolized section of the Jamaican population" owned slaves, often dressed and talked like the English, and over time displaced white boys from the schools. At the Woolmer's Free School in 1815, 3 "coloured" pupils studied with 111 whites; by 1832, 360 "coloureds" studied with only 90 whites.[17]

Jamaicans always enjoyed substantial cultural independence. But Jamaica—and all the West Indian islands—were ultimately money-making English colonies. The Crown used force whenever necessary to maintain control, and Jamaica's economy was tied so closely to Great Britain's that Jamaican prime minister Michael Manley later noted that Jamaica tried to move forward while chained to an imperial anchor: the island produced what others consumed and consumed what others produced. But England, even as it bled the economy dry, continued to add to the Jamaican mix. As late as the 1940s Jamaica absorbed the Chinese and the Indians, who, like the gypsies, found themselves exploited by the English and embraced by the Jamaicans. Nearly one in five Indians married a local, and curried goat flesh is a staple of the Jamaican diet.[18]

England exploited the world; it never wanted the world to live in the British Isles. Only seven thousand "coloureds" lived in Great Britain in 1939.[19] After World War II, the English very reluctantly admitted hundreds of thousands of West Indian immigrants. In an effort to resuscitate the empire, Churchill and his colleagues said that anyone in the Commonwealth enjoyed British citizenship. While even the British had a hard time keeping out their own citizens, the Conservative government did its best to keep the "coloureds" where they belonged, in the Caribbean, Africa, and South Asia. In the West Indies governors were instructed to tamper with shipping lists and schedules so that West Indian workers would find themselves at the end of the immigration line; they were also ordered to cordon off ports in order to prevent passport-holding stowaways from boarding ships and to delay the issuing of passports to migrants.[20]

Nothing worked. Coloured Commonwealth citizens continued to flow into the United Kingdom. So, using a variety of legal pretexts, Britain adopted what was effectively a zero immigration policy in the same year—1965—that the United States opened its doors to the world. West Indians began coming to the United States in large numbers because England had locked them out, because the island's economy was tethered to the mother country's, and because U.S. policy rarely did anything to help create self-sustaining Caribbean economies. When President Reagan imposed country quotas on

Caribbean sugar in 1982, he put, by one estimate, four hundred thousand people out of work. Washington's Caribbean Basin Initiative did create roughly 136,000 jobs, but that still left the Caribbean with a net loss of more than a quarter of a million jobs.[21]

The North American Free Trade Agreement (NAFTA) has also had a devastating effect on the Caribbean in general and on Jamaica and the Dominican Republic in particular. Mexico produces clothing at costs 25 percent below those in the Caribbean. Meanwhile, Jamaica and the Dominican Republic are to this day subject, as with sugar, to quotas that limit their exports to the United States. Post-NAFTA Mexico has no quota restrictions.[22]

Until the Caribbean becomes self-sustaining, West Indians will continue to migrate to the United States in large numbers. The West Indian community in Brooklyn numbers more than 750,000 people by some estimates; the one in Hartford contains more than 60,000. An exact count is impossible because, as with Mexicans, the West Indian population includes many undocumented Americans. They come to find opportunities, and they stay because that is the best way to help their families. The World Bank reports that no one in Latin America and the Caribbean sends more money home, per capita, than Jamaicans.[23]

Resistance and Assimilation

West Indians often struggle to make sense of life in the United States. At home, social class is often the key identifier. In meetings, for example, West Indian people address one another by "Mister" or "Miss"; even individuals with long-standing business and personal relationships generally avoid first names. Older professors complain that students come to their offices without academic robes; and I saw a close West Indian friend explode when a tradesman had the audacity to come to her front door. This otherwise charming and down-to-earth woman bridled at an offense whose significance would elude most Americans.

West Indians who disembark at JFK Airport may look for markers of social class, but, as one immigrant explains, this is what they find:

"You heard about crime but you didn't hear that you come here and you would be bombarded with this racial thing . . . I still see it as people against people. I find that American blacks, they talk about it, they see it in every incident that happens, it has to be race why this happen."

Many West Indians worry about their children catching the racial bug. "Well, no, I've never really told them because of black this and black that. Eventually you will start to become racial. At least I feel that. You see, I feel that it doesn't matter the color of your skin. And you know, the minute you will start to look at it, oh, he's white, they're black . . . you know, eventually it becomes you and humbles your thinking."[4]

Any sociologist, cleric, or political leader advocating assimilation into Anglo Protestant culture needs to consider this person's assessment. It comes from a West Indian woman who does not care about color. But we want her to. She is virtually color-blind, but we teach her to think in black and white. Worse yet, she understands that thinking of herself as black will "humble" her. She and her children will think less of themselves because of what they have learned in the process of assimilation into American life.

In response, West Indians sometimes use their accents to emphasize their "foreign" status. They vigorously protest any manifestation of skin color prejudice against themselves or other West Indians but, especially in the first generation, distance themselves from a culture that sees black and thinks white. In Hartford, for example, many African Americans and West Indians live on the "wrong side" of town. But there is a clear geographical boundary between the two communities; the proof is in signs indicating Caribbean or West Indian restaurants and the accents of people on the street.

Harvard sociologist Mary Waters quotes a West Indian from New York, who could also be living in Hartford or Miami. "I can't help them [African Americans] because they're so wrapped up in racism, and they act it out so often, they interpret it as such so often that sometimes they are not approachable. If they're going to teach anything and it's not black, black, all black, they are not satisfied you know . . . Sometimes I feel sorry for them, but you find that you just can't change their attitude because they tell you that you don't understand. You weren't here to feel what we felt."

African Americans get the point. When Waters asked about tensions and problems with West Indians, she got this response: "Oh yes. Oh my god. Are you kidding? This is ridiculous. I mean it's really ridiculous because a lot if it is pure ignorance . . . they don't like us. And myself included. We don't try to get out and do things for ourselves. We just sit back and complain about the white man."[25]

The white/black dichotomy turns one group of people against another. Meanwhile, whites sit on the sidelines, proclaiming that they harbor no prejudices against anyone but telling Waters and her associates that "they felt very uncomfortable with blacks, made negative judgments about black people as a whole, and evaluated their employees by the color of their skin all of the time."

This is not ancient history. Waters published her book in 2000. Whites retain their prejudices against blacks and, in a pernicious use of the dichotomy, ask West Indians to reaffirm and reinvigorate their prejudices against African Americans. The dead end reappears because West Indians become as much of a model minority for whites as Asians (see chap. 4). As Waters notes, given prejudice against blacks and an egalitarian value system, whites are "eager to find 'good blacks' whom they can trust and relate to as 'individuals' without the weight of guilt and 'chips on the shoulder' and past historical wrongs being thrown in their face."

West Indians are a prejudiced white person's dream come true. They work hard, do not obsess about race, and treat people like individuals if people treat them like individuals. The West Indian becomes the exception that whites cite as proof that they were right about "black people" all along.

This perverse logic highlights the negative power of the white/black dichotomy. After all, if dark-skinned Jamaicans or Trinidadians can neglect skin color and use ethnicity as an axis of identity, they prove that nothing insurmountable stands in our way. Moreover, are we really civilized if West Indians need to defend themselves against whites and blacks? What does it say about us that they arrive wanting to be Jamaican and we refuse to allow them to do so?

In summarizing her findings, Waters found three general responses to the United States. Recent immigrants happily accepted their foreigner status; they self-identified as Jamaican or Trinidadian and did not distance themselves from blacks. "Rather, their identities were strongly linked to their experiences on the island, and they did not worry much about how they were seen by other Americans, white or black."[26] This response represented 27 percent of Waters's sample.

A second group (31 percent) "adopted a very strong ethnic identity, which involved a considerable amount of distancing themselves from American blacks." These folks frequent the many West Indian social clubs in New York and Hartford. They hang with their own, and, at times, they adopt a stance that makes West Indians superior to blacks and whites. Like the South Asian Indians described in chapter 5, West Indians agree to work days and nights to get ahead economically; but, when it comes to culture, they embrace their own because it is love and because it is a strong shield against the hatreds they find in the United States.

The most common response (42 percent) of the sample was to assimilate, to become black. Ironically, social class affected the likelihood of this response; if you grew up in the inner city, if your parents lacked an education, if you were poor, if the schools were rotten, then you were much more likely to focus on skin color. These young men and women did not see their West Indian identities "as important to their self-images." On the contrary, the schools represented "white culture and white requirements," which meant that, as blacks, these formerly West Indian immigrants had to "act black."[27] In a worst-case scenario, they would adopt the attitudes of victimization and anti-intellectualism described by John McWhorter in *Losing the Race*. Then, fully assimilated, the West Indians who learned to be black could teach Caribbean newcomers how to "make it" in the United States.

West Indian culture poses truly important challenges to the American fixation on race. Tragically, we have so far neglected the Caribbean lesson and, instead, tried to teach people who have substantially transcended their colonial heritage to embrace ours. It is a world in which the last laugh still belongs to the slave traders who taught us to think in white and nonwhite categories.

Cubans: Tampa, Miami, and Whiteness

Here are two stories, separated by eighty years of American life. Evilio Grillo moved to Tampa from Cuba in the early 1920s. He got off the boat and into a line. "As Cubans entered Ybor City [the cigar making section of Tampa]," he writes in his memoir, *Black Cuban, Black American,* "they were sorted out. Black Cubans went to a neighborhood immediately east of Nebraska Avenue, inhabited by black Americans and a scattering of poor whites. White Cubans had a much wider range of choices, although most of them chose to remain in Ybor City."

Darker-skinned people still experienced discrimination in Cuba but nothing like the Jim Crow ugliness of Florida. Even in the twenties, affluent black Cubans managed to thrive among the island's elite structures in Havana or Santiago; commercial and government facilities were opened to everyone, and blacks used the same hospitals and clinics as whites. In fact, after Grillo's brother contracted tuberculosis, his mother finally sent him home to Cuba, "where medical care for blacks was vastly superior to that available in Tampa."[28]

Grillo explains that the level of discrimination in America was so great that no one shared any interest in his accent, language, or culture. "Being black was the *only* thing that really mattered in Tampa," he writes. As he grew up, he recognized that only one viable option existed: "Join the black American society, with its rich roots deep in this country, or have no American roots at all."

This dark-skinned Cuban lost his ethnic heritage and became black. He was treated as such when he joined the service. On the way to fight World War II, he discovered that "white troops had fresh water for showering; Black troops had to shower with sea water. White troops had the ample stern of the ship to lounge during the day. Black troops were consigned to the narrow bow, so loaded with gear that it was difficult to find comfortable resting places."

Meanwhile, white Cubans are almost entirely absent from Grillo's memoir. He never saw them because they assimilated by embracing Jim Crow, a force so powerful that it even erased "Cubanidad," or pride in culture above all else.

Joel Ruiz and Achmed Valdés both fled Fidel Castro's dictatorship in the 1990s. Almost like brothers in Cuba, they came to Miami on different rafts, and, like Evilio Grillo seventy years earlier, they were sorted into lines. Ruiz is dark skinned, while Valdés is much lighter. These two men who had been so comfortable with one another in Cuba learned to treat each other like strangers in Miami.

Valdés quickly assimilated. "He lives in an all-white neighborhood, hangs out with white Cuban friends and goes to black neighborhoods only when his job, as a deliveryman for Restonic mattresses, forces him to." Proudly wearing America's "invisible knapsack of privilege," Valdés rarely thinks about race. When he does, it is based on the lessons learned, not in Cuba, but in Miami. "American blacks, he now believes, are to be avoided because they are delinquent and dangerous and resentful of whites. The only blacks he trusts are those he knows from Cuba."[29]

Joel Ruiz left Cuba because of the lack of freedoms and opportunities. Except for the newspapers published by the Communist Party, fresh information is hard to find; the bookstore at La Casa de las Americas, once famous for serious intellectual discussions, contains more books about Che than anything else. Real access to the outside world is only available to Cubans who work in the tourist industry; they get to watch CNN and spend U.S. tourism dollars on consumer goods that create invidious distinctions in a theoretically classless society.

Ruiz loves *la patria* (the motherland), but politics pushed him on a raft, despite pleas from his mother. On her hands and knees, she begged him not to go. Arriving in Miami, he discovered that he had made a Faustian bargain with the descendants of Jim Crow. He got freedom of movement and freedom to order a steak whenever he wishes. But race is now such an important variable in his life "that he cannot forget about it." The dichotomy dominates his newly segregated life: his lifelong friendship with Valdés ended when they jumped off their respective rafts and moved into Miami's segregated neighborhoods. Today they can reminisce about their old life in a politically closed society but never discuss the consequences of their divergent paths of assimilation. Valdés says his old friend needs to leave his black neighborhood, forget about his needy relatives, and begin life on his own, to which Ruiz laments, "Achmed does not know what it means to be black."[30]

Separated by eighty years of social space, these two stories suggest a one-way street. When Cubans assimilate into American culture, they make race and skin color more important than being Cuban. In reality, the dynamic is much more complicated; in fact, like so many things in Cuba, this one begins with José Martí.

If Cubans in Miami and in Havana agree about anything, it is their reverence for José Martí, the nation's preeminent hero. Even Fidel Castro uses Martí's statue and museum as backdrop for his million-man speeches in La Plaza de la Revolutíon. A wall depicting Che is in the background; front and center is José Martí. Martí also dominates in Miami. Martí statues, portraits, and busts are everywhere, in universities and restaurants and libraries. He is the hero who, after a short stay in Brooklyn, literally rode a white horse into "Nuestra América." For Martí, our America began below the Rio Grande. Almost thirty years before Vaconcelos and Rivera in Mexico, Martí sought to create a sense of unity throughout Latin America, but especially in Cuba, by emphasizing *mestizaje,* the endless human and cultural combinations that characterize life in the Caribbean and Latin America. Martí believed in the universalizing ideal; but, equally important, he sought to create a renewed sense of "Cubanidad" in a late-nineteenth-century nation struggling to defeat the Spanish while somehow keeping "the giant colossus of the North" at arm's length.[31]

Martí, who was born in 1853, grew up in a Cuba overwhelmed by immigration, slavery, and imperialism. In 1757, the giant island was home to only 149,170 inhabitants. The Spanish had allowed their Caribbean colonies to languish, but, after a damning report on conditions in 1765, Spain decided to finally exploit Cuba as aggressively as it exploited Mexico. Offering everything from land grants to toleration of slavery, Spain was able to raise Cuba's population to 898,732 by 1846, a sixfold increase in 89 years. Even more to the point, the first 250 years of Spanish rule had brought 60,000 slaves to Cuba, whereas, between 1763 and 1865, while the rest of the world was debating abolition, Cuba's slave population increased to 636,465.[32]

While about a quarter of slaves worked on Cuban sugar plantations, another 18 percent worked on small properties in the countryside and fully 45 percent worked in homes and cities throughout
Cuba. Eduardo Torres Cuevas rightly emphasizes the enormous
impact of original African culture on Cuban life. Many slaves worked
and lived in people's homes, an intimacy that bred the transculturation celebrated by Fernando Ortiz and other Cuban social scientists.
However, Spanish imperial policy reserved the lion's share of political
and economic privileges for European landowners and merchants,
who lacked any ties to Cuba and its culture. Spain treated the newcomers like close members of the family. Meanwhile, "native" Cubans
got angry, and Martí tried to provide, through essays like "Nuestra
America," a synthesis that sustained the independence movement by
creating unity rooted in mestizaje, patriotism, and wariness of the
United States.[33]

In 1898, three years after Martí's death on the battlefield, the U.S.
Congress confirmed Cuban nationalists' worst fears. In a debate about
war in Cuba, President McKinley's opponents reminded Secretary of
State John Sherman about a speech he made in 1896. Sherman then
said that, "much to my surprise . . . they have gone through all the for-
mulae of self-government as fully and completely as the people of the
United States did at the beginning of the Revolution." In 1896 Sherman thought Congress must recognize the Cuban revolutionary government. Senator Henry Cabot Lodge of Massachusetts seconded this
suggestion. He said the Cubans had endured "a year of desperate and
successful fighting against heavy odds." The U.S. government should
recognize the independence of Cuba for two reasons: "it was reasonable and proper, and Lodge felt certain "that the American people
would sustain recognition of independence without a dissenting voice
and that the civilized world would applaud."[34]

In 1898 President McKinley refused to concede independence.
Disregarding the previous comments of his secretary of state, McKinley said that "such recognition is not due to a revolted dependency
until the danger of its being subjugated by the parent state has entirely
passed away." In addition, if the United States recognized the legitimacy of the revolutionary government, "our conduct would be subject

to the approval and disapproval of such government. We would be required to submit to its direction and to assume to it the mere relation of a friendly ally."[35]

With his refusal to concede independence, McKinley changed the Cuban War for Independence into the Spanish-American War. Martí wanted to create a united Cuba by marrying Cubanidad—the fierce and wonderful pride exhibited by Jésus in 2003—to an affirmation of mestizaje as the island's cultural soul. The new Spanish immigrants thought otherwise and so too the Americans, who, in the name of independence, retained the right to interfere in Cuba whenever they pleased.

In *On Becoming Cuban,* Louis Perez Jr. writes that the Americans "intruded themselves" at a "critical juncture" in Cuban history. Thanks to the revolutionary government, "the institutional basis of a more equitable society actually existed." Especially for the Spanish and other European immigrants, prejudice against darker-skinned Cubans flourished in public institutions and in private life; but "Cubans of color had distinguished themselves in all sectors of the separatist project. They had occupied positions in the provisional government and the Cuban Revolutionary Party; they were fully represented within the command structure of the Liberation Army."[36]

Cuba could move toward Martí's ideal or away from it. The Caribbean nation moved away from it because, with the Spanish defeated in war, the United States brought Jim Crow to the Caribbean. The U.S. military government that controlled the island for its first three years of independence "revived and reinforced many of the most deleterious aspects of race relations in the colonial regime." Perez notes that whites monopolized most of the appointments to government offices. Cuban blacks got few of the positions in the Rural Guard; they were "officially" denied commissions in the Artillery Corps; and, most important, "they were systematically excluded from political participation through narrow suffrage restrictions." Ultimately, Secretary of War Elihu Root congratulated General Wood "for the popular establishment of self-government, based on a limited suffrage, excluding so great a proportion of the elements that have brought ruin to Haiti and Santo Domingo."[37]

America demanded that Cubans disregard Martí's teachings. Cubans could disagree—and they did—but the United States held the keys to power, and they exerted that power even when Cubans refused to sanction the American takeover.

Remember not the Maine but Guantanamo. Cubans leaders never wanted Yankee bases on Cuban land. By October 1902, President Roosevelt told Secretary of State John Hay that "the naval stations are to be ceded and in the near future . . . the question is not a matter open to discussion by the Cubans. It is already in their constitution and no discussion concerning it will be entertained." When Cubans resisted— the constitutional clause was never their idea—Roosevelt suggested sending troops to take what the United States wanted. Finally, negotiators produced a face-saving deal. In exchange for the bases, the United States agreed to return title to the Isle of Pines, a twenty-by-fifty-mile appendage that, for centuries, rested under Cuban sovereignty. Not one Cuban leader appeared when Guantanamo formally changed hands on December 10, 1903. Cubans were angry about the bases and furious with a U.S. Congress that never returned title to the Isle of Pines. That occurred in 1925, a quarter of a century into Cuba's lauded independence.[38]

Americans and Cubans moved the nation toward Jim Crow and away from ideals espoused by the Mexicans. Light skin color was so esteemed that, by 1930, a North American dentist in Havana could blithely advertise "a practice confined to the white race." Even as Evillo Grillo's mother was sending her son back to Cuba because blacks still received better medical treatment on the island, U.S. citizens were demanding that Havana be more like Tampa. The Washington Saloon posted this large sign: "We Cater to White People Only." And the American Grocery advertised for a clerk to wait on customers: "Must be white." Finally, in sharp contrast to the intimacy that existed in the nineteenth century, "a family advertised for a neat girl (white) as cook and for general house work."[39]

As the tourist industry developed and relied on American customers, the same "whites only" preferences came to dominate. African American poet Langston Hughes already expected that the American steamship lines would refuse to sell colored people tickets to Cuba. He did not anticipate that, when he finally got to Cuba, he would be denied admission to tourist spots because, as in Atlanta or Miami, dark skin color meant that you belonged in the shadows of Cuban life.[40]

This history is relevant for at least three reasons. One, it indicates the Jim Crow culture inherited by the revolution. In 1957 black Cubans could not enter Veradero, the most important tourist spot on the island. Second, this history suggests who came to Miami because they fled Fidel Castro and his dictatorship. Today we see freedom fighters out to defeat communism and Castro. Then, the refugees significantly included those who adamantly supported Jim Crow; the Batista dictatorship; and, as the CIA stressed, the "gangsters" who worked for the United States and Cuban interests also supporting the political and racial status quo. Finally, the history matters because race was a very hot topic on the island when we spoke to academics at the University of Havana in 2003.

During a dinner hosted by faculty at the university, I told our hosts about the book I was writing and my African American students' delighted reaction to life on the island. How had the Cubans managed to do such a good job of eliminating Spanish, North American, and Cuban prejudices? Our Cuban colleagues explained that, while total elimination was an exaggeration, Cubans under Castro did learn to focus on Cubanidad rather than on the color of a person's skin. Those born after 1959 grew up in a world that, whatever the lack of everyday freedoms, genuinely tried to erase the racial past. However, with a sly smile, one fellow added that Fidel Castro had a secret weapon. "We sent all the rabid racists to Miami; we exported our problem to you and thus had the chance to work from a relatively clean slate."

The 2002 Pew Hispanic Center's *National Survey of Latinos* found that roughly 20 percent of Latinos identified as whites but 55 percent of Cubans did so.[41] No other Latino group approaches the Cubans in their willingness to use the white label. Can we blame the Cubans if, like the Arabs in the previous chapter, they once again identified with prejudiced white people rather than their national hero, José Martí?

In Cuba, in 2003, politicians and academics also talked about Martí as they debated the possible failure of the revolution. For example, in the center of Havana the El Presidente Hotel contains a wall full of photos of its important managerial personnel. No dark faces appear on the wall, and critics who call Castro a hypocrite and a racist underline the lack of dark faces in the nation's positions of power. Our Cuban colleagues noticed the same thing, but, instead of blaming Castro, they blamed everyone's failure to erase the institutional barriers to change. Unlike the Indians in 1948, Castro and colleagues focused on ideology; they tried to transform beliefs but never demanded that, for example, darker-skinned Cubans move to locations that easily offered access to education and social mobility. Given the segregation that existed in 1959, darker-skinned Cubans often lived in grossly underserved areas. Since the revolution never moved the people to the services, nor enough of the universities and other advantages to the people, darker-skinned Cubans experienced few prejudices but never the jump start necessary to leap over the institutional barriers that also prevented real equality and justice. Our Cuban colleagues blamed themselves and the revolution. Cuba needed to rectify it mistakes by marrying a change in beliefs to affirmative access to, among other things, the school systems that trained Cuban leaders.

Here, then, is the situation after a century full of change. Cubans raised under Castro arrive in Miami, where they learn that assimilation requires racial segregation, even in the twenty-first century. Meanwhile, ninety miles offshore, in a nation with precious few public freedoms and information, their fellow Cubans openly debate the failure of their revolutionary efforts to eliminate prejudices connected to race and skin color. All the while Cubans in both nations celebrate their version of Martí. It is a stalemate for them and for us. Instead of learning from history, we choose to repeat it, using black and white film from the early twentieth century.

Gracias a Gracia

Jorge Gracia is a Cuban immigrant who offers a vision of the future that is an imaginative process of cultural reconfiguration. In *Hispanic/Latino Identity*, Gracia roots himself in the Caribbean, offering fellow Hispanics a way to avoid America's interpretation of their past.

Gracia begins with an analysis of two words: Latino and Hispanic. He devotes significant attention to the names because "names serve to carve out the world"; accompanied by concepts, names teach us how to think about things and the properties we attribute to them. Names and concepts *"are windows to the world."*[42]

Gracia seeks to unite—over and against Anglo Protestant culture—people as different as Mexicans, Cubans, and Colombians. He therefore settles on Hispanic because it is a label that reidentifies the meaning and place of Caribbean and Latin American people in the Americas. "Hispanics are the group of people comprised by the inhabitants of the countries of the Iberian Peninsula *after 1492*." Hispanic also includes people raised "in what were to become the colonies of those countries after the encounter between Iberia and America took place." Finally, Hispanic also includes "the descendants of these people who live in other countries (e.g., the United States) but preserve some link to these people."[43] By this definition, even Spanish immigrants as removed from contemporary issues as my parents are Hispanics because they came from Iberia after 1492 and they proudly maintained a link with their homeland.

With his name and concept in place, Gracia opens his window by asking this question: Where do we come from? His answer is as creative as the Chicanos in the sixties and, implicitly, as assertive as those who speak about an occupied America.

No one discovered a new world. To Gracia, "discover makes sense only insofar as it describes what Europeans thought had happened, not what actually happened." Gracia uses the word *encounter* because it is neutral and because it makes all parties to the encounter equal participants. Those with guns and cannons did have more power, but none of the participants was inherently superior or inferior to the other. They encountered one another, and altogether Hispanics created new nations and cultures. Judgments about the value of those cultures will vary between and among, for example, Puerto Ricans or Chileans; the indisputable point is that all the creators deserve the name Hispanic.

Starting in Spain, Gracia reminds us that the English phrase "blue blood" originated from the Spanish term *sangre azul.* Spaniards worried about the purity of blood because they realized that the world already ran through their veins. They tried to do the impossible: find sangre azul in a world that contained no pure breeds, only endless combinations that began at the dawn of time.

When the Spaniards and other Iberians encountered the new world, they behaved like Cortez and Malinche. They intermingled with everybody, but "since conquest implies domination and domination requires identifying and labeling, naming is the first required step toward domination." We get Christians and heathens; whites and blacks; and, in Mexico, a list that requires a higher education to decipher. A mulatto had a European father and a Negra mother. A mestizo had a European father and an Indian mother. A Zambo had a Negro father and a mulatta mother. A Chino *claro* had a mulatto father and mestizo mother. A Chino *oscuro* (dark) had a mulatto father and a Chinese mother.[44]

Gracia stresses that the one-drop rule never dominated in Latin America. Equally important for all Hispanics, *mestizaje* never implied homogeneity, the racial purity imagined by Anglo Protestant culture. On the contrary, the elements in any combination were not "actually separable." Once united, *mestizaje* implies a fusion, something so new that "it can be a principle of union without implying the kind of homogenization that obliterates the contributions made by different ethnic and racial elements."[45]

Gracia uses the word *race* in its cultural rather than its biological meaning. He indicates that Fernando Ortiz discarded the biological concept of race in the early 1900s; and he uses race in its *raza*—its Spanish language—sense. *Race* means a group of people who think and act in a similar fashion.

Hispanics "cannot be understood apart from *mestizaje*." In addition, unlike the creation of a mythical Atzlán by Chicanos, Gracia seeks to root Hispanic in indisputable, historical facts. "The Spanish, the African, the Iberian, the Mexican, the Inca, the Amerindian—all these are myths if we mean by those names something pure, unmixed and separable. Indeed, they are at best abstractions and at worst nothing but fictional creations of the present based on nostalgic longings for the past or on political manipulation by power-seeking opportunists."[46]

Imagine this: forty million Hispanic Americans joining hands around recognition of mestizaje and the encounter with Europe, Africa, Asia, and Iberia. By definition, this union would require, as in Cuba or Puerto Rico, a "righting" of history. Since Europeans wrote most of the books, they talk about discovery while Hispanics talk about conquest and the need for a reconfiguration of contemporary American culture.

Potentially, Hispanic is a lovely window to the world, our world. The problem is that Gracia seeks to fuse a bond around mestizaje while the Census Bureau, in October 2004, talks about eliminating the "other race" category that is crucial to Hispanics. Our choice is clear: the Census Bureau or a Caribbean man who understands the lessons we can learn from the Spanish- and the English-speaking Caribbean.

Seven

The Question Marks

———— ✺ ————

Mixed-Race Americans

The Claremont Colleges Host the Eighth Annual
Conference on the Mixed Race Experience

They call them noisy minutes. To relieve stress after a pressure-packed week of schoolwork, students at California's Harvey Mudd College (one of Claremont's eight subdivisions) gather among the cinder-block residential halls on Friday nights and, using their dorm court-yards as a barbecue pit, torch anything they can find. Dictionaries, wooden palettes, an oven, a shopping cart, a scarecrow: these kids even burned a fountain.

Mudd students like flames. One fellow repeatedly ignites his hands with Ronson lighter fluid for Zippos; another boasts that he can light a whole book of cardboard matches and put them out in his mouth. Still others stockpile as many as twenty containers of 99 percent iso-propyl alcohol.

The flames often rise above the buildings. Naturally, university officials know about the noisy minutes. However, as dean of residential life Guy Gerbick stresses, "fires on the campus are encouraged for their warmth and social nature, not for any destructive purposes . . . we explicitly prohibit students from burning large objects and those that do not fit within a barbeque."[1]

In February 2004, four Mudd College students in search of spring break fun decided to steal a huge piece of art from a campus building. They dragged the piece—a ten-foot cross—to their common area and lit it up. The entire campus soon reeked of burning wood. As one of the perpetrators explained to the school newspaper, the *Student Life*, "When we stood it in the dorm courtyard, the towering ten-foot art piece screamed to us for a Mudderesque noisy minutes style touch. It was granted. We lit it, watched it burn, and marveled at the flames. When it was over, we went to sleep. At no point during this act did we stop to consider the political and social implications of burning a cross. At no point did we stop to think of a possible explanation for why the cross was there or to whom it belonged. This is the only possible explanation I have to offer you: boredom, stupidity, and lack of common sense."

Just a few weeks later, on March 9, 2004, vandals attacked a car owned by Kerri Dunn, a visiting professor of psychology. Three of her tires were slashed with a razor; her windshield was smashed, and the entire vehicle was spray painted with anti-Semitic and anti–African American slurs over her car.[2]

Claremont president David Oxtoby declared March 10 a day of reflection. Classes were canceled, teach-ins ran throughout the day, and that evening more than two thousand chanting students assembled. "Hey, hey. Ho, ho. Ignorance has got to go." Jewish students told the crowd, "we are here to say that we are scared. Swastikas and broken glass trigger potent memories for Jews." Professor Dunn, making her first public appearance since the attack, spoke to the crowd: "I can't tell you how it makes me feel to look out into the sea of you and know that you are here to support me and the larger issue of civil rights and equality." Students erupted with such passion that it took "two minutes for the crowd's explosive applause to die down."

But Dunn was about to go from campus hero to campus villain. The day after the rally, students told police that they had seen Professor Dunn defacing her own car. By April 1, the beginning of an intercollegiate mixed-race conference, Dunn found herself suspended with pay. Meanwhile, the FBI claimed to be following a trail that could lead to charges of a hate crime against the professor; and the campus tried to recover from two terrible incidents, one of utter stupidity, the other an apparently "well intentioned" effort to make students aware of Claremont's allegedly poisonous racial climate.

The mixed-race conference was a gathering of students from all over the United States. They occasionally met to strategize about the dilemmas of being multiracial in a society that demanded that they choose one and only one box. In a beautiful location, students hoped to share experiences and lines of attack. None expected that the host campus would be reeling from an incident that dramatized the problems of mixed-race Americans.

Walking through the dorms on the first day of the conference, I saw many windows still plastered with homemade signs: "I will not tolerate hate" and "Ponoma College [another Claremont subdivision] has no room for hate." Will Talbott ('05) told the *Campus Collage,* "no one wants to suggest that the solidarity expressed at the various rallies and teach-ins was misguided, but if the allegations turn out to be true, one has to recognize that as a campus we were deceived. And I think that deception generates a lot of frustration, and it's tough to know where to direct that frustration."

Offering a ready answer to Talbott, a student organization named SCRAP (Students Challenging Racism and White Privilege) wanted Claremont to erase the economic and social advantages that nurtured and sustained Claremont—and a legion of other ivy-covered universities. Michael Owen ('05) noted, "we are reviving SCRAP to address the need—particularly among students who are white or who benefit from white privilege—for self-education about racism, privilege and related systems of oppression."[3]

The mixed race conference also spotlighted white privilege. On a campus full of the incredible promises and depressing realities of U.S. life, two hundred American students expressed a level of frustration with white America that often exceeded the angst displayed by Claremont's battered and bewildered students.

The conference organizers included the following student activists, all of whom prominently cited their family backgrounds: Janiva

Cifuentes-Hiss, a "Colomgringa"; Michelle Vijerberg, "DutChinese"; Jun Stinson, "Japanese, German, and Scotch-Irish"; Alex Auerback, "Filipino and Caucasian"; Lakshmi Eassey, Indian/Russian/Polish/ Italian/French; Mariko Ferronato, "Hapa-haole"; and Vivian Ohtake-Urizar, "Jamalan (Japanese and Guatemalan)."

This diverse group hoped to represent the nearly seven million Americans of mixed racial origins. Their common cause was an unprecedented change in the 2000 census that allowed respondents to make one or more choices when describing their racial origins. These young activists sought to jump-start a radical redefinition of race and ethnicity in the United States. Their dream was that a revolution in racial thinking would forever eliminate the kind of ugliness experienced at Claremont and around the United States.

Conference organizer Matt Kelley spoke of the many mixed-race people "who recall actually thinking they *were* aliens—they thought they *had* to be. It is as if the world is moving on apparently oblivious to this dilemma that's earth shattering for you—the person in the middle of it. *Do I exist or do I not exist?*"[4]

In a room sporting a sign reading "In the event of an earthquake, don't panic!" organizers calmly told campus activists about a nationwide plan to force universities to comply with the wishes of mixed-race Americans. They wanted all universities to include a multiracial category on their admissions and other administrative forms. In the event that the universities refused, students were told to assert their civil rights. By all means, learn what they think of you; but never forget to define yourself as you see fit, that is, as a Jamalan, a Colomgringa, a Blackanese, a double, or a mixed-race American.

Keynote speaker Ramona Douglass, of the Association of Multiethnic Americans (AMEA), devoted her address to the question "What does it take to produce extraordinary results in the face of no agreement where matters of race/multirace are concerned?" Douglass is the intelligent, vibrant "grandmother" of the mixed-race conference. After founding AMEA in the 1980s, she lobbied Congress and the Census Bureau relentlessly in the 1990s to include a multiracial category in the 2000 tabulations. Douglass fully understands the need for inclusion and compliance with administrative procedures. But, as the young people acquire legitimacy and visibility, she hopes that their pleas for recognition produce a paradigm shift, a cultural revolution that uses the question "What are you?" to undermine five hundred years of U.S. history.

In 1997 Douglass testified before the House Subcommittee on Government Management and Technology, arguing that the concept of race is "real only in our speaking of it—not in science—and through our communications with one another we have the ability to transform the listening mentality and spirit of a nation." She wanted people to recognize that "the one drop rule is an irrational notion born out of greed, exploitation and repression."[5]

At the Claremont conference, Douglass told her audience that seven million mixed-race people share an awesome responsibility. As walking question marks, they had the power to help three hundred million Americans understand the pain and prejudice experienced by the multiracial community. However, along the way, they should never be selfish. "In the pursuit of justice for one community, *we must take a stand for securing justice for all communities.* Without that commitment and generosity of spirit we will remain slaves to our collective fears, doubts, racial misconceptions and what's expedient."

As the conference came to a close, the mixed-race students focused on developing a four-year strategy to force universities to recognize their existence and comply with demands for a multiracial box on admissions and other administrative forms. A few veterans of the movement suggested that such efforts would encourage not radical social change but traditional racial thinking; after all, if race was real only in our speaking of it, then using the word *race* only reinforced the existing cultural ugliness. The students politely listened to these warnings, but it was clear that they intended to devote their energies and scarce resources to winning inclusion in America's traditional racial mix.

They may succeed. Or, rather than wedge themselves in between white and black, the mixed-race students may ultimately decide that, however hard the task, they need to explode current categories rather than reform them.

The debate is on, in a society whose best universities experience rigid racial divisions, everyday tensions, cross burnings by the igno-rant, and faculty who stage hate incidents to help us love one another. If Claremont is a microcosm, America is what it represents.

A Matter of Life and Death

Bothered by some skin lesions on her face, Cathy Tashiro went to a der-matologist. The doctor gently assured her that "Asian women don't get skin cancer." When Cathy explained that her Irish mother had extremely fair skin, the doctor repeated himself: "Asian women don't get skin cancer." Cathy tried to leave the doctor's office as soon as she could, but his reaction is normal for many physicians. Like the rest of us, doctors learn to think in pure categories, so Cathy is Asian, and the truth is irrelevant when it comes to the "science" of race.

Take another case. The Howards, a family of four, seem to be living the American Dream. But six-year-old Nicole has leukemia. When her parents tried to find a bone marrow donor, they were shocked to dis-cover that Nicole did not exist. Physicians maintain monoracial donor lists, matching like with like. Since Nicole is a fusion of Japanese and European ancestries, the medical system had no list of possible donors. Distraught, her parents tried to locate a donor on their own, only to discover that no one knew how to find one, if they did exist. As her father told researchers Maria Root and Matt Kelley, "I learned how decades of being forced to check only one box had discouraged multiracial Americans from acknowledging their mixed race her-itage."[6]

Today the Seattle-based Mavin Foundation maintains the Match-maker Bone Marrow Project. At last count, over six thousand people stepped up to help Nicole and her peers. But her awful dilemma underlines the lethal consequences of living in a world of one and only one box. Nicole could have died because American society still teaches its doctors and their patients to focus on racial purity, a con-cept that only exists in the mind of the beholder.

Fused ancestry people often stumble over unique, ugly problems because, until very recently, American society championed the ideal of social mobility in a nation that simultaneously maintained castes based on color. Born poor, you could climb the ladder of success. Born white or black, you only married your own kind. Fully forty-one of the fifty states barred interracial marriage at one point or another because, as one Virginia judge told a white and black married couple on January 6, 1959, "Almighty God created the races white, black, yellow, malay, and red and he placed them on separate continents. And but for the interference with his arrangement there would be no cause for such marriages. The fact that he separated the races shows that he did not intend for the races to mix."7

This injunction is one reason mixed-race people hear the same question—"What are you?"—every day, week after week, year after year. It often comes from perfect strangers, gatecrashers who somehow believe they have the right to ask total strangers the most intimate questions about their family heritage.

People want to know because, according to American culture, mixed-race people should not exist. They represent the ultimate prohibition, and, if the Virginia judge's devilish thinking is more and more of an exception, the rest of us still learned to expect "pure" races. Recall, too, that large-scale migration of Asians, Indians, and Arabs is a very recent phenomenon. Americans kept the world at bay. We thrived on meat and potatoes, black on one side of the plate and white on the other.

On a deeper level, people ask "What are you?" because they see mixed-race people as threats to social order. Successful interactions can occur only when my assumptions match yours. For example, say "good-bye" when we first meet, and I have a problem. You are not doing what I learned to expect. But, if you extend your hand and shake mine as you say "glad to meet you," then all is well.

In relatively homogeneous states like Maine, Nebraska, Iowa, and Vermont, mixed-race people are still so out of the ordinary that their very presence sometimes sets off cultural alarms. Confronted with a Japanese/Guatemalan woman, white and black minds may be stymied. They are in the presence of a human conundrum. To get order in *their lives* they need a category so badly that otherwise polite white and black people may become extraordinarily rude.

One informant told me that his daughter-in-law was a fusion of Asian and Latino heritages. When his family had visited the Metropolitan Museum of Art in New York, they quietly and (they thought) unobtrusively strolled through the galleries, However, one older man kept staring at the young woman. Finally, he tapped her on the shoulder and said, "What are you?" The father-in-law was shocked, but the young woman was polite, gracious, and just a bit bored. She is asked the question so often that she has developed a form of permanent armor against the curious and sometimes dangerous intrusions into her private space.

Simple manners demand that men and women never approach a total stranger and ask, "What are you?" Yet it happens all the time; as I learned from Hilary on a Web page called "Swirl," "it is a big deal that people think they can be so blatantly rude to people like us. I have had many people come up to me and ask me if I'm mixed or what I am and they don't even ask for my name first." What is *our* problem? Why is it so urgent for us to get an answer that we disobey the most elementary forms of social etiquette?

A century ago, the sociologist Georg Simmel wrote, "All relations among men are determined by varying degrees of incompleteness." I can never see the core of your individuality because I also see you—all the time—generalized to some degree. If I introduce my friend Paul, I ask you to meet the unique person who is simultaneously a member of the social category of friend. If I show you a picture of our three children—Adam, Carrie, and Ben—I introduce three individuals who are also social categories—children—and, besides that, members of a group, our family.

Simmel argued that social identities place a veil over our individuality. These labels—friend, child, black, white, mixed race—make us something different, but, like it or not, society collapses without shared and approved social identities. White and black often act as a sure guide to interaction in 2006 because they provide a shared set of beliefs and values about me and about others. Whites know how to behave with blacks and vice versa.

Social order never implies social justice. The two may exist simultaneously, but that was not Simmel's concern. He only wanted to understand how society was possible, so he identified the social identities indispensable for successful interactions.

As walking question marks, mixed-race people offer no clues to interaction within a white/black dichotomy. I more or less urgently need a category as a guide to behavior, so when people rudely ask, "What are you?" it is because they need an answer in order to restore their sense of order. As Pearl Fuyo Gaskins has written, "we are inkblots . . . people see us and they project what they need onto us to make themselves feel comfortable."[8] Once the "inkblot" has been interpreted, a person can be placed in a known category—for example, half this, half that—and given a mask to wear. Of course, if the mixed-race person refuses to play this game, they may be seen as antagonistic or even engaging in disorderly conduct.

Our current form of society is impossible if mixed-race people refuse to play along. They can create new categories and demand that we either learn them or go bother somebody else. It is a continuing conversation, but before we examine the new categories, the everyday lives of mixed-race people also allow *them* to observe and analyze *us*. We inadvertently reveal a great deal about American society and ourselves when we interact with mixed-race people. In what follows, I use an analysis of roughly two hundred biographical statements to spotlight three issues that typify the multiracial person's experience with the rest of us.

Hyperexposure, Invisibility, and the Border Patrol

Donna Jackson Nakazawa writes that mixed-race people often feel that they are "hyper-exposed." Because their faces offer perplexing combinations to most Americans, these seven million men, women, and children are always on stage. On the subway, one young (Japanese and Colombian) woman found herself charged with treason. A Japanese woman—who was a total stranger—wanted to know why she surgically fixed her eyes. Was she ashamed of her obvious Japanese features?

Here are some additional examples of hyperexposure. Each focuses on a different side of the mixed-race experience. In New York, Adam Gelfand (Jewish and Japanese) grew up on a street with a code for identifying gang threats, "kids who were coming into our block and were beating us up." A one meant white, a two Hispanic, and a three black. Adam and his brother learned the code only to discover that they produced a new one. His friends said, "You guys are really dark like a code three, but you look like a code two, but you're a code one, but you are not really a code one. What in the world are we going to do with you?" A year later, they came back and said, "We have something very special for you. You are a code JJ. Code one Jap-Jew."⁹ In this example, Adam is hyperexposed because he first fits into no categories and then gets a new one, all his own. Unfortunately, Jap/Jew makes him more exposed than ever.

Writing for *Eurasian Nation,* Catherine Betts talks about "checking the 'other' box." She fears the experience because "checking the OT box is like walking into a room full of strangers and introducing myself as Barney. It is just as inconclusive and arbitrary." It also reduces the "many luxuries" of being multiracial. Catherine richly experiences life from at least two perspectives; without ever going abroad to expand her horizons, she gets to see the positives and negatives of being Japanese and European. The box not only locks her in, but it also creates a weighty sense of defeat. She surrendered because checking the box allows others with power to define her in a simple manner. "I wonder if my multicultural ancestors are rolling over in their graves. But, even more so, I wonder how long it will take for the box to be defeated, and I wonder if the other 'others' out there are having the same existential dialogue with themselves about a silly box."¹⁰

In this instance, Catherine is hyperexposed because of the "other" category and what it precipitates. Her monocultural friends check the appropriate box without thinking; they know who they are. Catherine, realizing how silly it is, nevertheless moderates an existential debate with a government-issue box that highlights her inability to fit into society's approved categories.

Julie Fischer, a student at the University of California, Davis, offers a final example of hyperexposure. She joined the university's hapa (Hawaiian for "half") club, eager to participate in the group's forums and other activities. However, at one event she eventually became so upset with the group that she loudly raised this issue. "Instead of asking ourselves, 'who am I?' we should begin with asking, 'Why am I?'" The final straw was "a weird revelation." Half of the panelists existed because of military base marriages. "No one even discussed that little point that they are existing in this world because of U.S. military power/imperialism and the consequential barbaric/exoticism complex that is strung along in the military mentality when interacting with the local women."

In the system of American cultural prejudices, the "oriental" is exotic. Julie felt that she and the other students in the group only exist because their Asian mothers were the object of a fetish for that exoticism. The fetish is so contagious that even hapa men contract it. At a potluck supper of the Hapa Issues Forum, "all of the hapa guys stared at me and you know what? I felt like they were basically just white guys who just happened to have an Asian parent at home—what makes their fetish with me, a hapa, any different than when it is coming from a full white guy. I was insulted."[11]

Here the hyperexposure turns into a personal trait. Given a peculiar, positive prejudice of American society, Julie stands out. She is exotic, a fetish that makes her as special as one of the toys at the local adult video store. She dates but never knows if anyone is interested in her or if it is just the exotic quality that always puts her in the limelight. She is even exotic when she parties with her "own kind."

Hyperexposure is one side of the multiracial experience. The other side is invisibility, a maddening paradox to the youngsters who must nevertheless endure it.[12] Invisibility occurs when presumably sympathetic people of color say no to a multiracial category. This is especially apparent if it is a fight between whites and blacks. Some blacks regard recognition of multiracial people as a "white conspiracy," another plot to divide and further conquer black people. Others say that one drop of black blood makes you black. Why invent a new category when you are and always will be only black to white people. But perhaps the most powerful resistance comes from minority-group leaders who fear that minorities will lose rights and entitlements if multiracial people are counted as a separate category.

Meanwhile, whites behave as badly toward multiracial people as blacks do. Jennifer Ho is a fusion of European (English, French, Irish, and Scottish) and Chinese ancestries. People tell her she is white, but making interaction impossible, Jennifer disagrees. If they say, "Yes you are," as they often do, the fight begins. Jennifer embraces all her heritages. Her antagonists want her to white out her double status and enlist in the best race of all. In fact, instead of asking why it is so important *to them* that Jennifer be white, her antagonists generally ask why she is making such a big deal out of it. "'You look white, so you are white.' I've even had people say that I am lucky I can pass for white— that I should be grateful." Jennifer thinks differently; she refuses to be invisible, but "I think that it makes these people really uncomfortable and I think that they would just prefer that I let them think that I'm white."[13]

Schools function as a powerful source of racial categorization. However, even the best elementary and high schools often treat the multiracial child as the invisible student in row E, seat 4. Following federal guidelines, some schools simply slide the multiracial child into the box that most closely reflects everyday American prejudices. Jennifer Ho would thus have to check the white box. But, because she and her friends demand recognition as multiracial people, the federal government offered this advice to school systems: Add a new category if the need arises, but let the youngster check this box "only when the data gathering agency is prepared to assign the persons choosing this response option to a standard category for purposes of presenting aggregated information."

Visible when she completes the form, Jennifer somehow becomes invisible by the time that form is counted. There is no discrimination because "interracial children are not discriminated against since they are not discriminated against *as a member of a majority or minority race*" (emphasis added). Put differently, they cannot be subject to discrimination because they do not exist in the first place.[14]

In November 2005 the Mavin Foundation published findings of

similar invisibility at the nation's universities, colleges, and community colleges. The cover of the study shows a smiling young woman wearing a T-shirt labeled "blaxican"; meanwhile, in an analysis of close to 300 schools (from Stanford University to Western Wyoming Community College) the foundation discovered that only 27 percent of the institutions even "allow prospective students to identify themselves as having mixed heritage on admissions forms." Moreover, when it came to actually encoding the information, more than 60 percent of the schools recoded the information into categories that made the person "monoracial." Only 9 of the 298 institutions actually "retained data on a student's *specific* racial/ethnic mixed heritage" (emphasis added). In the end the report's authors reluctantly confirmed their own invisibility: "Our report has found that the vast majority of institutions of higher education have failed to provide multiracial students with appropriate opportunities to identify their racial and ethnic heritages."[15]

One final example of invisibility occurred because of the reactions of family members. At the Claremont mixed race conference, a young man explained the consequences of his mother's Chinese and his father's Jewish ethnic roots. He explained that he had never even met his Jewish grandparents because they shunned him throughout his life. With tears in his eyes, he patiently explained the consequences of the mixed race experience. His grandfather had just died; he never met the man, and that loss and longing would be with him forever. Yet he still wanted to connect with the family that had treated him so badly.

The all-volunteer racial border patrol exists in all fifty states. In a conference workshop on Asian American identity, Kimiko Roberts (an Afro Asian) showed a baseball video that graphically illustrated her lack of acceptance by both the Chinese and the African American communities. Especially at the onset of adolescence, student racial police, without uniforms or badges, monitor the high school corridors. Since Kimiko involuntarily bats from both sides of the plate, she has no idea which side to use. Her classmates resolve the problem by telling her that she cannot play the all-American game. Her double racial status disqualifies herself from being a "whole" anything; she is a "half breed," shunned by her friends and sometimes even by her relatives. As Kimiko told the audience, one reason she created the video was to talk to her "racist" Chinese grandmother. She hoped that pictures would break down the borders created by her grandmother's aversion to the color of Kimiko's skin.

Racial police cordon off many areas of the multiracial child's life. First is physical appearance. Jamie Doyle (Japanese, Irish, and Caucasian) wanted to join the Asian group at her university. She went to a meeting only to discover that, because of her ambiguous looks, she was "*not* Asian enough to be part of their organization." Since Jamie lacked the "typical" features of Asian women, she failed the authenticity test as her cohort failed the decency test. They guarded the turf that only recognized pure people from pure races.[16]

Kevin Maillard is Native American and African American. He self-identifies as a Black Indian and notes that, since roughly 30 to 70 percent of African Americans possess Native American ancestors, to identify as a Black Indian is to have a mental attachment to a mixed ancestry. That is Kevin's opinion; he is proud of his fused roots, and in high school he only wanted to be a member of the crowd. Unfortunately, his everyday life "was horrible." Based on his features, multiple border patrols forced him to reach this conclusion: "It is a three pronged thing—you are not black, you are not white, you are not Indian. It comes from all directions."[17]

The racial police also patrol the way others speak. One of my students is often accused by her African American friends of trying to be white because she speaks with a proper West Indian accent. This is a common experience among multiracial children who may claim two heritages but find that only one is sanctioned. One white/black youngster learned the dozens as a means to acceptance by his black friends. But, when he sometimes spoke standard English, his pals accused him of trying to be fake. He had to pick a side and remain loyal to it and it alone.

Another area of border control revolves around the friends you can keep. Tatyana Ali, who played Ashley Banks on the TV sitcom *The Fresh Prince of Bellaire,* boasts a Panamanian mother and an East Indian father. She acted as a black person on the show but never denied nor denies her heritages. Meanwhile, one evening in New York, she dined with her white boyfriend. One of her black fans appeared and made this comment: "Tatyana, I want you to know that I watch your show all the time. But now that I see you letting this white man date you, I will never watch your show again."[18] This man patrolled borders that did not exist. He tried to keep Tatyana in the black circle when he really needed to offer a first-class ticket to the Caribbean. There she could easily find a Panamanian/East Indian spouse.

Racial policing is also geographical. You sit at one lunchroom table, with one racial crowd. Eat elsewhere and you can eat with them (the whites, the blacks) or you can eat alone. Who cares? You are no longer one of us. In a Manhattan high school, the patrolling reached such extremes that "White, Black, Latino and Asian students each exited the school from different doors."[19] Fused ancestry children therefore had two choices: They could sleep at school or walk out under the staring eyes of the whites, blacks, Latinos, and Asians. Pick a door and, if the guards let you through it, you pick your future, like it or not.

The border patrol even polices cultural capital. James Coley is a fusion of white and black who attended a predominantly white private high school. He did exceptionally well in his academic work, and his personality proved so appealing that he became class president. But James made his mark by using what others perceived as only white cultural capital. If he played great jazz, that was acceptable. But, as a successful scholar, he was told: "You know you are not really black—you are white because of all the accomplishments you have made." This was not an honorary membership in the white race. Instead, it closed the wagons around the achievements that only white people could make. James was the exception that proved the borderline rule.[20]

Even music and sports are subject to the scrutiny of the border patrol. One multiracial man liked the music of Barry Manilow. He had to hide his tapes or his Latino friends would angrily accuse him of being "too white." In another instance, a black/white fusion had the audacity to like hockey. He joined the school's squad, only to discover that, for his black friends, this made him a "white boy." Blacks apparently do not play hockey.

The combination of hyperexposure, invisibility, and the border patrol is a witch's brew. In their unmarked cars, the racial vigilantes are especially effective because no one knows when they will arrive. Just as the fused ancestry person is getting comfortable, a friend, family member, or antagonist whips out the race card in a discussion of anything from music to sports, from exit doors to the way you speak.

Young people are at once hyperexposed and invisible because many of us refuse to recognize the axis of their problem: race in America. Indeed, my interviews suggest that to many Americans fused ancestry people represent a group of whiners. Kids and adults have always been cruel to one another. What is so special about the daily dilemmas of mixed-raced Americans?

Mirror on the Wall

In Disney's movie *Snow White* the young woman's beauty forced her stepmother, the queen, to see herself in the mirror. What she saw there was not how she imagined herself. Mixed-race people are our Snow White. And only we can change the image that appears as a result of our reaction to a simple fact: Human beings fall in love, they have children, and we treat those children in an abominable manner.

Here, for example, is an interesting contradiction: Many of the most powerful people in America ask us to embrace globalization. Our very salvation allegedly rests on trading with the rest of the world. Yet, when we analyze the treatment of mixed-race Americans, we appear as one of the most insular, provincial people on the planet.

Recall (from chap. 6) the portrait of Jamaican people in the painting *Dance Hall.* A fellow with lovely Asian features is in the middle of the picture because the artist is comfortable with the fusions produced in Jamaica. Similarly, on one trip to Cuba, our guide through the periodical archives was Federico Chang. For all their other problems, Cubans generally remain quite comfortable with fused ancestry children. However, for us, the provincial, blinkered dominance of white and black is so great that it even acts as a bludgeon when mixed-race people suddenly find that they are "cool."

A young woman named Abbie (Miyabi) Modry writes that, in her circle of friends, "the values have become completely reversed to the point where people who don't come from a 'minority' culture start feeling as if they are no one, they are too bland. Being 'just white' is not cool or anything admirable anymore (though this still depends on your social circle)."[21]

Abbie's anger stems from a crucial insight: "The sad thing though is that the value reversal is entirely superficial because it still maintains the same mentality of neatly categorizing people along the same old lines." A mixed-race person is cool only in relation to the whites who are bland. White remains the designer original and, adding insult to injury, using whites to make others cool only "reinforces the feeling that the categorizations are authentic and natural." Even when people say something positive about mixed-race Americans, it stems from the white, nonwhite, people of color template. Somehow, we are to embrace the globe while still using the vocabulary of slave traders and Jim Crow America.

The mirror again suggests an observation made by Bruce Jacobs: "we strain our eyes looking for color and in the process lose all other senses." Fifty years after *Brown v. Board of Education,* sixty years after *Mendez v. Westminster,* and ninety-one years after a judge decided (in the Shahid case) that Jesus was not a white man, our behavior is a form of "public insanity."[22]

Built on the dichotomy and the concept of race, color sometimes appears to be a background issue. We think we are moving forward until, at the level of what makes society possible, seven million mixed-race people threaten to explode the dominating categories and colors. We do not know what to make of them so, rather than discard race and the dichotomy, we use those cultural tools to put mixed-race people in their place.

In the most intense instances, fused ancestry people drive categorical thinkers into a state of crisis. "The crisis is caused by the contradiction between how people have been trained to understand race and the fact that the multiracial person does not fit the scheme." Confronted with information that threatens their categories and beliefs, people imitate a boomerang. They come back on themselves, retreating to the safety of the white/black dichotomy; and, once there, they affirm the dichotomy with more passion than ever as a means of convincing *themselves* that they do in fact know the right rules about race, color, and mismatches.[23]

One conclusion is that we use the words and beliefs invented by the worst Americans, all the while allowing people in crisis to lead the charge as they reinforce and resurrect the past. Remember the black fan hassling (Panamanian and East Indian) Tatyana Ali. Color is such a necessity that we use it to castigate a woman based on a case of maliciously mistaken identity.

Even the most well-intentioned Americans lack an alternative grammar or code of conduct; we use words with color because that is our cultural inheritance. To escape from our self-imposed prison we turn to the efforts of people interested in self-preservation. We turn to the fused ancestry population that, given our behavior, seeks to create a new way of looking at all Americans.

The Doubles Who Live in Limboland

I was raised as a Roman Catholic and still recall the nuns teaching us about baptism and limbo. To wash away the stain of original sin, God used baptism. This divine dosing made us eligible to enter heaven and achieve the "beatific vision," the actual sight of father, son, and Holy Ghost. Unfortunately, infants sometimes died before they received the sacrament of baptism. God, in his mercy, did not want to send these infants to hell. But, with the stain of original sin still on them, they could not enter heaven. God therefore created limbo. But limbo was not a way station on the road to heaven. The nuns explained that the infants stayed in limbo forever. They were never punished nor did they receive any rewards.

Catholics erased limbo roughly forty years ago. Mixed-race people rediscovered and redefined it in their Web and other conversations. Limboland is a place where people take pride in their mixed-race ancestry. "It sounds like we do not know where we are going or where we came from, no direction, no future," one chat room correspondent commented. "That is incorrect. There is no consensus on who we

are, where we came from, what we are about, and where we are going."
Yet, in Limboland, "we are hotly debating all those issues (this is the
most exciting time for Mixies) and there are definite patterns of
thought . . . that are emerging from these debates."[24]

For a more pessimistic assessment of life in Limboland, consider
this metaphor from James McBride (a fusion of white and black):
"Being mixed feels like that tingly feeling you have in your nose when
you have to sneeze—you are hanging on there waiting for it to happen, but it never does."[25]

Fusions can be excited, frustrated, angry, confused, and ambiguous about life in Limboland. They can also experience those feelings
in combination, or they can experience different reactions on different days. How a person responds depends on a variety of variables.
Some are outside of the person's control. Some are not.

Fred McHenry Rabb (Japanese and African American) reflects a
distinction between being a "minority-majority" and a "minority-
minority."[26] The language underlines our public insanity; however,
the point is that a white/black fusion may experience even more tension and turmoil than an Asian/African American fusion. The latter
always gets it from both sides; you definitely know you are unwanted.
Meanwhile, the white/black person may receive a pass into mainstream America because of their partially white ancestry, only to be
rebuffed when the black ancestry is discovered. You suddenly have
that tingly feeling again because exposure reveals your true identity:
You are a mixed-race American.

Jennifer Poulson (Japanese and white) grew up in Japan. Many
people there expressed envy, seeing her whiteness as something positive. On the streets, other kids called her "*gaijin, gaijin.*" Dictionary
definitions for this word include "foreigner," but the negative meaning implied is "outsider," someone who can never be Japanese. But
although Jennifer was being sent these mixed messages, she was at a
distinct advantage in attending international schools. "I was surrounded by likeminded 'half' kids, as we referred to ourselves," she
writes. "I was not an anomaly or an aberration. I was one of many
mixed kids and everyone knew exactly what we were."[27]

School was a place to relax. That is a gift because fusions must deal—above all—with the issue of being half. As a (border patrol) axis of identity, "half" generates so much pain that it also produces a widespread consensus. Indeed, despite the many variables that help or hinder "adjustment," fusions can tell us precisely what they hate, exactly what Anglo Protestant culture needs to abolish.

Kanna Livingston (Japanese and white) talks about the people she continually meets. "Oh, so you're half Japanese, they'll say, their eyes shining with clarity. They will say 'half' exactly the way it is typed. And I wince at hearing those words, feeling somehow compressed, restricted, and excluded from the 'pure breeds.'"

Kanna gets no pedigree certificate because she is an impure mix. Yet, "if I am half Japanese, then where does that half end? Where do I begin not being Japanese? Would a bar of chocolate have to introduce itself as being 'half' chocolate, 'half' milk? Do people start off their conversations at sophisticated cocktail parties saying, Oh, I am half of my father's genes and half of my mother's? How about you?"[28]

Sometimes, a single encounter can be literally traumatic. "I still can't forget the shock I felt when I was nine and a friend drew an imaginary line that spilt me in half," Abbie Modry recalls. "How strange it must have been that somehow my right leg wasn't shorter than my left, and that my eyes weren't blue on the left and brown on the right . . . that was no joke and till today remains a vivid and hurtful memory fifteen years later."

The imaginary lines assume special significance when race is the issue. Millions of Americans can discuss, casually and often with great delight, ethnicities that include Finnish, Scottish, and English heritages without once asking the person to draw lines through their face. How absurd it would be if someone said, "The left eye is Irish; the right is definitely from Scotland."

Abbie continues, "Half makes you sound like you are only half a person, and therefore inferior to the non-half person." The defense that "I just wanted to know" holds no water when people ask the "What are you?" question with such frequency. If it does not matter, why ask? As Abbie sees it, whether it is the word *half* or the modern, neutral word *mixed*, the consequences for her remain the same. She notes that "it might help to see what the possible antonyms to mixed (or half) are: One possibility is "non-mixed" but there must be another more common word . . . Oh! Pure. That is it. No? But strange then, isn't the opposite of pure, impure, contaminated, diluted, etc. Yeah, well, that is often the connotation mixed (or half) carries."[29] When Abbie correctly feels angry and awful about other people's use of the word *half*, she is listening, in 2006, to a tape recording of the terrible testimony of so many congressmen during the immigration hearings in 1924.

Sometimes, even the fusions at times accept the language and beliefs that, instead of being anachronistic, are actually alive and well. In reading through the biographies of fused ancestry people, you often see this: Connor, Japanese + Caucasian + Native American. Alexis, Mexican + Caucasian. Will, African American + Caucasian + Blackfoot.[30] When fusions self-identify using the personal prejudices of a man obsessed with the Caucasus Mountains, the power of the operating system is vividly underlined.

In general, the young people debating their ancestry know what they oppose. The real problem is what they propose and how they can convince the rest of us to accept their proposals.

One often hears three examples of new social identities: swirl, double, and fusion. In one mixed race conference workshop, a father artfully transformed a gallon of ice cream into a teaching tool. Chocolate represented his daughter's African roots; strawberry represented her Native American heritage; and vanilla represented her European ancestry. He explained that he had told his daughter to put three scoops of ice cream in a bowl and combine them in a swirl of colors. Once fused, no one could separate the elements. So, why worry about purity, when swirls are the human norm?

It is an image that, as with Richard Rodriguez's *Brown: The Last Discovery of America,* focuses on combinations as the human norm but, unfortunately, still uses color to define human beings. Would swirls line up with whites, blacks, and nonwhites? Would swirl be better and the other colors worse? However lovely as an image, critics stress that swirl adds another colorful category rather than transcending those categories.

Double is another word with promise. Unlike swirl, it completely avoids, for almost the first time in five hundred years, the use of any suggestion of color. *Double* suggests the joining of ethnicities in a unique synthesis, but, in addition, it offers a sense of self-esteem that acts as a badge of pride when the border patrol agents appear. As one double emphasizes, "one thing I really like about the term 'double,' and where you can sense the warm gaze and encouraging attitude of the parent who first came up with the term is that it emphasizes that we are 'full' individuals in each and both of our communities, not only 'half.'"[31]

The word *double* reconfigures cultural elements in a manner that allows the person to transcend half and all its negative connotations. While that is an obvious benefit, debate participants also perceive problems. What do you do with people who have three or four ethnic heritages? Are they triples or even quadruples? And is a triple better than a double? The new language is necessary to achieve a sense of self-esteem in a society that denies it, but, in the process, no one wants to start a race in which some people get more self- and social esteem than others do. In addition, "double makes you sound like you are two people in one person's body and that you are more impressive than a non-double person. Strange, huh? As an extension of the strangeness, it also contains the problem of burdening yourself to be just as 'fully' one as the other."[32]

The last term, *fusion*, indicates the creation of something unique, and it never relies on race or blood to define or separate either individuals or groups of human beings. Mothers and fathers obviously provide the genes that make us look different; but what we think of those differences is a sociological, not a biological, fact. Fusions therefore believe that all people contain combinations of ancestries. Human life is a ceaseless series of fusions, none necessarily better than another. Fusions judge people on what they say and do, never because of prejudices rooted in an operating system that teaches about pure and impure, whole and half.

As Stefanie Liang (German + Chinese) puts it, "what is beautiful about us [about fusions] is that we embody harmony and we transcend racism in many ways." For a more down-to-earth definition, Lee Swift (Japanese + Black) says, "I feel like everything is just meshed together. There is nothing you can really separate. All my cultures and colors just mixed together . . . I even had the same food on one plate. Sometimes I had beans on the plate, and some kind of Japanese food. And that's how I felt about myself. It was all in my mind, all in one plate."[33]

Fusion avoids all the negative connotations associated with *half* or *mixed*. Once joined, nothing separates the ingredients. They fuse in a unique manner and affirm our shared humanity because all six billion of us represent more or less complex fusions. However, as the daily debate proceeds, fusions need to decide the exact nature of the fused ingredients. If those ingredients include races, fusion is an improvement that never challenges traditional conceptions. If, on the other hand, fusions deny the existence of races, they create a concept that focuses only on ethnic groups. Ultimately, saying that I have Chinese and German ethnicities could be as significant or as harmless as saying that I have an English and Italian background.

Swirl, double, fusion: Using Internet forums on an everyday basis, the thoughtful dialogue occurs in a society that, by definition, makes successful assimilation impossible. Seven million people remain forever outside the Anglo Protestant mainstream, so, as a response, some fusions express a sense of angst that borders on desperation. David Horowitz (white and Japanese) writes, "Some people never experience the differences that we encounter from being half-Asian, but these experiences have made me feel that I'm not really anything. But instead in my own world of culture that I have built as a result of isolation . . . I typically feel isolated from society because I don't feel like I fit into the mold of anything out there."[34]

Another, much more positive reaction is that of Chela Delgado. Her mother is European American (Scottish), and her father is African American (Jamaican, East Indian). Chela says that she and her "biracial" friend developed a strategy. They hate feeling like the only white people in a black meeting and the only black people in a white group. It is both boring and tiresome to be the outsider all the time. Their new philosophy is this: "Being biracial isn't hard because we are confused about our racial identity. It is hard because everyone else is confused. *The problem isn't us—it's everyone else.*"[35]

Chela's reaction promises the full-scale mutiny that is on the horizon. As their numbers increase, more and more fusions will unite and refuse to accept the sense of alienation and inferiority that comes with being "mixed race" in the land of the pure. However, until the rebels think their way out of Limboland, Anglo Protestant culture is their bane and our problem. In fact, contemporary society is such a danger to the health of children that the parents of fusions devise strategies to shield their daughters and sons from everyday life.

Survival Strategies

In his book "Mind, Self and Society," the social psychologist George Herbert Mead uses baseball as a metaphor for understanding the "successful" socialization of any child. To play well a person needs to understand themselves in relation to eight other players in the field, the batter, any runners on base, and the coaches giving orders from the sidelines. When I understand my role in the game and, simultaneously, the roles of at least nine other people, I can "play ball" because others successfully taught me the rules of the game.

For Mead baseball serves as a metaphor to underline the crucial significance of culture in shaping our beliefs, values, and practices. Whenever children learn something about themselves, they also learn something about others. It may be, as in baseball, how those others fit into something as innocent as a game, or it may be the less benign "game" of categorizing people based on race and the color of your skin.

For parents of mixed-race children one crucial issue always arises: How much do you tell them about the often ugly rules of the game? And what do you do when this happens to your child? As George Meyers (Japanese/Caucasian) explains it, he went to a Japanese school on Saturday mornings. His classroom contained a "huge rolling chair" and "when the teacher was not in the room kids would take turns riding in the chair around the class and they would punch me as they went by. I would curl up in a ball or try to run away, but the other kids would hold me down."[36]

In the seventies, many parents believed that love could solve everything. Ignore differences, never discuss racial issues, and the love and acceptance received at home would act as a shield against any prejudice the child experienced. In practice, love failed because the children inevitably learned how Americans played the game, and, in the absence of any discussion at home, the kids took the abuse on the streets and sometimes drew the conclusion that, despite the lip service paid to love, there was something wrong with them. They were so insignificant that no one took the time to discuss issues at the core of their identity and their everyday life.

Today parents of fusion children realize that "dialogue is everything." Their sons and daughters will inevitably experience a series of nasty incidents so, as parents, they must be available on an as-needed basis. Instead of a castle, home must be a sanctuary where the children feel comfortable enough to discuss issues that may hurt their parents as much as they hurt the children.

Some adolescents refrain from telling their parents what they feel because the kids know that their parents cannot change society or they hate to see their parents experience pain when the youngster explains an especially troubling incident. Somehow, parents need to create a sanctuary that is so comfortable everyone is willing to share their emotional lives. In a society where some argue that the significance of race is declining, one parent stresses that "this conversation is so ongoing in our house that when I ask my kids . . . questions like, 'What was school like?' or, 'Has anyone questioned you?' they know *exactly* what I'm talking about. They know why I'm asking, I'm not *looking* to find something, but they know that if something comes up, it is an open forum and we can discuss it as much as they want to."

Some parents provide what Maria Root calls a "Bill of Rights for Racially Mixed People." As a multiracial person I have the right "*not* to justify my existence in this world, *not* to keep the races separate within me, *not* to be responsible for people's discomfort with my physical ambiguity, and *not* to justify my ethnic legitimacy."[37] Using these rights, the child builds a sense of self-esteem only by ignoring Anglo Protestant culture. However, that culture still rules because the child requires a series of negative rights only because the larger society wants him or her to justify his or her existence and to keep the races separate.

These kids stick out by definition, yet, as Jamie Doyle (Japanese/Irish/Caucasian) writes, "my middle school was *not* diverse but I grew up in Southern California, which was very multicultural. We not only had all the races, there were also a lot of other multiracial Japanese/Caucasian families . . . That really helped to keep me from feeling like I was really weird, despite all the difficult things that were happening to me at school."

In the absence of other fusion children, one alternative is "a familiar consistent group of friends with whom a child develops strong emotional bonds, before racial awareness and a playground culture of cruelty . . . converge." While this suggestion assumes that the family remains in one location for a considerable period, friends love and value the child for who they are, not what they are. Obviously, the friends may also buy into the prejudices of the larger society, but, if parents can find open-minded families, children in isolated states at least have a welcome mat that is always available.

Donna Jackson Nakasawa notes that "among the most crushing experiences" she heard from multiracial children involved school systems and teachers who refused to validate what the children learned at home. Some teachers told the kids that they got a color identity and nothing more. Others "held stereotypical assumptions that black/white multiracial kids would under perform or that Asian/white kids would outperform because of gross stereotypes attached to students of these minority heritages."

Parents need to check on the content of the school's curriculum and they need to fight the school systems that deny their children's existence. In an ideal world, school administrators and teachers would support the parents, but this gargantuan task requires support from a communitywide if not a nationwide effort. While a lone parent can sometimes fight and beat city hall, the chances of success significantly decrease when the issue is a topic that cuts to the core of American culture. For example, one suggestion is to provide children with biracial heroes like Frederick Douglass. His father was white, but black studies programs appropriate him as a black and only a black man. To wage that battle in the classroom is to challenge the very structure of our cultural operating system. It is a crash that should occur, but it is hard to see how until and unless many of the rest of us *also* decide that fusions and their parents undeservedly carry the heaviest burden imposed by America's focus on race and skin color.

Fusion parents find themselves locked into a process where they continually play only defense. They shield the children from society as best as they can, fully aware that when they use labels like "multiracial" or "biracial" they feed into and even affirm the status quo. As Monina Diaz (African American/Puerto Rican) argues, "I think the worst thing to do would be to put a multiracial category in the census because, in effect, you would be buying into the system that you've detested all your life, a system that pressures you to fit into some group. So now you have a group, and now you fit into it, but what does that do for racial problems in America? I would hate to see the creation of more racial divisions."[38]

While parents understand the problem, the only alternative is to use labels that make their child a guinea pig for social change. Words like *double* or *fusion* house new beliefs, but fusions can never pleasingly interact with the rest of us if we refuse to reconfigure—consciously and voluntarily—American culture. At times, a parent's sense of frustration understandably produces raw and rough responses. Susan Fu (Caucasian) married a Chinese American man. They have three lovely children. Yet Susan fields "endless questions." In line with her daughter at a bagel store, another customer asked, "Is she one of the Children of China?" On another occasion, "a man actually asked me, 'Does she speak English?'" Finally, "another time a woman asked me where my children were from, and I told her 'they're mine,' and she said, 'I know they are *yours,* but where did they come *from?*' So I said, 'They're from my uterus.'"[39]

While that is a great answer, it makes no sense to the person asking the question. The problem is that, at the beginning of the twenty-first century, our racial operating system still makes it inconceivable to many Americans that Chinese people live in the United States and that they marry and have all-American children. Susan Fu endures the endless series of painful questions because she and her children are *impossible creations* from the perspective of the prevailing beliefs, values, and practices.

For serious change to occur, we all need to help fusions and their parents take the offensive. Fusions are an increasingly integral part of America's future. They walk alongside Chicanos, Latinos, Jamaicans, Asians, Arabs, and Indians. It is a new America, and it urgently requires another operating system if we are to eliminate race and the colorful dichotomy provided by slave traders and, more recently, Jim Crow.

Eight

A Heart Transplant

※

Galileo, Blumenbach, and Sociology

In 1616 priests issued a fiery threat to Galileo Galilei. His work argued that the sun, not the earth, was the center of the universe. At the time, the Catholic Church held that the earth was the center of the cosmos, created by God for man. Both earth and man stood at the axis of a sacred and closed universe. Galileo's theory threatened to place all human beings at the periphery of an infinite universe, created by God knows who, for only God knew what purpose. In 1633 the church formally declared the heresy of Galileo's theories and gave him two options. Burn or recant. No fool, Galileo publicly recanted, and, armed with his telescope, he continued to privately believe what he pleased.

In the twenty-first century, we face a sociological challenge as meaningful and important as Galileo's. We must decide the significance of skin color and race in deciding people's place, not in a sacred cosmos but in the disunited states of America. This requires us to radically reassess received cultural wisdom about assimilation and the melting pot. As the earlier chapters on Chicanos, Asians, Indians, Arabs, Caribbean, and mixed-raced people have shown, instead of that melting pot, non-European immigrants have found, and still find,

220

themselves excluded from "mainstream" American life. Instead of a sense of unity, we have developed a series of parallel monologues that often define the groups—for example, "Muslim first" or Hindutva—in a manner that divides us more than ever.

We can solve these problems because we are graced with social scientific tools as powerful in their way as Galileo's telescope. We have all the insights needed to assess our present position and then consciously ask where to begin.

The dichotomy is a problem in its own right. Tragically, it receives crucial support from the bad science that produced the concept of race. Thanks to "Caucasians" like Friedrich Blumenbach, race divides the world in general and Americans in particular. This prejudice teaches that biologically homogeneous groups of people exist; and it teaches that some groups of people are superior to others. In the United States, we actually argue that six billion people divide themselves into white and nonwhite human beings.

Galileo fought priests who fought science. Today, scientists opposed to the concept of race and the dichotomy often debate scientists who *agree* that science killed the concept of race! This is an odd dispute. Many supporters of racial thinking wholeheartedly accept that, as a scientific concept, race is as valid as the church's claim that the earth was the center of a finite universe. As Manning Marable has written, "We are mobilizing ourselves around a concept that is morally repugnant and should not exist. Yet even though race is social constructed, it nonetheless sets the parameters of how most Americans think about politics and power."[1]

Alternatively, some simply surrender to the supposedly daunting power of the conventional "wisdom." In academic language, "we should think of race as an element of social structure rather than as an irregularity in it; we should see race as a dimension of human representation rather than an illusion."[2]

Of course race is an element of human representation. But so are terms like *spic, kike, nigger, chink,* and *jap.* Would anyone argue that we should think of these labels as elements of social structure rather than a cancer to be excised? The inconsistency is to reject the ugly representations yet surrender to the underlying concept. The absurdity is to accept race as a fact and then place Caucasians at the center of the universe, with people of color at the distant periphery.

But if Galileo could fight the church, we can fight—and change—the beliefs and values of American society. Admittedly, we face the well-armed white and black border patrol, but the abolitionists can win because those who accept that race is a social construct ignore the emancipating effects of that conclusion.

Sociology is the most liberating discipline on earth. When we "discovered" that race and the dichotomy are social constructs, we conferred on ourselves the power to transform, consciously and creatively, our societies and ourselves. People are in command. Society is a human construction. It is a liberating insight because nothing necessarily stops us from changing unacceptable or false beliefs and values. We can always move into the future based on a shared and corrected past.

The rub is that people never inherit a clean slate. At birth each of us discovers an already established set of *approved* cultural beliefs, values, and practices. By definition our freedom to reconfigure social life is constrained because we learn and internalize a culture before we manifest a desire to change it. Equally important, we must use the inherited culture's words and ideas to transform the beliefs or practices that we find troublesome or, as with race, a 150-year-old falsehood.

Critics note that the concept of culture assumes a consensus that does not necessarily exist. Especially in a society as large and diverse as the United States, the culture received in New York may be very different from the offerings in Georgia or Kansas. While critics make a fair point, the beauty of our problem is that we focus on beliefs and concepts that, like a canopy, hang over each one of the fifty United States of America. From Hawaii to Florida, from Washington to North Carolina, from Kansas to New Jersey, from Texas to Vermont, I have never met an American who does not understand the white/black dichotomy and, as mental baggage, the concept of race and the outsider status of non-European immigrants to the United States.

Race, the white/black dichotomy, and the illusion of the melting pot are as close to American cultural universals as we are ever going to get. This puts those seeking social change at an enormous advantage.

For sure, the precise meaning and import of the dichotomy will vary from locality to locality and from person to person; but the most and least prejudiced Americans still understand where the other guy is coming from when they talk about the dichotomy and its linked beliefs, values, and practices.

The targets are in range, and we can fire at will. Yet the rub remains. We begin life with a received culture, we internalize that culture, and when we seek change we need to use the tools provided by the very culture we seek to change. It is a paradox. As adults, people are simultaneously free and socially determined. The culture first shapes us; and—here is the liberation promised by sociology—we can freely and consciously reconfigure the culture when we use the insights of men like George Herbert Mead.

With great force, Mead focused much of his work on the human consequences of a special ability: People possess the power to reflect on their experiences.[3] They can stop the action and look back at what they learned; and, even more important, people can consciously analyze how they reacted to what they learned. For Mead cultural emancipation is possible because we can see what we learned, understand how we reacted, and then decide if we want to continue thinking and acting as we do.

In chapter 2, I argued that the white/black dichotomy is a cultural dead end because, among other things, even those who despise Anglo Protestant culture still find themselves determined by it. When John McWhorter writes about "self sabotage in black America," he contends that many African Americans reject an education only because academic achievement is something that white people do and "blackness means opposition to whites at all costs." McWhorter makes an argument, and we can argue about the accuracy of his argument. It is, however, undeniable that he has stopped the action, has seen what "blacks" learn about themselves, and then has seen how they react to what they learned. If we accept McWhorter's analysis, liberation is possible because African Americans can transcend both their cultural inheritance and their reaction to it.

With great reluctance, Debra Dickerson offers similar possibilities in *The End of Blackness*. We need to transcend race because "there is no way to define blacks as the group owned by 'whites' without whites at the center of black agenda setting. It is a maddening but obvious choice."[4] It is maddening because transcending race potentially ignores the reprehensible behavior of whites. It is obvious because unless we transcend race and the dichotomy we remain the prisoners of our inherited culture and, like those Africans Americans who reject an education because it is white, our self-defeating reactions to that culture.

Liberation requires an intensive effort; we need to unlearn what we can never put, completely, out of our minds. We need to erase the significance of beliefs and values that, for more than four hundred years, have made America a nation of whites, blacks, and none-of-the-aboves. But, once we accept that race and the dichotomy are *both* social constructs, we either accept the wonderfully emancipating consequences of that insight or point the finger of blame in only one direction: at ourselves and at our unwillingness to accept the gift offered by a conjunction of social circumstances that allow us to reconfigure America in a revolutionary fashion.

The mutiny is already under way. Chapters 3–7 show that, in general, Latinos, Asians, West Indians, and seven million fusions refuse to accept either the dichotomy or the concept of race. Indians and Arabs offer responses that are more diverse, but, to the extent they assimilate as whites, they reaffirm the dichotomy and the prejudices that go with it. Does anyone want a society in which being American means self-segregating, as in chapter 6, one group of Cubans from another or, as with some Arabs, making the thought of marrying an African American so unthinkable that your parents would regard the suggestion as a joke?

We *can* do the job, if we are willing to learn as much from immigrants and fusions as they learn from us, if we are willing to analyze the black and white consequences of assimilation, and if we are willing to "right" history. We need to transform American culture and consciously create a set of beliefs rooted in new core identities. Following are my suggestions for a way to begin *re*constructing the social constructs that now provide America's operating system of "racial" and ethnic beliefs, values, and practices.

Race Is Crucial

In "Thinking Orientals," Henry Yu writes that, "even if every single American did stop thinking about race, this would not erase the legacy of a history of thinking about it and practicing it for so long that every element and relationship in society has been structured on its definitions. Indeed, forgetting about race would only freeze the historical inequities that existed because of racial thinking."5

Yu spotlights the problem: A contemporary cornerstone of the white/black dichotomy is the concept of race. In American history, the dichotomy preceded the concept, but, with the imprimatur of science, race entered U.S. culture in the nineteenth century and it instantly fit like a white glove over the traditional prejudices of slave traders, slave owners, and millions of complicit Americans. In the robber-baron era race became such a powerful force in American culture that, like an octopus, its tentacles grabbed every immigrant group, examined them, and sent them packing if—like the Chinese, Japanese, Indians, or Syrians—they came from inferior races. Even Jesus Christ was theoretically deported when Americans used race to order the world and its inhabitants.

Race remains such an important concept in U.S. life that the Census Bureau still seeks world order rooted in race and a glaring contradiction: Race supposedly refers to solid, empirically verifiable scientific categories, yet the Census Bureau changes its racial categories so often that prejudice rather than science dictates the number of races at any given point in time. In 1890 the census list included octoroon and quadroon; in 2010 it may or may not include an "other race" category. The Census Bureau also confuses race and ethnicity. Japanese, Chinese, Korean, and Samoan are all races in the bureau's latest version of world order.

Henry Yu is right: Race reaches into every nook and cranny of American society. It would be horrible to freeze the inequities that already exist. However, if we do not eliminate racial concepts from our thinking, then the only alternative is to freeze our minds, to teach the coming generations to think about one another using vague, subjective categories that supposedly reflect hard and fast scientific truth.

We would pass on to our children and grandchildren the concept of race *and* the inequities they produce.

Here is another option. Suppose we focus on the future, on the seven million men and women who confront racial vigilantes who, as if priests during the Inquisition, make it very difficult for them to have a good day. Let us think, too, about the Mexicans, West Indians, Puerto Ricans, Filipinos, Chinese, Indians, Cubans, and Arabs who also refuse to accept, or have serious reservations about, our racial thinking.

Abolishing race never means forgetting about it. On the contrary, to erase the concept of race, we need to think about it more than ever before. David Theo Goldberg, for example, argues that one of Europe's great problems with immigrants is that the concept of race is forgotten but exists; it is denied and so too the linking of race "to the intellectual and political histories of colonialism and racism." My argument is to do the opposite. To actually abolish—rather than to simply forget about—race, we need to spotlight it, especially in relation to political histories of colonialism and racism over and through time.[6]

Race will only disappear when we agree to think about it more than ever before so that, as a society of like-minded citizens, we eventually share an informed consensus about the illusion of race and the persisting reality of an illusion's positive (for whites) and negative (for people of color) political, economic, and personal consequences.

In burying race, we would never ignore the historical inequities or their persistence in our own time. On the contrary, as in chapters 2 through 7, any honest analysis of the consequences of racial thinking needs to right many historical wrongs because of what happened to—besides African Americans—Japanese, Chinese, Filipino, Mexican, Indian, and Arab Americans. With varying degrees of inequity, racial thinking affected—and affects—all these ethnic groups. No one can understand the identity Chicano without also analyzing what the Reagan administration identified as the "total dependence" of U.S. agriculture on Mexican workers. Similarly, to read the 1869 *Congressional Globe* debates about Chinese Americans is to gain some understanding of why we remain surprised that third- and fourth-generation Chinese Americans speak such perfect English.

We can get rid of race and right history if we do not put the cart before the horse. Many millions of Americans with a sense of fair play will be far more willing to make up for historical and persisting inequities if, as a civilization, we first achieve a lasting consensus about the historical and contemporary consequences of racial thinking. My contention is that, while never losing sight of issues like reparations or affirmative action, we first need to focus on the social construct that uses science to create a hierarchy that begins with the Caucasians who live on Mount Ararat.

Suppose, for example, that Blumenbach was in a different mood when he created his racial order. Suppose he decided to call his beautiful people Ararats instead of Caucasians. How stupid would that be? And, if we believed in Ararats, what would that say about us and our civilization?

Here is a specific proposal: Where President Clinton created a Commission on Race, we need to have a national debate not about race relations but about the concept of race itself, its impact on American thinking, and its role in the perpetuation of profound inequities.

To repeat, we would have this debate not because of the declining significance of race but because, in many ways—think of West Indians and African Americans—race is as much of a problem as it has ever been. Equally important, if we neglect to tackle the concept of race head-on, it may generate a boomerang effect of national significance. Confronted by more and more contradictions and challenges, Anglo Protestant culture could react by reinforcing and resurrecting the world that was. As an answer to the demands of America's seven million walking contradictions—not to mention Chicanos, Asians, Arabs, and Indians—Americans might decide to strengthen rather than destroy the great walls that "protect" one group from another.

If a sitting president or either major political party made this debate a national priority, the print and broadcast media would jump on the issue. Alternatively, or simultaneously, religious groups or universities could lead the way. Funded by foundations like Ford, Rockefeller, or MacArthur, universities across the country could sponsor widely publicized public forums about the concept of race.

My own very specific suggestion is this: Since California *is* the future, let's ask the people of California—who hold no less than fifty-three seats, or 12 percent, of the U.S. House of Representatives—to lead the way. Californians by themselves have enough political muscle to launch a national debate about the concept of race. It could even be headquartered at the University of California, Los Angeles, 45 percent of whose freshman boast "Asian" heritages of various kinds. A well-organized request from California would get a great deal of support from, among others, New York, Illinois, and New Jersey; and, altogether, representatives could begin the debate in the House that theoretically represents the will of the people.

However the debate begins, it need not be an acrimonious exchange between victims and victimizers. None of us is responsible for the culture we inherited, only for the culture we are willing to endure and sustain. The forums focus on everyone, on the uniting idea that there is only one race and that, while we might deny the future, we cannot stop it.

To jump-start the debate process, we can deliberately create what social movement theorists call a dramatic event. Sometimes, like the sinking of the *Lusitania* in May 1915, the events occur by accident. Sometimes, like draft card burning in the sixties, organizers stage the events. Either way, for social movements to gain national traction, dramatic events offer significant assistance. They momentarily monopolize our attention, and, with our eyes fixed, we can create the momentum needed for social movements of lasting significance.

Here is another suggestion. Fusions already manage national organizations. And with the incredible organizing power of e-mail and the Internet they can easily arrange dramatic events of historic significance. So why not imitate the example of countries like Latvia and Estonia? When the citizens of the Baltic countries wanted freedom from the Soviet Union, organizers staged a peaceful protest that caught the world's attention. Citizens lined up on the nation's highways, held hands from one end of the Balkans to the other, and made their demands for change using a backdrop of mass and peaceful support from the nation's men, women, and children.

Using the thousands of student groups that already exist on campuses throughout the United States, organizers could produce—on Blumenbach's birthday, for example—simultaneous demonstrations from California to Maine. Holding hands around the campus student centers or local city halls, organizers would draw attention to the need for a national debate about the concept of race and its consequences. They could distribute charts depicting the absurdity of the Census Bureau's shifting language from 1890 to 2000. They could deploy slogans like "One Race, United We Stand" or "People: The Fantastic Fusions." The possibilities are endless; the goal is to monopolize attention with one or a series of dramatic events and therefore attract the support necessary for Americans to join the movement and support it over and through time.

Any movement to abolish the concept of race already has fifty million potential members. From Chicanos to Arabs, from West Indians to fusions, the mutiny is already under way. With support from the president or Congress, the nation could deliberately and consciously emancipate itself from the concept of race and, over time, discover a new world, a world that glorifies not one group's ego but the worth of every individual, in all forms, in any of the fifty states.

Erasing the Dichotomy

In 1946 Fernando Ortiz's *El Engaño de las Razas* (The Deception of Race) argued that one of the most banal and vulgar ways to think about humanity was to call people white or "*de color*" (of color). Ortiz said this was an absurd dichotomy because anyone with two open eyes could see that whites were not white, blacks were not black, and the descendants of Cuba's Chinese population certainly never deserved the word *yellow*. If society's colorful labels actually rooted themselves in "logical rigor," the opposite of people of color was "*incoloro*" (colorless). Whites would be colorless, blacks would be colorful, and never non-white. Additionally, logical rigor produced a "double absurdity" because, if perceived as the color of light, black was not a color but the negation of all colors. As old and new encyclopedias stress, "black is the absence of light and therefore the absence of color." White, on the other hand, represents "the integration of colors" since it occurs when red, yellow, and blue are added in equal amounts.[7]

Twenty-four years later, Albert Murray published *The Omni-Americans,* a "counter-statement or restatement" to America's "race oriented propagandists." Murray wanted to shout it out: "The United States is in actuality not a nation of black people and white people. It is a nation of multicolored people. There are white Americans so to speak and black Americans. But any fool can see that the white people are not really white and that black people are not black. They are all interrelated in one way or another."[8]

If any fool can see it, why can't we?

Close to three hundred million Americans persist in vulgarities and nightmarish logic. If I was in a room and said to the audience that a red wall was purple, they would rightly assume that Fernandez has perceptual problems. However, if I call a tan person black, that somehow makes sense. When the Census Bureau says that dark-skinned Arabs are white, that also makes sense. And, when we meet darkskinned Indians or Pakistanis and do *not* call them black, that too makes sense. Using the dichotomy is institutionalized nonsense, all in the service of perpetuating divisions that, thanks to their slave-owning creators, produce everyday and historical tragedies.

Here is another specific suggestion for significant social change: Stop using the dichotomy and never use skin color as an axis of anyone's social or personal identity. The dichotomy defines us by what divides us, and simultaneously it excludes fifty million Americans who do not fit into the dichotomy. Activists try to include them by calling Indians or Chicanos "people of color," but that label only ensures white supremacy. First, people of color only exist in relation to whites, who are not a color yet receive our foolish permission to define the color of everyone else on earth. Whites silently sit on the sidelines and let people of color use them as the human archetype. Second, the label "nonwhite" diminishes anyone who uses it because, as Murray stressed, it nourishes and sustains all the fundamental assumptions of white supremacy and segregation.

To erase the dichotomy we need no national debate, no dramatic events, and no social movement. Like race, the words *white* and *black* are social constructs, created by one group of people to oppress and denigrate another group of people. Over time—and because of the concept of race—the dichotomy came to include whites and everyone else on earth. This absurdity eliminates itself in a simple manner: Each of us refuses to use color—and especially the words *black* and *white*—as a crucial means of group and personal identification.

Success is possible because this revolution is unique: It gives *everyone* something vital to do. Normally, leaders like Abraham Lincoln or Martin Luther King Jr. pave the way and the rest of us follow along. In the case of eliminating the dichotomy, our tremendous advantage is that each and every one of us can easily act like a leader. In sharp contrast to other liberation struggles, there is no need for violence, no need to attend a meeting, and no need to work a phone bank or send money. Anyone who wants change only needs to do one thing: prepare your mind to watch your mouth. Though tempted to use color as a means of identification—for example, "Do you remember that black guy we met last week?"—all Americans can refuse to focus on color, not because the world is color-blind but because it is as colorful as it ever was. However convenient color is as social shorthand, we can deliberately stop using the words *white, black, nonwhite,* and *people of color* because we refuse to support the beliefs, values, and inequities that the words condone as a matter of cultural fact. We can stop using the language because, after five hundred years of use, we finally agree to put an end to slavery's most lasting ideological legacy: the white/black dichotomy.

One final point. If words are unimportant—or, as some critics suggest, political correctness malarkey—why do we get so upset about the slurs (e.g., *spic* or *jap* or *nigger*) associated with prejudice against particular groups? As with the concept of race, the incredible inconsistency is to attack the slurs but not the white/black dichotomy that makes white the American default category for everyone on earth. At the 2005 Golden Globe awards, African American actor Jamie Foxx spoke about the "Caucasian" director of the film *Ray*. No one stood up in protest. *Spic* or *nigger* act like lightening rods, but meanwhile, behind the scenes, *white, black,* and *Caucasian* quietly and endlessly reaffirm the Eurocentric racial hierarchy envisioned by Friederich Blumenbach more than two hundred years ago.

In refusing to use the words *white, black, Caucasian,* and *people of color,* we deliberately run the risk of making social interaction impossible. Like the fusions that produce the question "What are you?" our unwillingness to support the dichotomy will produce another question from whites, blacks, and people of color: "What's with you?" or, in a different mood, "What the hell are you talking about?"

Making interaction impossible is the only way to achieve emancipation. The old language reaffirms what we already know. By asking for a general strike against the words *white* and *black,* we—at all times empathetically—ask others to join us in thinking more than ever before about the dichotomy and its consequences. Like the fusions, we may founder about looking for new words to describe ourselves; and, like many Asians or Latinos, we may only know what we oppose. The strike is simply a way to get other people's attention and begin, in millions of everyday interactions, a national conversation about the absurdity of the dichotomy and its provably poisonous consequences.

To the whites and blacks who wonder if we have problems, we can respond in the following manner: Yes, I do. The problem is Anglo Protestant culture, and I refuse to walk into the colorful dead end devised by slaver masters and Jim Crow. I want to move on, not stand still. And I even have some suggestions about the words that can replace *white, black,* and *people of color.*

When asked, "If you are not black or white, what are you?" I would answer with pride: "I am a fusion." And I would explain that I chose this new identity not to be troublesome but to use it as a way of telegraphing the beliefs and values contained within the word *fusion.*

- Fusion denies the concept of race. It accepts, with Diego Rivera, that *all human beings* are fusions, that is, ethnic combinations. It accepts that there is one race, the human race, and that the human race is, by definition, a ceaseless series of human unions.
- Fusion deliberately refuses to use skin color as a basic category of identity. Fusions think it is ridiculous to key on a physical attribute determined by less than .001 percent of our genes.

- Fusions believe that, instead of being self-segregating barriers to interaction, somatic differences are delightful and diverse manifestations of the underlying and indissoluble unity of six billion people.

- Fusion is a core identity that happily allows room for other forms of self and group expression. Fusions think of differences in nationality, religion, ethnicity, or geography as a potential source of interest rather than as a reason to discriminate or self-segregate.

- Fusions are individualists. They define us by what unite us: our membership in the human race. Fusions believe, with the sociologist Émile Durkheim, that by glorifying the individual in general you create a greater sympathy for all that is human and, as if joined at the hip, a greater thirst for social justice.

- Fusion fosters a shared sense of solidarity among Asians, Chicanos, Cubans, West Indians, Arabs, Indians, and Puerto Ricans. Members of each group will recognize that fusions refuse to think in black and white; equally important, fusions accept that others may have as much to teach Americans as Americans have to teach the world.

- For anyone who refuses to change, the word *fusion* deliberately waves the revolutionary flag: "I moved on; how about you?" Fusions proudly and assertively announce that they seek a future with this goal: Let us make the word *fusion* so commonplace that it acts no longer as an alarm but as a bedrock of a reconfigured, just, and truly *United* States of America.

Besides the word *fusion,* I would add *American.* It is a surprisingly underused word in the United States. Ask a person what they are, and they generally respond with a skin color or an ethnicity. Americans exist when we travel abroad, but we need to bring the word home and marry it to fusion.

I am an *American fusion.* In battling the concept of race and the dichotomy, I would appropriate the word *American* and use it to celebrate what Samuel Huntington calls the "American Creed." Simply defined, that creed applauds "the essential dignity of the individual human being"; the fundamental equality of all men and women; and everyone's "inalienable rights to freedom, justice, and a fair opportunity." As the chapters on African Americans, Chicanos, Asians, and fusions show, these marvelous ideals often have little to do with life as it is actually lived. An "American fusion" pays homage to the creed and asks that, instead of paying it lip service, we best acknowledge our debt to Jefferson, Paine, Franklin, and Washington by using "common sense."

In 1776 Thomas Paine wrote that "male and female are the distinctions of nature, good and bad the distinctions of Heaven; but how a race of men came into the world so exalted above the rest, and distinguished like some new species, is worth inquiring into, and whether they are means of happiness or of misery to mankind."9 Paine wrote about kings and subjects. Our focus is whites, blacks, and none-of-the-aboves. Using common sense, American fusions can imitate the patriots at the Boston Tea Party by throwing ugly social constructs overboard; and, this time, let us make the American Creed a living reality for everyone, even our most recent immigrants.

Historical Inequities

We must return to Henry Yu's point: Does eliminating race and the dichotomy freeze the inequities created over hundreds of years of oppression, prejudice, and discrimination? Why, for example, would African Americans agree to these changes if a color-blind world threatened to blur or hide the awful political, economic, and cultural consequences of history?

For two reasons. One is the future. Unless we change the language, white remains the designer original against which we judge everyone else on the face of the earth. Over time—another fifty years—the negative implications of blackness may dissipate, but the white/nonwhite division of humanity would still perpetuate all the fundamental assumptions of white versus black. In addition, our none-of-the-above population—150 million people by 2050—would continue to experience confusion, prejudice, and, worst of all, the need to assimilate by learning to think like whites and blacks. If that is a future with promise, the promise is more of the same, all in the name of white supremacy.

We need to change the language so that our grandchildren avoid slavery's most lasting ideological legacy. And, reason number two, we need to change the language as a way of using a different strategy to attack and eliminate institutionalized inequities. Leaders like Jesse Jackson want to hold on to traditional categories as a way of ensuring that, at a minimum, black power is neither diminished nor diluted by the recognition of a multiracial category by agencies like the Equal Opportunity Employment Commission. However pragmatic this concern may be, the reluctance to embrace revolutionary concepts perpetuates the racial status quo while enabling whites to feel victimized by blacks. It also alienates potential allies—for example, Chicanos, Puerto Ricans, Asians, Arabs, and Indians—who do not think in black and white and do not accept responsibility for the inequities experienced by African Americans.

But eliminating the dichotomy never means ignoring the inequities. On the contrary, it means thinking about them in a more forceful and just manner. By changing the words, we potentially make social interaction impossible; the revolution is perpetual because we ask anyone with whom we interact to rethink the beliefs and inequities buried in the words. We hope they respond in an empathetic manner, but, if they do not, we proceed with the peaceful revolution. We refuse to make skin color the axis of identity, and, like the mixed-race population, we will continue to live in limbo until we devise words, beliefs, and practices that offer justice, dignity, and self-respect to all Americans.

Challenging the words exposes one of the gravest of their consequences: the institutionalized inequities in anything from educational opportunities to hiring practices. In essence, as more and more fusions break out of the maze they unite and create a power block that transcends not only race and color but ethnicity, gender, and educational attainments. By definition, fusion denotes a new way of seeing self and society and a new means of coming together as a cultural and political force capable of honestly confronting inequities. African Americans stand to be among the biggest beneficiaries of this change because the refusal to legitimate skin color as an axis of identity contributes to our efforts to solve many contemporary problems. For example, university admissions policies typically place very different people in the same black box. In 2004 roughly 66 percent of Harvard's so-called black students actually traced their ethnic roots to Africa, the West Indians, or biracial parents.[10]

Since everyone who is not white is a person of color under this system, such dark-skinned students are taking spots supposedly reserved for African Americans. But, if social justice is the goal, why should the offspring of an African or a West Indian with a PhD be considered in the same light as a poor African American student from New Orleans? This kind of lunacy goes on every day in the United States. We turn privileged newcomers and their children into overnight minorities; a system designed to open up opportunities gives those opportunities to people who, in many instances, already have excessive amounts of social capital.

The American idea of race also turns some Caribbean or African immigrants into blacks, who in turn embrace the dichotomy and all its divisive consequences. In her February 15, 2007, editorial for the *Washington Post,* Marjorie Valbrun says she is a Haitian immigrant who proudly identifies as a black; and as a voter, she has no trouble understanding how a politician who reaches out to "them" can also include "us." Such an approach increases the number of black Americans as it simultaneously reinforces the white/black dichotomy. The result is diminished opportunities for African Americans: like the West Indians taking "black" seats at Harvard, Haitians in America are now black and only black.

In a world without race, African Americans would be seen as an ethnic group with a unique and terrible history of oppression in the United States. To those who suggest that African Americans are not an ethnic group, I would respond that many African Americans are themselves adopting the "ethnic" designation. Among African American observers of the 2008 presidential race, some have decided that Senator Barack Obama is not "one of us," emphasizing the senator's partial ethnic origins in Kenya disqualify him from being an African American.

I agree. Such thinking ignores race and the one drop rule. Using an ethnic lens, Senator Obama is *not* an African American—and that is exactly my point. By abolishing race and spotlighting African Americans, and not inflating their ranks with instant "people of color," we focus on the real issues, problems, and needs of people who have lived in the United States for more than four hundred years. Fusions will be far more open to righting the past than whites and made-in-America "people of color." In addition, American fusion is an identity that transcends both race *and* ethnicity. Right now, the four minority "food groups" self-segregate by using identities like Latino, Asian, Native American, and African American. At the Unity Conference for Minority Journalists held every five years in Washington, D.C., journalists bond with each other and focus on the institutionalized inequities that affect their groups. For example, as noted in our discussion of Detroit in chapter 5, blacks who dominate the city council seek to create an Africa Town using tax revenues that will freeze out the Arabs from Africa.

The entire debate takes place using the social constructs—the conceptual categories—created by white people for everyone else on earth. Does anyone believe that you will forcefully confront institutionalized inequities in a world where blacks tell Arabs that they come from the wrong part of Africa? Is the idea that whites who live in the high-end suburb of Grosse Point will frequent Detroit's casinos and provide the revenues to one "minority group" so that it can freeze out Arabs, who are "nonwhite," invisible, and eager to get their own minority food-group status?

Detroit is only one troubled city. But as Nicholás Vaca demonstrates in *The Presumed Alliance,* similar battles are going on in Los Angeles, Houston, Miami, and Compton.[11] Moreover, anyone who has spent time on this nation's campuses has witnessed the same battle for resources among the various ethnic groups. "Minorities" often spend as much time fighting among themselves as they do with the "white folks" who control the purse strings and our self-defeating manner of conceptualizing social problems.

Those who fear a conceptual revolution because it will ignore inequities need to use cities like Detroit as a question mark. If the bewildering number of minority groups continues to self-segregate and subdivide, where is the political muscle to achieve serious social change? American fusions offer a sense of unity that transcends the specific groups, rights history, and then seeks a redress of grievances rooted in a willingness to reconfigure the cultural and institutional consequences of the world created by white people for nonwhite people.

Ellis Island and the Statue of Liberty

In the decade 1821–30, 143,000 immigrants came to the United States. The figure for 1851–60 is 2.6 million immigrants; and for the decade 1891–1900, the figure is an astonishing 5.2 million immigrants.[12] On September 17, 1909, Israel Zangwill's new play *The Melting Pot* opened on New York's Yiddish Broadway. In the face of massive immigration, a Jewish playwright from London offered Anglo Protestant America a metaphor that explained how the new world welcomed immigrants from the old world. The main character is a Russian immigrant who, at the end of the third act with the upraised torch of the Statue of Liberty glowing in the background, makes this comment: "What is the glory of Rome and Jerusalem where all nations and races come to worship and look back, compared with the glory of America, where all nations come to labor and look forward."

Incredibly, the melting pot myth was born in the middle of an Americanization campaign that produced slogans like "The English language, if you don't know it, learn it, if you don't like it, move out."[13] Remember, too, the long series of court cases that denied citizenship rights to Chinese, Japanese, Syrian, and Indian immigrants. It was a time when a playwright like Israel Zangwill had to torture logic, sneaking Sicilians into the pot by calling them "dark whites."[14]

The Anglo pot *never* had room for most of the world, yet, into the twenty-first century, the myth survives, rarely challenged by the facts that explode it. As Randolph Bourne wrote in 1916, Americans forget history. The early colonists never came "to be assimilated into the American melting pot. They did not come to adopt the culture of the American Indian. They had not the smallest intention of 'giving themselves without reservation' to the new country." Bourne also stressed that "we act as if we want Americanization to take place only on our own terms, and not by the consent of the governed."[15] In 1924 Anglos formally closed the melting pot to everyone but their own kind. England, Ireland, and Germany received the lion's share of new immigration slots for more than forty years after the passage, in 1924, of the "Ethnic Origins" legislation. Our problem today is that we want to use the myth of the melting pot to absorb the very people whom we callously expelled during and after the very successful run of Israel Zingwill's play.

We can never create a sense of unity by using concepts that, by definition, exclude many of the people we supposedly want to include. Beyond this lies a still greater challenge: to determine our fundamental disposition toward the cultural differences that do indeed distinguish one group from another. Historically, we pushed people to assimilate or else; newcomers and especially their children generally accepted the culture of their adopted home. In a worst-case scenario, they also internalized the prejudices we taught them. Like some of the Cubans, Arabs, and West Indians discussed in the preceding chapters, they learned to think in white and black, to use the dichotomy to "understand" everybody from Chicanos to fusions to Indians.

In a society that affirms the American Creed, few people want newcomers to assimilate the prejudices of our culture. Some do so anyway. However, just as often, they resist assimilation and instead celebrate a process of transculturation, of reconfiguring American culture to their likes and desires. The Chicano notion of "Occupied America" is one example of a reconfiguration that creates disunity rather than solidarity. The Indian reaffirmation of Hindu culture is another. And the request of some Arabs for a new minority status is yet another effort to become American by embracing the dichotomy and its consequences.

Advocating the melting pot is like spitting in the wind. It ignores the many features of daily life that, in the twenty-first century, fuel resistance to assimilation: dual citizenship and the multicultural rhetoric that treats Europe and England as enemies; classroom lessons about American genocide of Native Americans and the continuing exploitation of Chicanos; and the need for a civil rights movement in a society that violently denied basic rights to African Americans.

Many immigrants are moved to ask, Do I want to become similar to these people? Do I want to become like the Japanese and Chinese who, after a hundred years in the United States, still get the same questions: Where did you learn to speak English so well? And how long is your visit to America?

The melting pot serves up a dish that needs to disappear. So, here is what I propose. Limit requests for similarity to the American Creed. As long as newcomers embrace our inalienable Bill of Rights, the essential dignity of every human being, and the U.S. Constitution, we will entertain a significantly different disposition toward beliefs and values that differentiate them in relation to attributes like religion, family, fashion, or food.

Instead of demanding cultural clones, we should think of the United States as a delightful banquet of cultures. We can sample a few dishes, taste them all, or leave the banquet and go to McDonald's for a hamburger and fries. The key is our positive disposition toward the cultural differences that obviously exist and the reasons for that positive disposition.

One reason is this: Exposure to other cultures shapes and broadens mind and character. As the United Nations Educational, Scientific, and Cultural Organization (UNESCO) put it in a recent publication entitled "All Different, All Unique," a willingness to learn from others is "a crucial factor in human and social development." Too often analysts focus on only economic or technological goals; they neglect that openness to other cultures also offers significant assistance as societies adapt to new possibilities, problems, and prospects. "It teaches us what other people believe needs to change to make the world a better place for themselves and for others"; and, perhaps most important, it nurtures and sustains all forms of creativity because "it widens the range of options open to everyone and gives us real choices for the way forward in the development of our societies."[16]

Throughout the United States, one university after another is urging its students to study abroad; from Augusta to Seattle, well-staffed offices of international education do everything possible to help students spend at least one semester in a foreign country. Their rationales range from the need to participate in a global economy to the desire that students learn to see self and society from fresh and provocative experiences.

If exposure to other cultures is a positive and increasingly required attribute for America's best and brightest, why not take advantage of the cultures that exist in our own backyards? The banquet metaphor sees the vital presence of immigrant communities as an easy and inexpensive means for all Americans to broaden mind and character by exposure to different cultures. It is a positive disposition toward difference because it assumes that all cultures and people can learn from one another and in the process enhance and nurture all forms of creativity.

The banquet metaphor works because we normally want to feast on the dishes offered. Wearing a smile, we volunteer to be there, and, even if we do not like some of the cultural dishes, we can put them aside and happily let others enjoy what we do not. The banquet metaphor implies the same openness toward religion or family that many of us have toward different foods. New York City, Chicago, or Los Angeles contains every imaginable ethnic cuisine. People literally "eat it up." So, using a banquet metaphor, we decide to open ourselves to the world rather than, as in 1924, locking the doors to the cultural differences that can stimulate Americans as much as Americans stimulate others.

As a possible ideal for the United States, consider this example from contemporary Norway. Describing state-sponsored classes in Norwegian for immigrants, American Bruce Bawer notes that as he learned the language "we also learned about Norwegian folkways and gained insights into our own and one another's native languages and cultures." Equally important, Bawer stresses that the classes produced such openness to difference that "our discussions brought into focus previously unexamined attitudes and assumptions that our native cultures had bred into us." Ultimately, "we laughed—laughed in easy self-mockery, and laughed, too, in celebration of the opportunity we'd been given to grow beyond our native cultures."[17]

Thanks to the immigrants we also have an opportunity to laugh, to grow, and to reconfigure our inherited culture. But the banquet metaphor is always a two-way street. If I am going to open my mind to the immigrants, they need to open themselves to me. Each of us uses empathy to understand the other person's culture, and everyone recognizes that empathy does not mean a suspension of judgment or a relativist repudiation of all standards by arguing that all cultures are equally good. After all, the person saying that all cultures are equally good just made a very strong value judgment.

Let me be quite specific. Given the immigration of millions of practicing Muslims, Europe now has to reconsider everything from school dress codes to the proper relationship between church and state. By definition "Islam is a holistic religion in which no distinctions exist between the realms of individual worship and community government, or between the realms of religion and politics." Since "there is no god but god," everything belongs to God, who through the gift of the Quran, provides a comprehensive guide to all aspects of life.[18] In Holland and Denmark, Islamic religious leaders adamantly claim jurisdiction that runs against the authority of the secular political state.

In the United States, Muslims now outnumber Presbyterians and Episcopalians. In addition, some Christian groups also make sweeping claims for the blessed and mandatory role of God in political as well as personal matters. In *American Theocracy*, Kevin Phillips claims that America contains perhaps forty million Americans who wish to see Jesus take a much more active role in political affairs. Many seek to reserve voting rights for Christian males; others wish to superimpose the Bible on the Constitution; and extremist Christian reconstructionists even advocate that homosexuals, prostitutes, adulterers, and drug users also be executed.

The banquet metaphor opens itself to empathizing with Islamic, Christian, or any religious beliefs. But, given the fundamental and indispensable primacy of the American Creed, anyone's right to be an atheist or gay is just as worthy of respect as anyone's right to be a member of a specific religion. The creed "glorifies the individual in general," and if there is a conflict between the inalienable rights of the individual and the credo of a particular religion, "the individual in general" receives primacy and the political state must ensure that, in this world, it is the sole and sovereign authority over civil rights and the political guarantees that include free speech, free assembly, and a free press.

From this perspective, a respect for the American Creed is the sacrosanct means we use to discuss our positive disposition toward the many cultures that now exist in the United States of America. We guarantee the rights of everyone, and, as we debate our shared destinies, the banquet metaphor resolves the traditional battle between assimilation, cultural pluralism, and multiculturalism by choosing "none of the above."

The banquet metaphor endorses an open road—what Nobel laureate Amartya Sen calls "cultural liberty"—because it recognizes that, given the unalterable realities associated with transculturation, all Americans now live between past and future. In this incredibly exciting social space, we can consciously reconfigure Anglo Protestant culture based on welcome additions from Americans of all ethnicities. Rooted in the American Creed, we can sit down with the newcomers, compare and contrast our contributions to the banquet, and altogether reconfigure a culture that eagerly globalizes not the economy but our beliefs and values about the world and about ourselves.

The Contemporary "Screw Loose" Immigration Debate

I—we—cannot talk about a banquet of cultures unless we include the eleven million illegal immigrants. Many are here to stay, and if the last century is any guide, millions more are on the way. So, let us begin with a 1928 conversation (already cited in chap. 3) between Congressman Bird J. Vincent and District Director of Immigration Grover Wilmuth.

Congressman Vincent: The very fact that you had, say, a dozen Mexicans herded in some place and that you gave them a chance to go back to Mexico and they said they would not go, and then you very politely turned them loose, that would indicate to their mind that there was a screw loose somewhere, would it not?

Grover Wilmuth: Yes sir: that is a natural inference.

On June 19, 2006, Richard Stana, director of Homeland Security and Justice, appeared at Senate hearings entitled "Immigration Enforcement at the Workplace: Learning from the Mistakes of 1986." In his prepared statement Mr. Stana said this: "if investigative agents arrest unauthorized aliens at worksites, the aliens would likely be released because the Office of Detention and Removal detention centers do not have sufficient space to house the aliens and they may re-enter the workforce, *in some cases returning to the worksites from where they were originally arrested*" (emphasis added).[19]

The Senate is presumptuous; as a nation we cannot learn from the mistakes of 1928, much less those made in 1986. Illegal immigration is, and has been for almost a century, an institutionalized part of American life. But, instead of rooting policies in structural realities, the 2005–2006 debates show that we are endlessly repeating history, all in the service of politics, vested interests, and hypocrisy. As General Clark Kent Ervin (the former inspector general of the Department of Homeland Security) recently told Congress, "Einstein said insanity is doing the same thing over and over again and expecting a different result. They never learn anything. It's just crazy."[20]

Consider information Congress commissioned from the U.S. Government Accountability Office (GAO). In 1996 Congress passed legislation that established a "Basic Pilot Program" to monitor employer verification of potentially illegal workers. Participation is voluntary, so, as of June 2006, .0015 percent of America's employers (8,600 firms out of a total pool of 5,600,000) actually use the government's program. As the National Border Patrol Council stressed to Congress on July 5, 2006, "as long as employers are allowed to continue to hire illegal aliens without any meaningful consequences, only a handful of them will participate in a legal program. Expecting them to do so would be as ridiculous as expecting people to wait in line to use a sophisticated security gate when everyone else is walking around because there is no surrounding fence."[21]

Despite the few firms (4,600 of the 8,600) that "actively" use the program on a regular basis, there are times when someone spots an illegal immigrant. Unfortunately, a new problem then arises because the United States Citizenship and Immigration Service (USCIS) often refuses to provide any information to Immigration and Customs Enforcement (ICE), relocated by the Bush administration in the Department of Homeland Security. In explaining its reluctance to share information, the USCIS is quite clear: "They have concerns about providing ICE broader access to Basic Pilot Program Information because it could create a disincentive for employers to participate in the program, as employers may believe that they are more likely to be targeted for a worksite enforcement investigation as a result of program participation."[22]

In reality employers need not worry because actual work site enforcement is the bureau's lowest priority. For example, with an estimated ten to eleven million illegal immigrants, notices of *intent* to fine employers dropped from 417 in 1999 to 3 in 2004. Arrests dropped from 2,849 in 1999 to 445 in 2003, and that is good news for the bureau because it openly admits that it lacks the staff to monitor "a significant number of new employers." Of course, it would not share that information with the Department of Homeland Security, and, even if it did, there is "no detention space" to house additional illegal immigrants.[23]

In hearings before the House of Representatives in November 2005, Congressman Howard L. Berman (D-California) called enforcement sanctions "a joke"; many of his colleagues seemed to agree, yet, in focusing on sending troops to guard the border and a proposed seven-hundred-mile wall between Mexico and the United States, the president, the House of Representatives, and the Senate neglect another study commissioned from the GAO. In an analysis entitled "Overstay Tracking," the GAO stresses that "a substantial proportion" of illegal immigrants arrive legally; they overstay their visas to such an extent that, instead of the 30 percent figure cited by the USCIS, the actual number of overstays could be 57 percent or more of the nation's total illegal immigrant population. Those overstays have a 2 percent chance of apprehension if only because "historically . . . over five times more resources in terms of staff and budget have been devoted to border enforcement than . . . to interior enforcement."[24]

The border is political theater. With well-publicized crackdowns like Operation Gatekeeper, federal officials grandstand about their expensive efforts to stop illegal immigration. The endlessly peculiar result is that Congress puts five times fewer resources in a search for the majority who continue working even though they can be easily apprehended; after all, we know exactly where the illegal immigrants are—at construction sites, in our homes, on lawns, in hotels, in restaurant kitchens, and on the docks collecting merchandise made in China and delivering it to the local Wal-Marts. As Bill Brush of Customs and Border Protection put it in June 2006, "if you were to make a firm policy that, say, Los Angeles and Long Beach had to check the immigration bona fides of every trucker, you'd have a major trucker shortage. You'd have a trade breakdown."[25]

Meanwhile, after spending more than twenty billion dollars to guard the border since 1996—and that includes a wall that is already sixty-six miles long—a GAO study (released on August 2, 2006) indicates that in many instances people never try to climb the walls; they simply walk right past the border guards. In 2006 "on three occasions—in California, Texas and Arizona—GAO agents crossed the border on foot. At two of these locations—Texas and Arizona—CBP [the border patrol] allowed the agents entry into the United States without asking for or inspecting any identification documents." The head of the National Border Patrol Council summed up the situation by telling Congress [in July 2006] that "front line agents estimate that for every person they apprehend, two or three successfully enter the United States illegally."

Even when agents catch illegal entrants, this is often the result. As Congressman Henry Bonilla (D-Texas) told his colleagues, in the past agents actually hunted the illegal immigrants; now, when folks cross the Rio Grande "they look for the Border Patrol, throw their hands up, knowing full well they're going to get a meal. They are going to get a place to sleep. They are going to get medical care . . . and then they [the Border Patrol] set them free with court papers, claiming that they don't have the detention space."

The immigrants come because of a fact openly accepted by Congress and editorial writers from one end of the country to the other. That is, the nation needs the illegal immigrants as much as the immigrants need the work. Listen to three members of Congress in November 2005 and to New York mayor Michael Bloomberg on July 5, 2006.

Steve Pearce (R-New Mexico): If you deport folks in Palm Springs that closes the city down. I mean it would just close down. All of the work is being done by a combination of legal and illegal immigrants in Palm Springs, and I have to tell you the hotels and the chambers of commerce, etcetera, are not willing to give that up. And they're not going to give it up.[26]

Luis Gutierrez (D-Illinois): Mexican immigrants today fill almost half of the blue collar, service related and unskilled jobs in my city [Chicago]. It is not an exaggeration to say that our cities would grind to a halt without these workers.

Michael Bloomberg: Although they broke the law by illegally crossing our borders or overstaying their visas, our City's economy would be a shell of itself had they not, and it would collapse if they were deported. The same holds true for the nation.[27]

John Hostettler (R-Indiana): I think the reason is, of course, that many of our industries depend upon that kind of labor. But we must answer to the American people . . . and make sure that our employers follow the law. But there are industries that are totally dependent.[28]

Total dependence is nothing new. President Reagan received the same message in 1986, and, after noting the complaints of his constituents, Congressman John Carter (R-Texas) told his colleagues that "these are ranchers that have lived on that border for four generations and had these illegals walk through for four generations of his family."[29]

Four generations and we still criminalize the workers; turn a blind eye to the employers; and ignore a point emphasized by an October 31, 2005, editorial in Tucson's *Arizona Daily Star:* "Eleven million people do not establish themselves as an integral part of a national economy without the tacit approval of society as a whole."[30]

In 1885 George Washington Cable criticized the North and Midwest for its "virtual consent" to the South's creation and maintenance of the Jim Crow laws. Will we do it again? Will we, in 2007 and beyond, tacitly consent to totally depend on illegal labor yet tell that labor to move to the back of the bus when it comes to equal rights and opportunities? As the *Milwaukee Journal Sentinel* put it in a 2005 editorial, "it is simply un-American to tell immigrants you are good enough to work for us but not good enough to be one of us."

Based on an analysis of documents at his presidential library, Ronald Reagan honestly and sincerely tried to resolve the nation's dilemma. Far more than his predecessors and successors, he worried about the claim of being a nation of laws, in the face of flagrant employer and employee violations of the law, "one generation after another." He also knew that if we made it too easy for workers to become legal "we would be rewarding those who have been here illegally and encourage others to continue coming."

The president understood the problems associated with an amnesty; he also understood the nation's reliance on illegal labor; and he respected and admired the work ethic, dreams, and tenacity of the vast majority of illegal immigrants. Ronald Reagan wanted to square the circle, but, in trying to "insulate" employers from the law, he ultimately bowed to the political pressures exerted by the supporters of both political parties. Like those who sent telegrams to then Senator Lyndon Johnson in the 1950s, employers (who also offered political contributions) made it clear to the president's staff that they wanted the stream of immigrants to continue swimming north with no fear of meaningful employer sanctions.[31]

Businesses are not going to give up their reliance on undocumented labor. And neither are the rest of us. The folks mowing the lawns at our Connecticut University are Latinos; I do not ask about their status and neither do the students sunbathing on the manicured lawns.

The American way to regularize the situation is to bring our desires in line with their needs. We own the contradiction, and amnesty is not a gift; it is the long-term worker's earned right. In the name of a century of justice denied, immediately offer amnesty (with no mention of a fine) to the long-term illegal immigrants. As President Ronald Reagan knew from his experiences in California, they are hard-working, family-oriented, and religiously devoted human beings.

They are also an integral part of America's future. As the *Des Moines Register* put it on August 28, 2005, "the numbers are irrefutable. Births of Hispanic babies in the state rose 358% between 1990 and 2004, while births of non-Hispanic babies dropped 8%." So, as the editorial stresses, "if Iowa wants to grow, welcoming newcomers from other countries is the best hope."[32]

And, if America wants to grow, offering amnesty provides the best kind of family reunification. The illegal parents can openly sit at the same table as their born-in-America children; and then we can altogether embrace the "cultural liberty" that allows us to radically reconfigure American culture.

Kingston, Jamaica, and Laredo, Texas

Dancing in Kingston

I recently attended the fortieth anniversary celebration of the National Dance Theater Company of Jamaica. The black-tie dinner took place in a theater very close to the center of Kingston, a city with a mountain of problems. Even locals avoid walking through many of its streets. Kingston manifests substantial poverty and, as a consequence of that poverty, an infrastructure in urgent need of major overhaul.

More than four hundred people attended the banquet and an exquisitely choreographed performance by the company. The troupe has always been run entirely by volunteers; the dancers sometimes receive food and other expenses, but most work for the love of their art. To be a member of the company is a badge of prestige in Jamaican society.

That evening's performance involved about thirty dancers. Their skin color included every shade of humanity. But what I found most impressive was that two of the lead dancers were Cuban. They had immigrated to Jamaica for the artistic opportunities, and they ultimately came to love the culture so much that they applied for citizenship and established Cuban/Jamaican families. No one talked about mixed races, and no one used skin color as a primary means of identity. These thirty Jamaicans proved that, whatever was happening in the center of Kingston, they were living the nation's motto: out of many, one people.

Out of many, a so-called developing country used pride in nationality to welcome people with different languages and different beliefs. Nobody asked the Cubans to be similar. Their required contribution was creativity, a willingness to work hard, and a disposition to learn from Jamaicans as Jamaicans learned from them.

Exercising the next morning, I walked in a guarded hotel parking lot rather than through the unguarded streets. Kingston is a rough city. But, with so many Jamaicans practicing what they preach, civilization somehow wins the day. You leave Jamaica knowing that it is possible to create a society in which race and skin color are peripheral facts of everyday life. You leave Jamaica with a realizable goal for the United States: "e pluribus unum," one out of many, a nation of creative fusions.

Laredo, May 1, 2006

Like Kingston, Laredo is a city with problems, from pollution to drugs, poverty to urban sprawl. Move out of the downtown and you encounter concrete boxes, surrounded with thousands of parking spaces. Laredo shops and eats with the rest of us. At Mall del Norte you can walk from the Olive Garden or Fuddruckers to J. C. Penney or Sears. The main drag, called San Bernardo, is arguably as ugly a stretch as any in America.

But the beauty becomes evident when people start talking. Laredo is a bilingual (bicultural) city. Eavesdrop on diners in a restaurant and you immediately notice that men, women, and children are moving effortlessly from Spanish to English and back again. They are all Americans who effortlessly speak two languages, and stereotypes offer little help this close to the Mexican border. In one hotel a large group of literal Marlboro men sit in their best gear: monogrammed shirts, multicolored boots, handlebar mustaches, toothpicks dangling from their lips, and white cowboy hats to protect their weathered faces. My Northeast stereotypes said southern drawls and prejudice, but I heard instead friendship, conviviality, and a mixture of accents, all seamlessly speaking Spanish and English. Some of the cowboys were Mexican Americans, but, whatever their ethnicity, their huge belt buckles announced that they worked for the Department of Agriculture. On horseback, these men chased not illegal immigrants but stray cattle, and they displayed a degree of interethnic comfort that, according to locals and the professors at Texas A&M, is characteristic of Laredo and its people.

Given this admirable state of relations, I expected a huge turnout for the "A Day without Mexicans" strike on May 1, 2006. At 5:00 p.m., the protesters planned to march from Laredo's Civic Center to the brand-new Webb County Justice Center. The television news vans dutifully appeared, but the crowd numbered a mere 150 at best, and that was after organizers brought all the children in town. With attendance surpassing half a million at similar protests, the terrible turnout called for an explanation. One was quickly provided by a local police officer. He explained that "Across the nation, people are afraid of losing their jobs. But here in Laredo, a boycott doesn't really make sense. Why would you walk out on your own people?" he said. "We are all one and the same."

This unself-conscious sense of unity is perhaps the most powerful response we can muster to Randolph Bourne's question, "What shall we do with our America?" In 1924 we answered that question by closing our doors to most of the world. We deliberately discriminated against virtually everyone in order to, as Congressman Albert Johnson stressed, discredit "the myth of the melting pot." The United States belonged to white people. As Johnson and his colleagues noted, "We intend to maintain it so."[33]

The people of Kingston and Laredo suggest a different answer to Bourne's wonderful question. Jamaicans prove that skin color and the poisonous dichotomy only matter if we say they do. And the laudable sense of comfort evident in Laredo argues that we can reconfigure the culture if we define ourselves by what already binds three hundred million people.

At this banquet, we are one race, united in peace and driven by our desire to celebrate a nation of all-American fusions.

Epilogue

—— ❋ ——

Our Fusion Family

Ken and I are both grandfathers. We both come from Brooklyn, both are second-generation Americans. Ken was born in 1940, and I arrived in 1944. He experienced prejudice because he was a Japanese American growing up in an America that sponsored "relocation camps." I was always a *spic,* heir to the slurs directed at Puerto Ricans and other Latino immigrants in 1950s New York.

We both managed not only to survive but to achieve the American Dream. After a life of hard work, Ken now lives in a high-end retirement community, while I, the son of a father who never had the chance to learn to read and write, claim one of the most privileged jobs in America: full-tenured professor.

Ken met his wife, Pepa, a first-generation immigrant from war-torn Colombia, in New York. They fell in love, got married, took on two jobs, bought a house in Queens, and successfully reared three children.

Our son Adam married their daughter, and, on November 15, 2005, Jacob Morton Fernandez was born. Look at him and you will see elements of Ken's handsome face and, at least so far, a head of reddish hair. He is a fantastic fusion who inextricably combines at least five ethnic heritages: Colombian, French, Irish, Japanese, and Spanish.

Jacob obviously knows nothing of the society he has inherited. But his parents do. To the extent they can, they will protect him from an America that will negatively judge him by his "mixed race" roots; the world is in Jacob's face, but too many Americans will struggle for positive words to describe him. He has done absolutely nothing to deserve this obscene question: What are you?

Jacob is an all-American fusion. Bad-mouth that boy and you will answer to our family because it is past high time to face it and move on: races do not exist; white people are beige; and if we are ever going to define ourselves by what unites us, we urgently need to snap the chains that bind us in mental slavery.

We can overcome. And I will tell you how: be selfish! If you are unwilling to radically reconfigure American culture for the sake of our grandchild, do it for your own.

Notes

Introduction

1. Emilie Hammerstein, "Sticky Rice at Yom Kippur," *Eurasian Nation: The Best of Both Worlds* (November 2002): 1, http://www.eurasiannation.com (accessed February 11, 2003).

2. For example, Eric Liu, *The Accidental Asian* (New York: Vintage Books, 1998), 188.

3. For example, Helen Hatab Samhan, "Not Quite White: Race Classification and the Arab American Experience," in Michael Suleiman, editor, *Arabs in America: Building a New Future,* 209–26 (Philadelphia: Temple University Press, 1999); quote appears on p. 209.

One

1. Iris Chang, *The Chinese in America* (New York: Viking, 2003); the ad appears in illustrations at the center of the book; for the farm labor figures see p. 72.

2. Ibid., 477.

3. House Committee on Immigration and Naturalization, *Restriction of Immigration: Hearing before the Committee on Immigration and Naturalization,* 68th Cong., 1st sess. (Washington, D.C.: GPO, 1924), 96–97.

4. John Higham, *Strangers in the Land: Patterns of American Nativism, 1860–1925* (New Brunswick: Rutgers University Press, 1963).

5. "The Road to Final Passage," pp. 61–62, White House Central Files, Legislative Background, Immigration Law, 1965, box 1, Lyndon Baines Johnson Library, Austin, Texas.

6. Speech of Attorney General Katzenbach, Cultural Heritage Dinner, San Francisco, Hilton Hotel, April 3, 1965, p. 3, Johnson Library.

7. "Road to Final Passage," pp. B6–B7.

8. Norbert Schlei, oral history interview, Kennedy Presidential Library; the interview dates from 1968, p. 36.

9. Senate Committee on the Judiciary, *Immigration: Hearings before the Subcommittee on Immigration and Naturalization of the Committee on the Judiciary,* 89th Cong., 1st sess., (Washington, D.C.: GPO, 1965), 256.

10. Ibid., 387.

11. House Committee on the Judiciary, *Immigration: Hearings before Subcommittee Number 1,* 89th Cong., 1st sess. (Washington, D.C.: GPO, 1965), 23.

12. Senate Committee on the Judiciary, *Immigration,* 267, 276.

13. Schlei, Oral History Interview, p. 40.

14. For the latest numbers see Rob Paral, *The Growth and Reach of Immigration: New Census Bureau Data Underscore Importance of Immigrants in the U.S. Labor Force* (American Immigration Law Foundation, August 16, 2006), 1, http://www.ailf.org/ipc/policybrief/policybrief_2006_81606.shtml; see also U.S. Census Bureau, *The Foreign-Born Population in the United States* (Washington, D.C.: GPO, March 2002), 1; and Steven Camarota, *Immigrants at Mid-decade* (Center for Immigration Studies, Washington, D.C., December 2005), http://www.cis.org (accessed February 2, 2006).

15. Camarota, *Immigrants at Mid-decade,* 1.

16. U.S. Census Bureau, *Current Population Survey,* March 2002, Ethnic and Hispanic Statistics Branch, Population Division, Internet Release Date, March 10, 2003; Camarota, *Immigrants at Mid-decade,* 1.

17. U.S. Census Bureau, *Foreign Born Population,* 1.

18. Camarota, *Immigrants at Mid-decade,* 13.

19. Steven Camarota, *Immigrants in the United States, 2000* (Center for Immigration Studies, January, 2001), www.cis.org (accessed December 20, 2003), 8.

20. U.S. Census Bureau, "Immigrants Admitted by Type and Class of Admission, Fiscal Year, 2004," table 5, in *Current Population Survey* (Washington, D.C.: GPO).

21. Jeffrey Passel, *The Size and Characteristics of the Unauthorized Migrant Population in the United States* (Pew Hispanic Center, March 7, 2006), i–iii.

22. U.S. Census Bureau, "Foreign Born Population Living in U.S. Regions by Sex and World Region of Birth, 2002," table 3.14, in *Current Population Survey* (Washington, D.C.: GPO, 2004).

23. Camarota, *Immigrants in the United States, 2000,* 5.

24. *La Presencia China in Cuba* (University of Havana: Fernando Ortiz Institute, 1975).

25. The concept of transculturation belongs to Fernando Ortiz. See Fernando Ortiz, *Etnia y Sociedad* (La Habana: Editorial de Ciencias Sociales, 1993), esp. 144–48; and Fernando Ortiz, *Cuban Counterpoint: Tobacco and Sugar* (Durham: Duke University Press, 1995), esp. 97–103. The definitions of transculturation are my own.

26. Alejandro Portes and Rubén Rumbaut, *Legacies: The Story of the Immigrant Second Generation* (Los Angeles: University of California Press, 2001), 45, 52.

27. Nathan Glazer, *We Are All Multiculturalists Now* (Cambridge: Harvard University Press, 1997), 14.

28. See Web page of the Charlotte-Mecklenburg School System, especially section 1, "Academic Achievement," http://nt.5.scbbs.com/cgi-bin/om_isapi .dll?clientID=275403&advqu (accessed January 14, 2005).

29. For example, Ronald Fernandez, *Cruising the Caribbean: U.S. Influence and Intervention in the Twentieth Century* (Monroe: Common Courage Press, 1994), esp. chap 1.

30. J. Jorge Klor de Alva, "The Invention of Ethnic Origins and the Negotiation of Latino Identity, 1969–1981," in Mary Romero, Pierrette Hondagneu-Sotelo, and Vilma Ortiz, editors, *Challenging Fronteras*, 55–74, esp. 60 (New York: Routledge, 1997).

31. See the tables titled "Immigrants Admitted by Type and Class of Admission," http://www.uscis.gov/graphics/shared/statistics/ index.htm. For 2004, see Office of Immigration Statistics, U.S. Citizenship and Immigration, *Characteristics of Family-Sponsored Legal Permanent Residents: 2004* (Washington, D.C.: GPO, 2005), http://www.uscis.gov/graphics/shared/statistics/publications/ FSFamSponsoredLPR2004.pdf .

32. Peggy Levitt and Rafael de la Dehesa, "Transnational Migration and the Redefinition of the State: Variations and Explanations," *Ethnic and Racial Studies* 26, no. 4 (July 2003): 587–611; on Portugal, see especially Jorge Malheiros, "Portugal Seeks Balance of Emigration, Immigration," *Migration Information Source,* Migration Policy Institute, http://www.migrationinformation.org.

33. *Takao Ozawa v. United States,* 260 U.S. 178 (1922); 67 L.ED. 199; 43 S. Ct. 65, available at http://chnm.gmu.edu/eoc/resources (accessed September 21, 2003); see p. 17 of the decision.

34. Sue-Yun Ahn, "Citizen Colored: Asian American Immigration and the Legal Construction of White National Identity," Senior thesis, New York University, 25, available at www.nyu.edu/gsas/dept/politics/undergrad/ research/ahn.pdf (accessed February 27, 2005).

35. Helen Zia, *Asian American Dreams: The Emergence of an American People* (New York: Farrar, Strauss, and Giroux, 2000), 27.

36. Suzanne Oboler, *Ethnic Labels, Latino Lives: Identity and the Politics of (Re) Presentation in the United States* (Minneapolis: University of Minnesota Press, 1995), 156.

37. Matthew Kelly, "At Princeton We're Mixed, at Georgia Tech We're Multiracial and at WPI We're Mutants," *Mavin* 1 (1999): 20–21.

Two

1. Ian F. Haney Lopez, *White by Law: The Legal Construction of Race* (New York: New York University Press, 1996), 213. See appendix B for the full ruling; see pp. 215 and 217 for the other quotes.

2. Ibid., 215.

3. Debra Dickerson, *The End of Blackness* (New York: Pantheon, 2004), 15.

4. George Washington Cable, "The Freedman's Case in Equity," *Century* 29, no. 3 (January 1885): 409–18; see p. 416 for the information offered; all subsequent quotes appear on pp. 410–13. I learned about this article from Grace Elizabeth Hale, *Making Whiteness: The Color of Segregation* (New York: Pantheon, 1998).

5. Henry W. Grady, "In Plain Black and White: A Reply to Mr. Cable," *Century* 29, no. 6 (April 1885): 909–18; the additional quotes appear on p. 912.

6. Stephen Jay Gould, *The Mismeasure of Man* (New York: Norton, 1996), 401.

7. Gould, *Mismeasure of Man,* 411.

8. Ian Haney Lopez, *White by Law,* especially the selection of cases included in the appendix; see pp. 209–25; for the later quotes see pp. 209, 210, 212.

9. Richard Hofstadter, *Social Darwinism in American Thought* (Boston: Beacon Press, 1955).

10. Ellis Cose, *Color Blind: Seeing Beyond Race in a Race Obsessed World* (New York: Harper, 1997), 2.

11. Johnathan Marks, *Human Biodiversity: Genes, Race and History* (New York: Aldine, 1995), 52.

12. Christopher Wills, "The Skin We're In," in Richard Delgado and Jean Stefanic, editors, *Critical White Studies,* 12–16 (Philadelphia: Temple University Press, 1997); quote appears on p. 13; see also Mark Nathan Cohen, *Culture of Intolerance* (New Haven: Yale University Press, 1998), esp. 47–48.

13. Marks, *Human Biodiversity,* 130; also Marvin Harris, *Our Kind* (New York: Harper, 1989), 107.

14. Harris, *Our Kind,* 107–8.

15. Michael Alan Park, *Biological Anthropology* (Mountain View: Mayfield, 1996), 301; see also Stephen Molnar, *Human Variation: Races, Types and Ethnic Groups,* 3d ed. (Englewood Cliffs: Prentice Hall, 1992).

16. Jared Diamond, *Guns, Germs, and Steel: The Fates of Human Societies* (New York: W. W. Norton, 1998), chap. 19, esp. 377 (emphasis added), 380–81.

17. Michael Omi and Howard Winant, *Racial Formation in the United States: From the 1960's to the 1990's,* 2d ed. (New York: Routledge, 1994), 55.

18. Ronald Fernandez, *America's Banquet of Cultures: Harnessing Ethnicity, Race and Immigration in the Twenty-first Century* (Westport: Praeger, 2000), 145.

19. Paul Hendrikson, *Sons of Mississippi: A Story of Race and Its Legacy* (New York: Vintage, 2003), 135, 295.

20. Edward Glaeser and Jacob Vigdor, *Racial Segregation in the 2000 Census: Promising News,* Center on Urban and Metropolitan Policy, Brookings Institution, April 2001.

21. Bruce A. Jacobs, *Race Manners: Navigating the Minefield between Black and White Americans* (New York: Arcade, 1999), 27.

22. Peggy McIntosh, "White Privilege and Male Privilege," in Margaret L. Andersen and Patricia Hill Collins, editors, *Race, Class and Gender,* 97–98 (New York: Wadsworth, 2001).

23. Albert Murray, *The Omni-Americans: Black Experience and American Culture* (New York: De Capo Press, 1970), 79; the next quote is also from p. 79.

24. Jan Nederveen Pieterse, *White on Black: Images of Africa and Blacks in Western Popular Culture* (New Haven: Yale University Press, 1992), 27–28.

25. In this section I relied on Scott Malcomson, *One Drop of Blood: The American Misadventure of Race* (New York: Farrar, Straus, and Giroux, 2000), 149–50; Pieterse, *White on Black,* makes the same point, see pp. 25–29. For the Malcomson quotes that follow, see pp. 277–81, 291, 282, 288.

26. Lawrence Steinhorn and Barbara Diggs-Brown, *By the Color of Our Skin: The Illusion of Integration and the Reality of Race* (New York: Plume Books, 1999), 13.

27. Joe Feagin and Eileen O'Brien, *White Men on Race: Power, Privilege and the Shaping of Racial Consciousness* (Boston: Beacon Press, 2003), 25 and 67. The Notion of Sincere Fictions is also derived from Feagin and O'Brien.

28. Steinhorn and Diggs-Brown, *By the Color of Our Skin,* 29.

29. Both quotes are from Dickerson, *End of Blackness,* 92.

30. This report was commissioned by the Department of Justice. See KPMG Consulting, *Analysis of Diversity in the Attorney Workforce,* June 14, 2002, 33; see also 53–54. I downloaded this report from the Memory Hole, www.thememory-hole.org/Fesldoj-attorney-diversity-unredacted.pdf (accessed March 15, 2005).

31. These assessments come from thirty years of personal experience. I got my own job, for example, because a good friend fixed it with the chair of the department.

32. For an overview of all the issues, see Charles Lawrence III and Mari Matsuda, *We Won't Go Back: Making the Case for Affirmative Action* (Boston: Houghton Mifflin, 1997).

33. Feagin and O'Brien, *White Men on Race,* 138, 140.

34. U.S. Census Bureau, *The Two or More Races Population: 2000* (Washington, D.C.: U.S. Department of Commerce, November 2001), 7.

35. For example, John McWhorter, *Losing the Race: Self Sabotage in Black America* (New York: Harper Collins, 2000).

36. See http://www.joannejacobs.com for more than thirty pages of commentary about Cosby and his speech. This comment appears on p. 9; see also the very similar comments of a responder called "CB" on p. 14 or "Regiwi" on p. 21 (accessed May 30, 2004; pagination is from my download of the extensive commentary).

37. John McWhorter, *Authentically Black: Essays for the Black Silent Majority* (New York: Gotham Books, 2003), 2.

38. Dickerson, *End of Blackness,* 18.

39. Ibid., 213.

40. Karl Mannheim, *Ideology and Utopia: An Introduction to the Sociology of Knowledge* (New York: Harcourt Brace and World, 1936).

41. Cornel West, *Race Matters* (Boston: Beacon Press, 1993), 28.

42. John McWhorter, *Losing the Race: Self Sabotage in Black America* (New York: Perennial, 2000), 26; for the next quote see p. 27.

43. Ibid., 27.

44. W. E. B. Du Bois, *The Souls of Black Folk* (New York: Signet Classics, 1995), 45.

45. Murray, *Omni-Americans,* esp. 22–38.

46. Ibid., 23.

47. McWhorter, *Losing the Race,* 2.

48. Jacobs, *Race Manners,* 33.

49. McWhorter, *Losing the Race;* Dickerson, *End of Blackness,* 52.

50. McWhorter, *Losing the Race,* 44; Dickerson, *End of Blackness,* 134.

51. http://www.joannejacobs.com, 11.

52. McWhorter, *Losing the Race,* 152 (emphasis added).

53. *Washington Post*/Kaiser Family Foundation/Harvard University, "African American Men Survey," June 2006, 17, 22, http://www.kff.org/kaiser polls/upload/7526.pdf (accessed, June 30, 2006).

54. Dickerson, *End of Blackness,* 138.

55. Nicolás Vaca, *The Presumed Alliance: The Unspoken Conflict between Latinos and Blacks and What It Means for America* (New York: Harper Collins, 2004), 190–91.

Three

1. Florence Christman, *The Romance of Balboa Park,* 4th ed. (San Diego: San Diego Historical Society, 1985), 36; additional park quotes come from 58–59 and 39.

2. Desmond Rochfort, *Mexican Muralists* (San Francisco: Chronicle, 1993), 87; see also Pete Hamil, *Diego Rivera* (New York: Harry Abrams, 1999).

3. Steven Camarota, *Immigration from Mexico: Assessing the Impact on the United States* (Washington, D.C.: Center for Immigration Studies, July 2001); Ilan Stavans, *Spanglish* (New York: Harper Collins, 2003), 14.

4. White House Staff and Office Files, Ralph Bledsoe Files, Series 1, Subject Files, President Ronald Reagan Library, Santa Barbara, California (emphasis added).

5. Francisco E. Balderrama and Raymond Rodríguez, *Decade of Betrayal: Mexican Repatriation in the 1930's* (Albuquerque: University of New Mexico Press, 2006), 25.

6. "Immigration and Refugee Policy," Francis Hodsoll Files, 1981, series II, box 13, Reagan Library.

7. Rep. Ted Poe, *Congressional Record,* 109th Cong., 1st sess., November 16, 2005, H10366.

8. Senate Committee on Land and Public Welfare, *Migrant and Seasonal Farmworker Powerlessness: Hearings before the Subcommittee on Migratory Labor,* 91st Cong., 1st and 2nd sess., May 1969, p. 1973; see pp. 1973 and 1975 for the next quotes.

9. House Committee on Immigration and Naturalization, *Temporary Admission of Illiterate Mexican Laborers,* 66th Cong., 2nd sess. (Washington, D.C.: GPO, 1920), 61, 80.

10. David Montejano, *Anglos and Mexicans in the Making of Texas, 1836–1986* (Austin: University of Texas Press, 1987), 51, 58, 73–74.

11. Ibid., 108–9; see also Gilbert Gonzalez and Raul Fernandez, *A Century of Chicano History: Empire, Nations and Migration* (New York: Routledge, 2003), esp. chap. 1.

12. Montejano, *Anglos and Mexicans*, 181.

13. John G. Bourke, "The American Congo," *Scribner's* 15, no. 5 (1894): 591–610, esp. 594, 606.

14. Tomás Almaguer, *Racial Fault Lines: The Historical Origins of White Supremacy in California* (Berkeley: University of California Press, 1994), 53–54; also Earl Shorris, *Latinos: A Biography of the People* (New York: Avon Books, 1992), esp. 167–68.

15. Gonzalez and Fernandez, *Century of Chicano History*, 13; Rodolfo Acuña, *Occupied America: A History of Chicanos*, 5th ed. (New York: Pearson, Longman, 2004), 77–78.

16. House Committee on Immigration and Naturalization, *Seasonal Agricultural Workers from Mexico: Hearings before the Committee on Immigration and Naturalization*, 69th Cong., 1st sess. (Washington, D.C.: GPO, 1926), 34; quoted in Ronald Fernandez, *America's Banquet of Cultures* (Westport: Praeger, 2000), 39.

17. House Committee on Immigration and Naturalization, *Immigration Border Patrol: Hearings before the Committee on Immigration and Naturalization*, 70th Cong., 1st sess. (Washington, D.C.: GPO, 1928), 10; on the labor recruiters, see George Sánchez, *Becoming Mexican American: Ethnicity, Culture and Identity in Chicano Los Angeles, 1900–1945* (New York: Oxford University Press, 1993), 51.

18. Balderrama and Rodríguez, *Decade of Betrayal*, 151, for the estimate of one million people repatriated; p. 266 for the percentage of U.S. citizens.

19. U.S. Senate, Agricultural Committee, *Investigation of Farm Labor Conditions: Hearings before the Special Committee to Investigate Farm Labor Conditions in the West*, 77th Cong., 2nd sess. (Washington, D.C.: GPO, 1942), 11. A superb book about the Bracero Program is Kitty Calavita, *Inside the State: The Bracero Program, Immigration and the I.N.S* (New York: Routledge, 1992).

20. U.S. Senate, Subcommittee of the Judiciary, *Admission of Foreign Agricultural Workers: Hearings before a Subcommittee of the Judiciary*, 81st Cong., 1st sess. (Washington, D.C.: GPO, 1949), 11–12.

21. Subject Files, 1958, container 605, U.S. Senate, 1949–61, Johnson Library.

22. Carlos Muñoz Jr., *Youth, Identity, Power: The Chicano Movement* (New York: Verso, 1989), 19.

23. See *Mendez v. Westminster* (1946), 64 F. Supp. 544, available at http://www.learncalifornia.org (accessed June 6, 2004). I first learned about this case from reading Nicolás C. Vaca, *The Presumed Alliance* (New York: Rayo, 2004), chap. 3.

24. Muñoz, *Youth, Identity, Power*, 49.

25. Ernesto Chávez, *My People First!—Mi Raza Primero!* (Berkeley: University of California Press, 2002), 14–16.

26. Richard J. Jensen and John C. Hammerback, editors, *The Words of César Chávez* (College Station: Texas A&M Press, 2002), 9.

27. T. R. Fehrenbach, *Fire and Blood: A History of Mexico* (New York: Da Capo Press, 1995), 209.

28. Sacramento March Letter, March 1966, in Jensen and Hammerbach, *Words of César Chávez*, 15.

29. See, Muñoz, *Youth, Identity, Power*, 61–62.

30. Ibid., 63.

31. José Vasconcelos, "La Raza Cósmica: Misión de la raza iberoamericana" (1925; repr., Mexico City: Universidad de Varsovia, 1993), 5, available at http://www.analitica.com (accessed February 15, 2003). All translations from Spanish are my own.

32. Ibid., 8.

33. Muñoz, *Youth, Identity, Power*, 76.

34. Klor de Alva, "Invention of Ethnic Origins," 55–80, esp. 60.

35. Ian F. Haney López, *Racism on Trial: The Chicano Fight for Justice* (Cambridge: Harvard University Press, 2003), 208, 220.

36. Ibid., 211. See also Oscar Zeta Acosta, *The Autobiography of a Brown Buffalo* (New York: Vintage, [1972] 1989).

37. López, *Racism on Trial*, 211.

38. "El Plan de Santa Barbara," April 1969, 1–2, available at http://www2.sjsu.edu/orgs/mecha/elplan_sb.html (accessed January 28, 2004).

39. Muñoz, *Youth, Identity, Power*, 81.

40. Albert Murray, *The OmniAmericans: Black Experience and American Culture* (New York: Da Capo, 1970), 79.

41. Douglas Massey, Jorge Durand, and Nolan Malone, *Beyond Smoke and Mirrors: Mexican Immigration in an Era of Economic Integration* (New York: Russell Sage Foundation, 2002), 45.

42. On the president's comment, see memo from Michael Uhlmann to Edwin Meese, June 23, 1982, p. 2, Michael Uhlmann Files, OA9445, Reagan Library; on insulating the employer, see memo from Uhlmann to Meese, February 23, 1982, p. 2, Reagan Library.

43. Letter, June 23, 1982, p. 3, Michael Uhlmann Files, OA9445, Reagan Library.

44. "Immigration Legislation," memo to Charles Hobbs from Charles Smith, October 20, 1986, Collection of Jan Mares, File Folder Immigration Legislation Memo, p. 1, Reagan Library.

45. Memo, October 20, 1986, p. 6, Alan Charles Raul Collection, File Folder Immigration Bill, Reagan Library.

46. Ibid., 1.

47. Massey, Durand, and Malone, *Beyond Smoke and Mirrors*, 90.

48. See Gonzalez and Fernandez, *Century of Chicano History*, 59.

49. Mile Davis, *Magical Urbanism: Latinos Reinvent the U.S. City* (New York: Verso, 2000), 18.

50. See Smith's letter to Congressman Rodino, July 27, 1983, p. 2, Jan Mares Files, Reagan Library.

51. U.S. Government Accounting Office, *H-2A Agricultural Guest Worker Pro-*

gram, GAO/HEHS-98-20 (Washington, D.C., December 1997), esp. 22–23, 49.

52. Massey, Durand, and Malone, *Beyond Smoke and Mirrors,* 131.

53. Victor Davis Hanson, *Mexifornia: A State of Becoming* (San Francisco: Encounter Books, 2003), 97, 99.

54. For a fine overview of what is happening throughout the country, see Héctor Tobar, *Translation Nation: Defining a New American Identity in the Spanish-Speaking United States* (New York: Riverhead Books, 2005).

55. Pew Hispanic Center/Kaiser Family Foundation, *2002 National Survey of Latinos* (Washington, D.C.: 2002), 31.

56. Richard Rodriguez, *Brown: The Last Discovery of America* (New York: Penguin, 2002), xi, also 132–33.

57. Mike Davis, *Magical Urbanism: Latinos Reinvent the U.S. City* (New York: Verso, 2000), 18.

Four

1. Gil Asakawa, *Being Japanese American* (Berkeley: Stone Bridge Press, 2004), 14; also Rudi Williams, "The 'Go For Broke' Regiment Lives Duty, Honor, Country," U.S. Department of Defense, http://www.defenselink .mil/news (accessed August 19, 2004).

2. Helen Zia, *Asian American Dreams: The Emergence of an American People* (New York: Farrar, Straus, and Giroux, 2000), 43.

3. Asakawa, *Being Japanese American,* 3.

4. House Committee on Immigration and Naturalization, *Restriction of Immigration,* 107.

5. Jan Nederveen Pieterse, *White on Black: Images of Africa and Blacks in Western Popular Culture* (New Haven: Yale University Press, 1992), 20, 22.

6. Deepika Bahri, "With Kaleidoscope Eyes," in Dhingra Shankar and Rajini Srikanth, editors, *A Part, Yet Apart: South Asians in Asian America,* 25–48 (Philadelphia: Temple University Press, 1998); the quote appears on p. 27.

7. David Theo Goldberg, "Racial Europeanization," *Ethnic and Racial Studies* 29, no. 2 (March 2006): 331–64, esp. 352.

8. Yen Le Espiritu, *Asian American Panethnicity: Bridging Institutions and Identities* (Philadelphia: Temple University Press, 1992), 32.

9. Chang, *Chinese in America,* 26. Paul R. Spickard, *Japanese Americans: The Formation and Transformation of an Ethnic Group* (New York: Twayne, 1996), 10; see also Sucheng Chan, *Asian Americans: An Interpretive History* (New York: Twayne, 1991).

10. Quoted in Vijay Prashad, *The Karma of Brown Folk* (Minneapolis: University of Minnesota Press, 2000), 13.

11. Robert Nisbet, *The Present Age: Progress and Anarchy in Modern America* (New York: Harper & Row, 1989), 29; see also Michael H. Hunt, *Ideology and U.S. Foreign Policy* (New Haven: Yale University Press, 1987).

12. Samuel Huntington, *Who Are We? The Challenges to America's National Identity* (New York: Simon & Schuster, 2004), 38–39.

13. U.S. Senate, *Congressional Globe*, 40th Cong., 3rd sess., February 9, 1869, 1030–31. I first learned about these debates in Haney Lopez, *White by Law;* the additional congressional quotes appear on pp. 1031, 1032, 1034.

14. Peter Kwong and Dušanka Miščević, *Chinese America: The Untold Story of America's New Community* (New York: New Press, 2005), 45.

15. Kwong and Miščević, *Chinese America,* 70.

16. Huntington, *Who Are We?* 61.

17. Stanley Karnow, *In Our Image: America's Empire in the Philippines* (New York: Random House, 1989), 108.

18. U.S. Senate, *Congressional Record,* 56th Cong., 1st sess., February 9, 1899, 1446–47.

19. Karnow, *In Our Image,* 164.

20. For Taft, see Karnow, *In Our Image,* 173–74; for Senator Wolcott, see U.S. Senate, *Congressional Record,* February 9, 1899, 1451.

21. Karnow, *In Our Image,* 213.

22. U.S. Senate, *Congressional Record,* February 9, 1899, 1447.

23. Veltizesar Bautista, *The Filipino Americans: Yesterday and Today,* http://www.filipinoamericans.net, 11 (accessed August 30, 2004); on Watsonville riots, see Richard Meynell, *Remembering the Watsonville Riots,* http://www.modelminority.com, 1–8 (accessed August 31, 2004).

24. Patricia Justiniani McReynolds, *Almost Americans: A Quest for Dignity* (Santa Fe: Red Crane Books, 1997).

25. This section is firmly rooted in Henry Yu, *Thinking Orientals: Migration, Contact and Exoticism in Modern America* (New York: Oxford University Press, 2002). Ronald Fernandez, *Mappers of Society: The Lives, Times and Legacies of Great Sociologists* (Westport: Praeger, 2003).

26. For example, Edward Hartman, *The Movement to Americanize the Immigrant* (New York: Columbia University Press, 1948).

27. Robert Park and Ernest Burgess, *Introduction to the Science of Sociology* (Chicago: University of Chicago Press, 1921).

28. Yu, *Thinking Orientals,* 40.

29. David K. Yoo, *Growing Up Nisei: Race, Generation, and Culture Among Japanese Americans of California, 1924–49* (Urbana: University of Illinois Press, 2000), 137.

30. Yu, *Thinking Orientals;* for the preceding quotes see pp. 54, 67, 68, 63.

31. Espiritu, *Asian American Panethnicity,* 29.

32. Peter Kwong, *The New Chinatown* (New York: Hill and Wang, 1996), 26.

33. Chang, *Chinese in America,* 204; the following quotes about 1930s Chinatowns, also from Chang, *Chinese in America,* appear on pp. 204, 205, 206, and 207.

34. U.S. Census Bureau, *American Fact Finder: United States 1997 Survey of Minority Owned Business Enterprises* (Washington, D.C.: GPO, 1997).

35. Yu, *Thinking Orientals*, 159.

36. U.S. Citizenship and Immigration Services, *Fiscal Year 2002 Yearbook of Immigration Statistics*, historical table 2; for the complete list see http://www.infoplease.com (accessed September 2, 2004).

37. Frank H. Wu, *Yellow: Race in America beyond Black and White* (New York: Basic Books, 2002), 95.

38. Michelle Malkin, *In Defense of Internment: The Case for Racial Profiling in World War II and the War on Terror* (Wasington, D.C.: Regnery, 2004), 84.

39. See Wu, *Yellow*, 99.

40. Hung C. Thai, "Splitting Things in Half Is So White," *Amerasia Journal* 25, no. 1 (1999): 53–88; quote appears on pp. 67–68.

41. Stephen Steinberg, *Turning Back* (Boston: Beacon Press, 1995), 13; see also Fernandez, *America's Banquet of Cultures*, 167.

42. Thomas Sowell, *Migrations and Cultures: A World View* (New York: Basic Books, 1996), 4–5. On the numbers from India, see Wu, *Yellow*, 53; for a theoretical analysis of why immigrants "succeed," see Alejandro Portes and Rubén Rumbaut, *Immigrant America* (Berkeley: University of California Press, 1996), esp. chap. 3.

43. This list is based on the analysis provided by Portes and Rumbaut in *Immigrant America*.

44. On Korean communities, see Pyong Gap Min, *Caught in the Middle: Korean Communities in New York and Los Angeles* (Berkeley: University of California Press, 1996); also In-Yin Hoon, *On My Own: Korean Business and Race Relations in the United States* (Chicago: University of Chicago Press, 1997).

45. See Chan, *Asian Americans*, 168–69.

46. Peter Kwong, *Forbidden Workers: Illegal Chinese Immigrants and American Labor* (New York: New Press, 1997), 35; on wages, see Kwong, *Forbidden Workers*.

47. Yu, *Thinking Orientals*, 190.

48. Wu, *Yellow*, 67–68.

49. Liu, *Accidental Asian*, 79.

50. Espiritu, *Asian American Panethnicity*, 33.

51. Caroline Aoyagi, "Parcells' Use of Jap Highlights Continued Efforts to Rid Texas of Racist Road Names," *Pacific Citizen*, 1, http://www.imdiversity.com (accessed September 5, 2004).

52. Japanese American Veterans Association, "Twelve Year Quest to Change the Name of Jap Road," 1–4, http://www.javadc.org (accessed September 5, 2004).

53. Meggy's story appears in Vickie Nam, editor, *Yell-Oh Girls!—Emerging Voices Explore Culture, Identity, and Growing up Asian American* (New York: Quill, 2001), 9–13; for similar experiences, see Joann Faung Jean Lee, *Asian Americans* (New York: New Press, 1992).

54. Sam Chu Lin, "Big Trouble in Arizona," *Asian Week*, September 3, 2004, http://www.news.asianweek.com (accessed September 5, 2004).

55. Kwong and Miščević, *Chinese America*, 341.

Five

1. "Is the Turk a White Man?" *New York Times,* September 30, 1909, 8.

2. Helen Hatab Samhan, "Not Quite White: Race Classification and the Arab American Experience," in Suleiman, *Arabs in America,* 217.

3. Therese Saliba, "Resisting Invisibility: Arab Americans in Academia and Activism," in Suleiman, *Arabs in America,* 311.

4. Samhan, "Not Quite White," 219–26; quote appears on p. 218.

5. Ibid., 319; Suleiman draws a similar conclusion in his introduction to *Arabs in America,* 12–13.

6. Suad Joseph, "Against the Grain of the Nation—The Arab," in Suleiman, *Arabs in America,* 257–71, esp. 260.

7. Samhan, "Not Quite White," 209.

8. Joseph, "Against the Grain of the Nation," 259.

9. See Jennifer Baum, "A Word from the Editor," *The Forum: A Contemporary Journal Celebrating Arab America* 1, no. 9 (October 7, 2004): 3.

10. Murray, *The OmniAmericans,* 77.

11. Karen Rignall, "Building the Infrastructure of an Arab Identity in Detroit: A Short History of ACCESS and the Community It Serves," in Nabeel Abraham and Andrew Shryock, editors, *Arab Detroit: From Margin to Mainstream,* 49–59 (Detroit: Wayne State University Press, 2000); Shams Alwujude, "Daughter of America," in Abraham and Shryock, *Arab Detroit,* 383.

12. Nadine Naber, "Arab San Francisco: On Gender, Cultural Citizenship, and Belonging," PhD diss., University of California at Davis, June 2002, 223.

13. Alwujude, "Daughter of America," 386.

14. Naber, "Arab San Francisco," 162.

15. Yvonne Yazbeck-Haddad and John Esposito, "The Dynamics of Islamic Identity in North America," Arab World Project, http://arabworld.nitle.org (accessed May 31, 2004). The essay is divided into nine parts. See p. 1 of the section "Islamic Identity and the American Experience."

16. Naber, "Arab San Francisco," 33.

17. Ibid., 63 (emphasis in original).

18. Ibid., 69.

19. Ibid., 78.

20. Sharkey Haddad, "The American Journey of a Chaldean from Iraq," in Abraham and Shryock, *Arab Detroit,* 205–17, esp. 207.

21. Naber, "Arab San Francisco," 94.

22. Ibid., 205 (emphasis in original).

23. Ibid., 206.

24. Ibid., 210.

25. *United States v. Macintosh,* 283 U.S. 605 (1931), available at http://religious freedom.lib.virginia.edu, 1 (accessed October 23, 2004). On Sutherland's naturalization, see Lopez, *White by Law,* 92.

26. *Takao Ozawa v. United States,* 16–17.

27. *United States v. Bhagat Singh Thind,* 261 U.S. 204 (1923), available at

http://www.pbs.org/rootsinthesand (accessed September 21, 2003); see p. 2 of the ruling.

28. Shekhar Deshpande, "The Nowhere Man," *Little India,* October 3, 2004, 5, http://www.littleindia.com (accessed October 3, 2004).

29. Biju Mathew and Vijay Prashad, "The Protean Forms of Yankee Hindutva," *Ethnic and Racial Studies* 23, no. 3 (May 2000): 516–34, esp. 522–23.

30. Vinay Lal, "A Political History of Asian Indians in the United States," *Punjabilok,* http://www.punjabilok.com/heritage, 1 (accessed June 17, 2004).

31. Lavina Dhingra Shankar and Pallassana R. Balgopal, "South Asian Immigrants before 1950," *Amerasia Journal,* 27, no. 1 (2001): 55–85.

32. Lavina Melwani, "Eating Their Hearts Out," *Little India,* June 2004, 3, http://www.littleindia.com (accessed June 16, 2004).

33. "Indians in the U.S.A.," NRILinks, http://www.nrilinks.com/us/indians/default.htm (accessed October 24, 2004); see also Wu, *Yellow,* 53.

34. Lavina Melwani, "Underground Tales," *Little India,* May 2004, http://www.littleindia.com (accessed June 16, 2004).

35. Melwani, "Eating Their Hearts Out," 1, 3.

36. Achal Mehra, "Mix and Match," *Little India,* June 18, 2004, http://www.littleindia.com, 1–2 (accessed June 18, 2004).

37. Prashad, *Karma of Brown Folk,* 93.

38. David Hollinger, *Postethnic America* (New York: Basic Books, 1995), 153.

39. Prashad, *Karma of Brown Folk,* 103.

40. Melwani, "The In-Between Generation," *Little India,* June 17, 2004, 3.

41. Prashad, *Karma of Brown Folk,* 104.

42. Deshpande, "The Nowhere Man," 5.

43. Arvind Rajagopal, "Hindu Nationalism in the United States: Changing Configurations of Political Practices," *Ethnic and Racial Studies* 23, no. 3 (May 2000): 467–96, esp. 472.

44. Vasant Kaiwar, "The Aryan Model of History and the Oriental Renaissance: The Politics of Identity in an Age of Revolutions, Colonialism and Nationalism," in Vasant Kaiwar and Sucheta Mazumdar, editors, *Antinomies of Modernity: Essays on Race, Orient, Nation,* 13–61 (Durham: Duke University Press, 2003), 23.

45. Ibid., 24, 41.

46. Ibid., 39.

47. Sucheta Mazumdar, "The Politics of Religion and National Origin: Rediscovering Hindu Indian Identity in the United States," in Kaiwar and Mazumdar, *Antinomies of Modernity,* 245.

48. Ibid., 241.

49. Trisha Pasricha, "A History Lesson," *Samskar: A Publication of the Hindu Students Council* (Winter 2003): 12–13, http://www.hscnet.org (accessed October 10, 2004).

50. Ibid., 13.

51. Bahri, "With Kaleidoscope Eyes," 25–48, esp. 41.

Six

1. Rex Nettleford, *Inward Stretch, Outward Reach: A Voice from the Caribbean* (London: Macmillan, 1993), 9.

2. Rachel Swarns, "Hispanics Resist Racial Grouping by Census," *New York Times,* October 24, 2004, 1; see also José Itzigsohn, Silvia Giorguli, and Obed Basquez, "Immigrant Incorporation and Racial Identity: Racial Self-identification among Dominican Immigrants," *Ethnic and Racial Studies* 28, no. 1 (January 2005): 50–78, esp. 59, 64, 75.

3. Swarns, "Hispanics Resist Racial Grouping," 1.

4. Carlos Antonio Torre, Hugo Rodríguez Vecchini, and William Burgos, editors, *The Commuter Nation: Perspectives on Puerto Rican Migration* (San Juan: Editorial de La Universidad de Puerto Rico, 1994).

5. Irving Rouse, *The Taínos: Rise and Decline of the People Who Greeted Columbus* (New Haven: Yale University Press, 1992); José Luis González, *El País de Cuatro Pisos* (San Juan: Huracán, 1985).

6. Arturo Morales Carrión, *Puerto Rico: A Political and Cultural History* (New York: Norton, 1983), 37.

7. Angel G. Quintero Rivera, *Patricos y Plebeyos* (Rio Piedras: Huracán, 1988). My interpretation is based on Quintero's superb analysis.

8. James Deitz, *Economic History of Puerto Rico* (Princeton: Princeton University Press, 1986), 31, 36.

9. William Willoughby, *Territories and Dependencies of the United States: Their Government and Administration* (New York: Century Co., 1905), 86; see also William Willoughby, "The Executive Council of Porto Rico," *American Political Science Review* 1 (1907), esp. 561.

10. Carlos Romero Barcelo, *Statehood Is for the Poor* (San Juan, 1978), 11.

11. Deitz, *Economic History,* 275.

12. Juan Flores, *Divided Borders: Essays on Puerto Rican Identity* (Houston: Arte Público, 1993), 187 (emphasis added).

13. Leonardo Rodríguez, *They Have to Be Puerto Ricans* (Chicago: Adams Press, 1988), 3.

14. Flores, *Divided Borders,* 188.

15. Mary C. Waters, *Black Identities: West Indian Immigrant Dreams and American Realities* (Cambridge: Harvard University Press, 1999), 68.

16. Richard D. E. Burton, *Afro-Creole: Power, Opposition and Play in the Caribbean* (Ithaca: Cornell University Press, 1997), 21, 14–15. See also Mavis C. Campbell, *The Maroons of Jamaica, 1655–1796* (Trenton: Africa World Press, 1990).

17. Burton, *Afro-Creole,* 36–37; for a more general view of the Caribbean and especially the West Indies, see Eric Williams, *From Columbus to Castro: The History of the Caribbean, 1492–1969* (New York: Vintage, 1983); finally, see Eric Williams, *History of the People of Trinidad and Tobago* (Brooklyn: A&B, 1942).

18. Verene Shepherd, *Transients to Settlers: The Experience of Indians in Jamaica, 1845–1950* (Warwick: University of Warwick Press, 1993), 206.

19. Ian R. G. Spencer, *British Immigration Policy since 1939* (London: Routledge, 1997), 3.

20. Ronald Fernandez, *America's Banquet of Cultures* (Westport: Praeger, 2000), 205.

21. Fernandez, *Cruising the Caribbean*, 417.

22. This was a very hot topic year after year when I attended conferences sponsored by Caribbean and Latin American Action, a Washington-based lobbying group for business interests.

23. Pablo Fajnzylber and J. Humberto López, *Close to Home: The Developmental Impact of Remittances in Latin America* (Washington, D.C.: World Bank, 2006), 4.

24. This section relies on Waters, *Black Identities*, and on my own experiences with West Indians; quotes are from Waters, *Black Identities*, 149, 150.

25. Ibid., 133.

26. Ibid., 288.

27. Ibid., 287–88.

28. Evilio Grillo, *Black Cuban, Black American* (Houston: Arte Público Press, 2000), 7, 25.

29. Mirta Ojito, "Best of Friends, Worlds Apart," *New York Times,* June 5, 2000, A20.

30. Ibid., A20.

31. For example, José Martí, *Nuestra América* (Havana: Casa Editora Abril, 2001); see also Pedro Pablo Rodríguez, "Una en alma e intento: Identidad y unidad latinoamericanas en José Martí, Debates Americanos," *Casa de Altos Estudios, Don Fernando Ortiz* 2 (July–December 1996): 12–33, esp. 18–19.

32. Eduardo Torres-Cuevas, "En Buscar de Cubanidad (II) Debates Americanos," *Casa de Altos Estudios, Don Fernando Ortiz* 2 (July–December 1996): 3–11; see p. 5 for the statistics.

33. Ibid., 5.

34. This is from U.S. Senate, *Congressional Record,* February 28, 1896; see Fernandez, *Cruising the Caribbean*, 11–12.

35. Fernandez, *Cruising the Caribbean*, 11.

36. Louis Perez Jr., *On Becoming Cuban: Identity, Nationality and Culture* (New York: Harper Collins, 1999), 322; see also Jules Robert Benjamin, *The United States and Cuba* (Pittsburgh: University of Pittsburgh Press, 1986); finally, see Louis Perez Jr., *Cuba under the Platt Amendment* (Pittsburgh: University of Pittsburgh Press, 1986).

37. Perez, *On Becoming Cuban*, 322.

38. Fernandez, *Cruising the Caribbean*, 40–43.

39. Perez, *On Becoming Cuban*, 323–24.

40. Ibid., 324.

41. Pew Hispanic Center, *2002 National Survey of Latinos* (Washington, D.C.: Pew Research Center, 2002), 32, available at http://www.pewhispanic.org (accessed July 20, 2003).

42. Jorge Gracia, *Hispanic/Latino Identity: A Philosophical Perspective* (Malden: Blackwell, 2000), 39 (emphasis added).

43. Ibid., 48.

44. T. R. Fehrenbach, *Fire and Blood: A History of Mexico* (New York: De Capo Press, 1995), 238–39.

45. Gracia, *Hispanic/Latino Identity,* 109.

46. Ibid., 120.

Seven

1. Lori DesRochers, "HMC Fire Culture Becomes Hot Topic," *Student Life,* February 27, 2004, 1.

2. Jay Antenen, "Dunn under Fire for Allegations," *Student Life,* April 2, 2004, 1, 4.

3. Ibid., 4.

4. Donna Jackson Nakazawa, *Does Anybody Else Look Like Me? A Parent's Guide to Raising Multiracial Children* (Boston: Peresus, 2003), 140–41.

5. See House Committee on Government Reform and Oversight, *Testimony of Ramona E. Douglass, President of the Association of Multiethnic Americans, before the Subcommittee on Government Management and Technology,* 105th Cong., 1st sess. (Washington, D.C.: GPO, 1997), 1.

6. Cathy Tashiro, "Health Issues Facing Mixed Race People," in Maria P. P. Root and Matt Kelley, editors, *Multiracial Child Resource Book: Living Complex Identities,* 27–31 (Seattle: Mavin Foundation, 2003); quote appears on p. 27; for the Howards, see p. 26.

7. *Loving v. Virginia,* 388 U.S. 1 (1967), 2, available at http://www.multiracial.com (accessed November 16, 2003); on state laws, see Renee C. Romano, *Race Mixing: Black-White Marriage in Postwar America* (Cambridge: Harvard University Press, 2003), 7.

8. Pearl Fuyo Gaskins, editor, *What Are You? Voices of Mixed Race Young People* (New York: Henry Holt, 1999), 20.

9. See Fusion Series, "Generations of the Mixed Race Experience," Panel Discussion, pt. 1, p. 2, http://www.fusionseries.com (accessed February 27, 2004).

10. Catherine Betts, "Checking the 'Other' Box," *Eurasian Nation,* http://www.eurasianation.com (accessed February 11, 2003).

11. Julie Fischer, "Without/Within: Hapas and Their Own Fetish," available at Swirl chat group at http://www.swirlinc.org (accessed November 16, 2003).

12. Jackson Nakazawa, *Does Anybody Else Look Like Me?* 140.

13. Fuyo Gaskins, *What Are You?* 34.

14. Jane Ayers Chiong, *Racial Categorizations of Multiracial Children in Schools* (Westport: Bergin and Gravey, 1998), 56–59, 65.

15. Alfredo Padilla and Matt Kelley, "One Box Isn't Enough: An Analysis of How U.S. Colleges and Universities Classify Mixed Heritage Students," Mavin Foundation and the Level Playing Field Institute, November 9, 2005, 7, 8, 12, available at http://www.mavinfoundation.org/projects/index.html.

16. Jackson Nakazawa, *Does Anybody Else Look Like Me?* 152–53.

17. Kevin Maillard, "We Are Black Indians," in Fuyo Gaskins, *What Are You?* 81–86, esp. 86.

18. See "The Fresh Princess," *Mavin,* no. 3 (Fall 1999): 27.

19. Root and Kelley, *Multiracial Child Resource Book,* 22.

20. Mariko Kawabori, "Census 2000: The Beginning of the Blend," *Mavin,* no. 4 (Spring 2000): 47.

21. Abbie (Miyabi) Modry, "The Problem with Terms and Labels," *Eurasian Nation,* http://www.eurasiannation.com (accessed April 1, 2003), p. 4 of the biographical statement.

22. Jacobs, *Race Manners,* 27.

23. For the crisis comment, see Fuyo Gaskins, *What Are You?* 21; on the boomerang effect, see, for example, Leon Festinger, *A Theory of Cognitive Dissonance* (Stanford: Stanford University Press, 1957); see also Leon Festinger, *Conflict, Decision and Dissonance* (Stanford: Stanford University Press, 1964).

24. This is from a Swirl chat room debate. The e-mail is dated September 20, 2004, and the intensity of the discussion easily produced ten to twenty back-and-forth responses.

25. Claudine Chiawei O'Hearn, *Half and Half: Writers on Growing Up Biracial and Bicultural* (New York: Pantheon, 1998), 184.

26. Root and Kelly, *Multiracial Child Resource Book,* 200–203.

27. Jennifer Poulson, "My Glass Is 'Half' Full: Being Racial Overseas," *Mavin,* no. 7 (2003): 29.

28. Kanna Livingston, "My Half Identity," *Eurasian Nation,* http://www .eurasiannation.com (accessed February 10, 2003), 1–2.

29. Modry, "Problem with Terms and Labels," 3.

30. Root and Kelley, *Multiracial Child Resource Book,* 42, 33, 1.

31. Modry, "Problem with Terms and Labels," 3.

32. Ibid.

33. Fusion Series, "Generations," 7.

34. David Horowitz, "Real Life Musings," *Eurasian Nation,* 1–2, http://www.eurasiannation.com (accessed February 2, 2003).

35. Chela Delgado, "I Don't Think of Biracial as a Burden," in Fuyo Gaskins, *What Are You?* 15 (emphasis added).

36. Jackson Nakazawa, *Does Anybody Else Look Like Me?* 78–79. This section relies on Jackson Nakasawa's book; the next quotes appear on pp. 96, 158.

37. Root and Kelly, *Multiracial Child Resource Book,* 32.

38. Fuyo Gaskins, *What Are You?* 54.

39. Jackson Nakasawa, *Does Anybody Else Look Like Me?* 56.

Eight

1. Manning Marable, "Beyond Color-Blindness," *Nation* 267, no. 20 (December 14, 1998): 30.

2. Michael Omi and Howard Winant, *Racial Formation in the United States* (New York: Routledge, 1994), 55.

3. George Herbert Mead, *Mind, Self and Society* (Chicago: University of Chicago Press, 1956); see also Fernandez, *Mappers of Society.*

4. Debra Dickerson, The End of Blackness (New York: Pantheon, 2004), 134.

5. Yu, *Thinking Orientals,* 11.

6. See David Theo Goldberg, "Racial Europeanization," *Ethnic and Racial Studies* 29, no. 2 (March 2006): 331–64.

7. Fernando Ortiz, *El Engaño de las Razas* (1946; repr., Havana: Editorial Ciencias Sociales, 1975), 57; for the information on colors, see "The Science of Color," http://www.webopedia.com (accessed October 10, 2004).

8. Murray, *The Omni-Americans,* 3.

9. Howard Fast, editor, *The Collected Works of Tom Paine and Citizen Paine* (New York: Modern Library, 1943), 11.

10. Sara Rimer and Karen W. Arenson, "Top Colleges Take More Blacks, but Which Ones?" *New York Times,* June 24, 2004.

11. Nicholás Vaca, *The Presumed Alliance: The Unspoken Conflict between Latinos and Blacks and What It Means for America* (New York: Rayo, Harper Collins, 2004).

12. United States Citizenship and Immigration Services, *Fiscal Year 2003 Immigration Statistics,* table 1, http://www.uscis.gov.

13. Ray H. Abrams, *Preachers Present Arms* (New York: Round Table Press, 1933), 116.

14. David Roediger, *Working toward Whiteness: How America's Immigrants Became White* (New York: Basic Books, 2005), 135.

15. Randolph Bourne, "Trans-National America," in Carl Resek, editor, *War and the Intellectuals,* 107–23 (New York: Harper Torch, 1964); quotes appear on pp. 109, 108. The original essay was published in 1916.

16. UNESCO, "All Different, All Unique: Young People and the UNESCO Universal Declaration on Cultural Diversity," Project of UNESCO and the Oxfam International Youth Parliament (New York: UNESCO, 2004), 14, http://portal.unesco.org/culture/en/ev.phpURL_ID=20381&URL_DO=DO_ TOPIC&URL_SECTION=201.html (accessed April 6, 2006).

17. Bruce Bawer, *While Europe Slept: How Radical Islam Is Destroying the West from Within* (New York: Doubleday, 2006), 36.

18. For example, Reza Aslan, *No God but God: The Origins, Evolution and Future of Islam* (New York: Random House, 2006); John L. Esposito, *The Islamic Threat: Myth or Reality* (New York: Oxford University Press, 1999); Mir Zohair Husain, *Islam and the Muslim World* (New York: Mc Graw Hill, 2006), esp. 23.

19. Senate Committee on the Judiciary, *Testimony of Mr. Richard Stana, Director of Homeland Security and Justice, before the Subcommittee on Immigration, Border Security and Citizenship on "Immigration Enforcement at the Workplace: Learning from the Mistakes of 1986,"* 109th Cong., 1st sess., June 19, 2006, 20, http://judiciary.senate.gov/schedule.cfm.

20. House Committee on Government Reform, *Waste, Abuse and Mismanagement in Department of Homeland Security Contracts,* July 2006, 5, http://www. demo crats.reform.house.gov/Documents/20060727092939-29369.pdf.General

Erwin was commenting on a two-billion-dollar border patrol contract in which Homeland Security asked prospective bidders to "tell us how to do our business."

21. House Committee on International Relations, *Hearings of T. J. Bonner, National President, National Border Patrol Council of the American Federation of Government Employees, AFL-CIO, before the Subcommittee on International Terrorism and Nonproliferation,* 109th Cong., 1st sess., San Diego, July 5, 2006, 7, http://wwwc.house.gov/international_relations/109/bon070506.pdf.

22. U.S. Government Accountability Office, "Immigration Enforcement: Weaknesses Hinder Employment Verification and Worksite Enforcement Efforts," GAO-06-895T, June 19, 2006, 9–10.

23. Ibid., 9–10, also 13, 20.

24. U.S. Government Accountability Office, "Overstay Tracking: A Key Component of Homeland Security and a Layered Defense," GAO-04-82, May 2004; for the last quote, see p. 18; for the chance of arrest, see p. 19; for the estimates, see p. 10.

25. William Finnegan, "Watching the Waterfront: How Vulnerable Is New York's Port?" *New Yorker,* June 19, 2006, 61.

26. House Committee on the Judiciary, *How Illegal Immigration Impacts Constituencies: Perspectives from Members of Congress: Hearings before the Subcommittee on Immigration, Border Security and Claims,* 109th Cong., 1st sess., pt. 1, November 10, 2005. For Pearce's comment see p. 41; for the next quote from Guiterrez, see p. 24.

27. Senate Committee on the Judiciary, *Field Hearing—Comprehensive Immigration Reform: Examining the Need for a Guest Worker Program,* Philadelphia, http://judiciary.senate.gov/hearing.cfm?id=1983.

28. House Committee on the Judiciary, *How Illegal Immigration Impacts Constituencies,* pt. 2, November 17, 2005, 4; for U.S. Census Bureau confirmation of this dependence, see Rob Paral, *The Growth and Reach of Immigration: New Census Bureau Data Underscore Importance of Immigrants in the U.S. Labor Force,* American Immigration Law Foundation, August 16, 2006, 1, http://www.ailf.org/ipc/policybrief/policybrief_2006_81606.shtml.

29. House Committee on the Judiciary, *How Illegal Immigration Impacts Constituencies,* pt. 2, 12.

30. Ibid. This is from an appendix with hundreds of editorials, p. 74 for the *Arizona Daily Star.* The *Milwaukee Journal Sentinel* May 15, 2005, editorial is at p. 190.

31. See Demetrios G. Papademetriou, *Europe and Its Immigrants in the 21st Century: A New Deal or a Continuing Dialogue of the Deaf* (Washington, D.C.: Migration Policy Institute, 2006). In his introduction to this book Papademetriou stresses that in working to create effective immigration policies nations need to work with rather than against the markets. Otherwise, as in the United States leaders create powerful "resisters" in their own countries.

32. House Committee on the Judiciary, Part 1, from the appendix of newspaper editorials, 141.

33. Quoted in Roger Daniels, *Guarding the Golden Door: American Immigration Policy and Immigrants since 1882* (New York: Hill and Wang, 2004), 55.

Select Bibliography

The following sources are more or less important sources for the ideas expressed in this book. Anyone who wants a more exhaustive version of the notes should contact me at fernandezr@ccsu.edu.

Berger, Peter, and Thomas Luckmann. *The Social Construction of Reality*. Garden City: Doubleday, 1967.

Bourne, Randolph. "Trans-National America." In *War and the Intellectuals*, edited by Carl Resek. New York: Harper Torch Books, 1964.

Chang, Iris. *The Chinese in America*. New York: Viking, 2003.

Cose, Ellis. *The Rage of a Privileged Class*. New York: Harper Collins, 1993.

Daniels, Roger. *Guarding the Golden Door: American Immigration Policy and Immigrants since 1882*. New York: Hill and Wang, 2004.

Diamond, Jared. *Guns, Germs and Steel: The Fates of Human Societies*. New York: W. W. Norton, 1998.

Dickerson, Debra. *The End of Blackness*. New York: Pantheon, 2004.

Dyer, Richard. *White*. London: Routledge, 1997.

Feagin, Joe, and Eileen O'Brien. *White Men on Race: Power, Privilege and the Shaping of Racial Consciousness*. Boston: Beacon Press, 2003.

Fernandez, Ronald. *America's Banquet of Cultures: Harnessing Ethnicity, Race and Immigration in the Twenty-first Century*. Westport: Praeger, 2000.

Flores, Juan. *Divided Borders: Essays on Puerto Rican Identity*. Houston: Arte Público, 1993.

Fuentes, Carlos. *El Espejo Enterrado*. Mexico City: Taurus, 1997.

González, José Luis. *El País de Cuatro Pisos*. San Juan: Huracán, 1985.

Gould, Stephen Jay. *The Mismeasure of Man*. New York: Norton, 1996.

Gracia, Jorge. *Hispanic/Latino Identity: A Philosophical Perspective*. Malden: Blackwell, 2000.

Grillo, Evilio. *Black Cuban, Black American*. Houston: Arte Público Press, 2000.

Hacker, Andrew. *Money: Who Has How Much and Why.* New York: Simon and Schuster, 1998.

Haney López, Ian F. *White by Law: The Legal Construction of Race.* New York: New York University Press, 1996.

Hollinger, David. *Postethnic America.* New York: Basic Books, 1995.

Huntington, Samuel P. *Who Are We? The Challenges to America's National Identity.* New York: Simon and Schuster, 2004.

Kwong, Peter, and Dušanka Miščević. *Chinese America: The Untold Story of America's New Community.* New York: New Press, 2005.

Malcomson, Scott. *One Drop of Blood: The American Misadventure of Race.* New York: Farrar, Straus, and Giroux, 2000.

McWhorter, John. *Losing the Race: Self Sabotage in Black America.* New York: Harper Collins, 2000.

Mead, George Herbert. *Mind, Self and Society.* Chicago: University of Chicago Press, 1962.

Montejano, David. *Anglos and Mexicans in the Making of Texas, 1836–1986.* Austin: University of Texas Press, 1987.

Murray, Albert. *The Omni Americans: Black Experience and American Culture.* New York: De Capo, 1970.

Naber, Nadine. "Arab San Francisco: On Gender, Cultural Citizenship, and Belonging." PhD diss., University of California at Davis, 2002.

Naber, Nadine. "Ambiguous Insiders: An Investigation of Arab American Invisibility." *Ethnic and Racial Studies* 23, no. 1 (January 2000): 37–61.

Nakazawa, Donna Jackson. *Does Anybody Else Look Like Me? A Parent's Guide to Raising Mutliracial Children.* Boston: Peresus, 2003.

Nettleford, Rex. *Inward Stretch, Outward Reach.* London: Macmillan, 1993.

Ortiz, Fernando. *Cuban Counterpoint: Tobacco and Sugar.* Durham: Duke University Press, 1995.

Pieterse, Jan Nederveen. *White on Black: Images of Africa and Blacks in Western Popular Culture.* New Haven: Yale University Press, 1992.

Portes, Alejandro, and Rubén C. Rumbaut. *Immigrant America.* Berkeley: University of California Press, 1996.

Prashad, Vijay. *The Karma of Brown Folk.* Minneapolis: University of Minnesota Press, 2000.

Rodriguez, Richard. *Brown: The Last Discovery of America.* New York: Penguin, 2002.

Roediger, David R. *Working toward Whiteness: How America's Immigrants Became White.* New York: Basic Books, 2005.

Root, Maria P. P., and Matt Kelley, editors. *Multiracial Child Resource Book: Living Complex Identities.* Seattle: Mavin Foundation, 2003.

Santa Ana, Otto. *Brown Tide Rising: Metaphors of Latinos in Contemporary American Public Discourse.* Austin: University of Texas Press, 2002.

Steinberg, Stephen. *Turning Back.* Boston: Beacon Press, 1995.

Vaca, Nicolás C. *The Presumed Alliance.* New York: Rayo, 2004.

Waters, Mary C. *Black Identities: West Indian Immigrant Dreams and American Realities.* Cambridge: Harvard University Press, 1999.

Wu, Frank H. *Yellow: Race in America beyond Black and White*. New York: Basic Books, 2002.

Yu, Henry. *Thinking Orientals: Migration, Contact and Exoticism in Modern America*. New York: Oxford University Press, 2001.

Zia, Helen. *Asian American Dreams: The Emergence of an American People*. New York: Farrar, Straus, and Giroux, 2000.

Index

277